SHARED GROUND
AMONG JEWS AND CHRISTIANS
A SERIES OF EXPLORATIONS

VOLUME II

Jesus' Jewishness

Exploring the Place of Jesus within Early Judaism

Editor
James H. Charlesworth

THE AMERICAN INTERFAITH INSTITUTE

CROSSROAD • NEW YORK

1991
The Crossroad Publishing Company
370 Lexington Avenue, New York, NY 10017

Printed in the United States of America
Typesetting output: T$_E$XSource, Houston

Library of Congress Cataloging-in-Publication Data

Jesus' Jewishness : exploring the place of Jesus within early Judaism
    / editor, James H. Charlesworth.
        p. cm. — (Shared ground among Jews and Christians ; v. 2)
    Includes bibliographical references and indexes.
    ISBN 0-8245-1061-5
    1. Jesus Christ—Jewishness. 2. Jesus Christ—History of
doctrines—Early church, ca. 30–600. 3. Judaism—History—Post-
exilic period, 586 B.C.–210 A.D. 4. Christianity—Origin.
5. Christianity and other religions—Judaism. 6. Judaism—
Relations—Christianity. I. Charlesworth, James H. II. Series.
BT590.J8J44 1991
232.9—dc20   90-44118
                                                                CIP

Contributors

James H. Charlesworth
George L. Collord Professor of
New Testament Language and
Literature
Editor, Dead Sea Scrolls Project
Princeton Theological Seminary
Princeton, New Jersey

Harvey Cox
Victor S. Thomas Professor of
Divinity
Harvard Divinity School
Cambridge, Massachusetts

David Flusser
Professor of History of Religion
Hebrew University
Jerusalem, Israel

Daniel J. Harrington, S.J.
Professor of New Testament
General Editor, *New Testament
Abstracts*
Weston School of Theology
Cambridge, Massachusetts

Hans Küng
Professor of Ecumenical Theology
Director, Institut für
ökumenische Forschung
University of Tubingen
Germany

John P. Meier
General Editor, *Catholic Biblical
Quarterly*
Professor of New Testament
Biblical Studies Department
Catholic University of America
Washington, D.C.

Alan F. Segal
Professor of Religion
Barnard College
Columbia University
New York, New York

Ellis Rivkin
Adolph S. Ochs Professor of
Jewish History
Hebrew Union College-Jewish
Institute of Religion
Cincinnati, Ohio

Geza Vermes
Reader in Jewish Studies
The University of Oxford
The Oriental Institute
Oxford, England

Contents

Illustrations
(pages 137–152)

Foreword

Irvin J. Borowsky

I am pleased to recognize Jesus as a Jew. I admire those who are obedient to the teachings of Jesus of Nazareth, the Galilean prophet of long ago. It is also, however, important to be clear and honest with the reader: I have no desire to become a Christian.

I am appalled at the way "Jews" are referred to in the New Testament. As an example, John 5:16 reads, "And therefore did the Jews persecute Jesus, and sought to slay him, because he had done these things on the sabbath day." In fact, accuracy and truth to ancient texts are better served when the sentence states, "And therefore did the *authorities* persecute Jesus, because he had done these things on the sabbath day."

Children's Bibles are even more inflammatory. Their derogatory and fearful references teach Christian children at the most impressionable time of their lives to distrust and hate Jews. Here are just a few examples. *My First Book of Bible Stories* (copyrighted in 1988) contains many statements similar to this one on page 54:

> ... but the leaders of the synagogue, the Jewish church, were jealous and afraid of Jesus because he was so popular, and they plotted to kill him.

The Children's Bible in 365 Stories (copyrighted in 1985) also contains numerous statements such as this one on page 330:

> If these charges were true, Jesus would be sentenced to death, but Pilate was certain that the Jewish leaders had trumped up the charges, because they were jealous of him.

International Children's Bible (copyrighted in 1988) contains many shocking headlines such as those appearing on pages 802 and 807:

> The Jews Try to Arrest Jesus
> The Jews against Jesus
> The Day the Jewish Leaders Started Planning to Kill Jesus

Nowhere do these authors or translators inform young people that all the founders of Christianity were Jewish. Instead, they portray the Jews as the people who killed Jesus; children are given the impressions that "Jews" are a people to be despised for all eternity. It is this portrait that is the genesis of the virulent anti-Jewish poison that has been passed down from generation to generation for almost 2000 years. As a result, untold millions of innocent people have been uprooted from their families and communities, to be tortured, to be killed. The contemporary Jewish people are survivors of the hatred that has devastated their co-religionists.

The Jewishness of Jesus must not be denied. Christians affirm, often without reflection, that God chose a young Jewess among all the women on earth to be Jesus' mother. Christian leaders need to clarify and emphasize that all the founders of Christianity were Jewish and that the distrust and hatred vented toward Jews is anti-Christian.

Today, the irrefutable facts, the information, and the structure needed to foster understanding and communication are in place. I salute those righteous people who are now striving to remove distrust and hatred from Christian theology. Clearly, true Christians have no desire to further decimate the remaining small number of Jews who have survived centuries of persecution. They, too, each had a mother of the same faith as Jesus.

Preface

James H. Charlesworth

To me as a scholar *Jesus' Jewishness* seems redundant. Obviously Jesus was a Jew; hence, what does it mean to refer to his "Jewishness?" Is it not tantamount to discussing Hillel's Jewishness?

But, I am not only a scholar. I live in the twentieth century, and dare never forget that my century is one marred by nuclear bombs, barbed wire fences to keep people in (when barriers were intended to keep undesirables out), and technologies to expedite not only killings but also the intentional and systematic extermination of people because of their nationality or race. A new obscenity, genocide, sadly appeared for the first time in human consciousness around the middle of this century.

Even more sadly, some of this gross alienation and massive hatred has resulted from a crass misinterpretation of Jesus of Nazareth. Riding on the crest of optimism the nineteenth century created waves that were heralded throughout the Western world as magnificent advances: the marvelous manuscript discoveries (especially in St. Catherine's Monastery); the identification of the Middle East especially through its gigantic pyramids and the beginnings of sensational archaeological discoveries in the Holy City, Jerusalem (thanks primarily to Napoleon and the British Empire, respectively); the breaking of myths by D. F. Strauss, F. W. Nietzsche, and C. Darwin; the prophetic voices of F. Engels and K. Marx; the founding of psychoanalysis by S. Freud; the all-encompassing philosophical system of G. W. F. Hegel; and marvelous industrial inventions, such as the typewriter, the radio, the telephone and telegraph, the light bulb, the railroad, the automobile, and the prototype of the airplane.

Amazing. Understandably, the Victorians felt they were ushering in a new and unbelievable Golden Age. But, all that momentarily sparkles may not be gold; and it may mask something horrible.

That something undid the optimism of Western civilization. It is not so much that the industrial revolution eventually gave us the Bomb. It is something more sinister, a swirling subliminal undercurrent, unrecognized until it seeps to the surface in the home, the marketplace, and even the Church.

Running within the development of Western culture and bobbing to the surface especially at the end of the last century, which as indicated essentially defined and shaped this century, was a three-pronged ideology that like the devil's pitchfork gouged the West and especially the body of Jesus' followers, the Church. The three points were the denigration of the "Old Testament" and its replacement by the revelations of the "New Testament"; the galvanizing of hatred for Jews through the neologism "anti-Semitism"; and concomitantly in the highest halls of academia the preposterous tendency to assume that "Jesus was no Jew," which is H. St. Chamberlain's proud conclusion in his *Foundations of the Nineteenth Century*, a popular book, originally published in German and often then heralded as the finest product of nineteenth-century historical research.

Only a few decades later diabolical demagogues shredded the historical facts. The Jewish man, Jesus of Nazareth, was transformed into an Aryan. Those who killed him were "Jews." It is obvious why the word "Christ" sticks in the throats of some of our contemporaries: they first heard the title through the slanderous claim that they were "Christ killers."

Who can create more wretched perversions? Jesus, the Jew, was crucified by Roman soldiers. All the evangelists agree on this part of the story of Jesus. As Professor Rivkin demonstrates in his essay on the following pages, we should probe records of the first century in search of *what*, not who, crucified Jesus.

The nineteenth century and its twentieth-century aberrations, in a very real sense, are still with us. In their wake are left deposits that are far too influential and devastating to ignore. Many Christians still harbor the fantasy that Jesus does not fit into first-century Judaism (and certainly not into "Judaism" as we know it today). They regard "Jesus Christ" first of all as "unique," although most somehow know better than to say "totally unique," not so much for grammatical reasons, but because of their creedal stress that Jesus was "fully human." Far too many New Testament scholars still fail to scrutinize the presupposition that the historical Jesus is unknowable and lost forever behind the creative editing of the evangelists. The dark side of Christology continues often unperceived; it is the contention that Jesus is solely and categorically the heavenly and preexistent Christ, the risen Lord, who is triumphant, transcendent, and timeless. These docetic acids eat away the earthly dimensions, including the Jewish beliefs of Jesus and his earliest followers.

So, at the end of the twentieth century we must weed from our minds some growths planted in our collective consciousness throughout the course of Western civilization. We must discard the presupposition that Jesus was not a Jew.

Scholars trained in significantly different schools and representing virtually every option for belief or disbelief have independently arrived at what may now be described as a consensus among Jewish and Christian *historians*: Jesus of Nazareth was a Jew; he was, moreover, a Jew who lived in Palestine before the destruction of the Jerusalem Temple by Roman soldiers in 70 C.E.; and, perhaps more significantly, his thought was shaped by the dynamic currents within that Judaism.

The present volume, *Jesus' Jewishness*, brings together, with some of my own work on this subject, the selected best recent publications on the Jewishness of Jesus. Represented are the findings of a Protestant minister (Charlesworth), Roman Catholics (Küng, Meier, and Harrington), and Jews from Israel (Flusser), Europe (Vermes), and the United States (Segal and Rivkin). All have published independent research showing why it is now obvious and undeniable that Jesus was a Jew and that his life and thought are properly understood within the cosmopolitan, creative, and diverse groups that shaped pre-70 Judaism.

These studies were not intended for this book; they were produced over the last two decades by distinguished scholars employing the so-called disinterested method of historical inquiry. The essays originally appeared elsewhere, but are republished now with appropriate corrections and additions. These studies are scientific and critical; they reflect the integrity of internationally renowned scholars. The American Interfaith Institute issues this book in partial fulfillment of a dream: *now* interconfessionally, and out of a plurality that condemns no one, we can look forward to the dawning of a new century, which, once rid of all forms of hatred, may herald the beginning of a better age. In the words of the *Shemone Esre* (The Eighteen Benedictions) and of Jesus, may the next decade and century more clearly reveal the reign and coming of the Kingdom that belongs to and comes from God alone.

J. H. C.
Princeton
October 6, 1990

Acknowledgments

We wish to express appreciations to the following authors, editors, and publishers for allowing us to reproduce the articles or chapters, usually in a revised form, in this volume.

Harvey Cox, "Rabbi Yeshua ben Joseph" (chapter 5) and "Introduction: Jesus and Dialogue" (chapter 1), from his *Many Mansions: A Christian's Encounter with Other Faiths* (Boston, 1988), appear here slightly edited and combined into a single essay, with the kind permission of Beacon Press. (The Editor wishes to acknowledge the editing by Frank X. Blisard in preparing this essay for republication in the present volume.)

James H. Charlesworth, "The Foreground of Christian Origins and the Commencement of Jesus Research in the 1980s," originally two articles, reprinted in a slightly revised form from *Proceedings of the Irish Biblical Association* 10 (1986) 40–54 and the *Princeton Seminary Bulletin* 6 (1985) 221–30. Permission obtained from the Irish Biblical Association and Princeton Theological Seminary.

John P. Meier, "Reflections on Jesus-of-History Research Today." An abridged version of this chapter appeared under the title, "Jesus among the Historians," in the Sunday Book Review of the *New York Times*, December 21, 1986, pp. 1, 16–19; that portion reappears with permission from the *Times*. Now for the first time the full original version is published.

Geza Vermes, "Jesus the Jew," reprinted in a significantly revised form, with permission, from *Jesus and the World of Judaism* by Geza Vermes (London, 1983) pp. 1–14. Permission granted by SCM Press.

Daniel J. Harrington, "The Jewishness of Jesus: Facing Some Problems," reprinted from *CBQ* 49 (1987) 1–13. Permission received from the Catholic Biblical Association.

David Flusser, "Jesus, His Ancestry, and the Commandment of Love," a new translation, reprinted in a revised form from *Jesus in Selbstzeugnissen und Bilddokumenten* by David Flusser (Hamburg, 1968; E.T. New York, 1969) pp. 7–24, 64–72. Permission obtained from Rowohlt Taschenbuch Verlag GmBH.

James H. Charlesworth, "Jesus, Early Jewish Literature, and Archaeology," reprinted in a slightly revised form from the *Princeton Seminary Bulletin* 6 (1985) 98–115. Permission granted by Princeton Theological Seminary.

Alan F. Segal, "Jesus, the Jewish Revolutionary," reprinted, by permission, from *Rebecca's Children: Judaism and Christianity in the Roman World*, by Alan F. Segal, Copyright © 1986 by the President and Fellows of Harvard College. Cambridge, Mass.: Harvard University Press, 1986; pp. 68–95.

Ellis Rivkin, "What Crucified Jesus?" reprinted from *What Crucified Jesus?* by Ellis Rivkin. Copyright © 1984 by Ellis Rivkin. Revised and updated by permission of the publisher, Abingdon Press.

Hans Küng, "Christianity and Judaism," reprinted in a slightly revised form from *On Being a Christian* by Hans Küng (Garden City, N.Y., 1984) pp. 166–74. Permission granted by Doubleday & Co., Inc.

Dr. Jin Hee Han helped in preparing this book.

Also, we acknowledge our indebtedness for some photographs in this volume to the following:

Doubleday & Co., Inc., for the artistic rendering of *yšu'* on an ostracon.

The Israel Museum in Jerusalem, for permissions to publish the inscription *šlby dwd*, discovered in 1971 in Jerusalem, and the inscription from Caesarea with the name of Pontius Pilate.

Elizabeth M. Ely and Leslye Borden of PhotoEdit, 6056 Corbin, Tarzana, CA 91356, for help in obtaining many of the illustrations.

Alan Oddie, professional photographer.

Erich Lessing, Culture and Fine Arts Archives, Vienna, Austria.

Zev Radovan, professional photographer in Jerusalem, Israel.

The Metropolitan Museum of Art in New York City, for permission to publish the depiction of Samuel anointing David King of Israel, according to a seventh-century silver dish found on Cyprus.

The Zuckermanns and the West Semitic Research Project, for the photograph of Qumran Cave IV.

Abbreviations

I. Modern Publications

AB	Anchor Bible
BJRL	*Bulletin of the John Rylands Library*
BTB	*Biblical Theology Bulletin*
BZ	*Biblische Zeitschrift*
BZRG	Beihefte der Zeitschrift für Religions- und Geistesgeschichte
CBQ	*Catholic Biblical Quarterly*
CRINT	Compendia rerum iudaicarum ad novum testamentum
EI	*Eretz-Israel*
ETR	*Études théologiques et religieuses*
ExpT	*Expository Times*
FRLANT	Forschungen zur Religion und Literatur des Alten und Neuen Testaments
FrRu	*Freiburger Rundbrief*
FZPT	*Freiburger Zeitschrift für Philosophie und Theologie*
HibJ	*Hibbert Journal*
HTR	*Harvard Theological Review*
HUCA	*Hebrew Union College Annual*
IEJ	*Israel Exploration Journal*
IMJ	*Israel Museum Journal*

JBL	*Journal of Biblical Literature*
JJS	*Journal of Jewish Studies*
JQ	*Jerusalem Quarterly*
JSJ	*Journal for the Study of Judaism in the Persian, Hellenistic and Roman Period*
JSNT	*Journal of the Study of the New Testament*
JTS	*Journal of Theological Studies*
KG	*Der katholische Gedanke*
RB	*Revue biblique*
SBT	Studies in Biblical Theology
SNTS MS	*Studiorum Novi Testamenti Societas* Monograph Series
SJ	Studia Judaica
SPB	Studia postbiblica
VoxT	*Vox Theologica*
WUNT	Wissenschaftliche Untersuchungen zum Neuen Testament

II. Ancient Documents

Bible and Apocrypha

Gen	Genesis	2Ezra	2 Ezra
Ex	Exodus	Tob	Tobit
Lev	Leviticus	Jdt	Judith
Num	Numbers	AddEsth	Additions to Esther
Deut	Deuteronomy	WisSol	Wisdom of Solomon
Josh	Joshua	Sir	Sirach
Judg	Judges	1Bar	1 Baruch
Ruth	Ruth	LetJer	Letter of Jeremiah
1Sam	1 Samuel	PrAzar	Prayer of Azariah
2Sam	2 Samuel	Sus	Susanna
1Kgs	1 Kings	Bel	Bel and the Dragon
2Kgs	2 Kings	1Mac	1 Maccabees
1Chr	1 Chronicles	2Mac	2 Maccabees
2Chr	2 Chronicles	Mt	Matthew
Ezra	Ezra	Mk	Mark
Neh	Nehemiah	Lk	Luke
Esth	Esther	Jn	John
Job	Job	Acts	Acts
Ps(s)	Psalms	Rom	Romans
Prov	Proverbs	1Cor	1 Corinthians
Eccl(Qoh)	Ecclesiastes	2Cor	2 Corinthians
	(Qoheleth)	Gal	Galatians
Song	Song of Songs	Eph	Ephesians
Isa	Isaiah	Phil	Philippians
Jer	Jeremiah	Col	Colossians
Lam	Lamentations	1Thes	1 Thessalonians
Ezek	Ezekiel	2Thes	2 Thessalonians
Dan	Daniel	1Tim	1 Timothy
Hos	Hosea	2Tim	2 Timothy
Joel	Joel	Tit	Titus
Amos	Amos	Phlm	Philemon
Obad	Obadiah	Heb	Hebrews
Jonah	Jonah	Jas	James
Micah	Micah	1Pet	1 Peter
Nah	Nahum	2Pet	2 Peter
Hab	Habakkuk	1Jn	1 John
Zeph	Zephaniah	2Jn	2 John
Hag	Haggai	3Jn	3 John
Zech	Zechariah	Jude	Jude
Mal	Malachi	Rev	Revelation

Pseudepigrapha

2Bar	2 (Syriac Apocalypse of) Baruch
3Bar	3 (Greek Apocalypse of) Baruch
1En	1 (Ethiopic Apocalypse of) Enoch
2En	2 (Slavonic Apocalypse of) Enoch
HistRech	History of the Rechabites
SibOr	Sibylline Oracles
TIss	Testament of Issachar
TMos	Testament of Moses
TZeb	Testament of Zebulun
TDan	Testament of Dan
TMos	Testament of Moses
AsMos	Assumption of Moses

Other Writings

Dead Sea Scrolls

1QH	Thanksgiving Hymns *(Hodayoth)*
1QM	The War Scroll
1QS	Rule of the Community; Manual of Discipline
1QPrNab	Prayer of Nabonidus
11QMelch	Melchizedek text from Qumran Cave 11
11QTemple	The Temple Scroll from Qumran Cave 11

Josephus

Ant	Jewish Antiquities
War	Jewish Wars

Early Fathers

1Clem	1 Clement
DialTrypho	Justin, *Dialogue with Trypho*

Did	Didache
HE	Eusebius, *Historia ecclesiastica*

Rabbinics

b.	Babylonian Talmud
Ber	Berakot
Hag	Hagigah
m.	Mishnah
Pes	Pesahim
Sanh	Sanhedrin
Sukk	Sukkah
t.	Tosephta
Ta'an	Ta'anit
Yom	Yoma

Additional Abbreviations

E.T.	English translation
Gk.	Greek
N.F.	neue Folge
NT	New Testament
OT	Old Testament
par.	parallels (usually to other related traditions)

CHAPTER ONE

Rabbi Yeshua Ben Yoseph: Reflections on Jesus' Jewishness and the Interfaith Dialogue

Harvey Cox

I. My Israeli Odyssey

Introduction

It happened during a long ride in a battered orange minibus from Jerusalem up to the Galilee: I discovered that the dialogue between Jews and Christians had entered a whole new phase. I was making my first visit to Israel, and I had arrived alone and unannounced. After years of reading and hearing stories and songs about what I was taught to call "the Holy Land," I had finally decided to see it for myself, not as a guest scholar or visiting lecturer but as a pilgrim. I reveled in the marvelous anonymity. No one met me at the airport. No one in the decrepit old hotel I stayed at inside the old city knew, or cared, who I was. For three days I had explored old Jerusalem and its environs on foot. I stood on the Mount of Olives, attempting to ignore the local children hawking trinkets and souvenirs. I walked slowly around the circumference of the entire old walled city. I watched, first with amusement and then with revulsion, as the clerical guardians of the Holy Sepulcher, representing rival Christian factions, bickered with each other. I stood quietly near the Wailing Wall while a family who had flown in from New York celebrated their son's bar mitzvah on the site of Solomon's Temple, now within a few steps of the Dome of the Rock and the Mosque of Al-Aqsa.

But Jerusalem is a jittery place, and it does not take long for a visitor to realize that the traditional interpretation of its name as "city of peace" is an empirical as well as an etymological error. (It really means "place of Shalem," the local pre-Israelite deity.) For Jerusalem is not serene. Israelis, Arabs, and foreign tourists brush each other in its narrow alleys but often avoid eye contact. It is a layered city, with strata dating back to ancient times and beyond and piled with deposits from the biblical period, the Roman Empire, the Muslim Caliphate, the Crusaders' Kingdom, the Turkish Empire, the British Mandate, and the new Jewish state of Israel. But despite the confusion and the blatant modernity that often leap out unexpectedly from a movie poster or an ear-splitting transistor radio, nothing can completely eradicate the aura. I know that Muslims also revere it as their third holiest city, and I look forward to the day when the access of the children of all three of the Abrahamic faiths is settled for good. But for me Jerusalem is the city of David, Solomon, the prophets, and Ezra. And, of course, it is the city where Jesus came to celebrate Passover and where he taught, was betrayed, and met his earthly end. Obviously it was not a particularly peaceful city then either.

My Worst Nightmare

In keeping with the edgy atmosphere, my visit to Jerusalem was also not a fully serene one. Whatever tranquillity there might have been was shattered on the third evening when I ran into another American visitor at a shop where I was buying extra film. He wore a yellow sports jacket, sharply pressed slacks, and mirrored sunglasses, and, when he heard me speak English to the proprietor, he introduced himself to me as an independent Christian evangelist. He had come to Jerusalem, he said, to make contact with those Israelis who were looking forward to the rebuilding of the Temple and the reinstitution of the animal sacrifices that had ended when Herod's temple was destroyed by the Romans in 70 C.E.

At first I was incredulous and asked him quite innocently why anyone would want to do such a bizarre thing. Then it was his turn to be incredulous. Surely I knew, he said, his brow furrowing, that the Book of Daniel and the Book of Revelation both clearly predicted the rebuilding of the Temple as one of the sure signs that we were entering the Last Days. After the reconstruction, he assured me — in tones that somehow combined both a conspiratorial breathiness and an anyone-should-know-this rebuke — the sacrifices of calves and sheep and pigeons would resume. Why, there were Jews from the ancient priestly line who even now, he said, were perfecting the nearly forgotten sacrificial techniques. After all these preliminary steps, he added, referring quickly to a jumble of texts from the prophetic and apocalyptic parts of Scripture, an evil empire would attack Israel, which would then be abandoned by its erstwhile but cowardly allies. Then, just when everything looked dark and hopeless, there would be a titanic battle at Armageddon, and God would intervene on Israel's behalf by sending Christ himself to lead the forces of righteousness. Christ would win, of course, whereupon all Jews everywhere would recognize that the Messiah they have awaited for so long was none other than Jesus Christ himself. The Jews would be converted en masse, and thousands of them would then encircle the globe as powerful evangelists winning the lost to Christ.

I was appalled. A strange impulse to reach out and strangle my new unsought acquaintance rose in me, then subsided. Then I wanted to argue. I wanted to try as hard as I could to prove to him that the texts he so craftily recited out of context and inserted into his phantasmagoric endtime scenario had to do with events that had already occurred millennia ago, that they were not predictions about our time. I had heard comparable interpretations before, and I knew that they sprang from that unlikely fusion of biblical literalism, holiness perfectionism, and the occult that we now call "dispensationalist fundamentalism." I remembered that the Scofield Reference Bible I was awarded as a boy for perfect Sunday School attendance advanced one form of these theories in elaborate footnotes and paragraph headings. I even knew that this fatalistic theology of history had been widely popularized in America a decade ago by Hal Lindsey's best-seller *The Late Great Planet Earth*. Lindsey is hardly subtle: "There remains but one more event to completely set the stage for Israel's part in the last great act of her historical drama. This is to rebuild the ancient Temple of worship upon its old site. There is only one place that this Temple can be built, according to the Law of Moses. This is upon Mt. Moriah. It is there that the two previous Temples were built." These are Lindsey's words, and even printed on the page of a paperback they had seemed grotesque to me — grotesque, but not ominous. This, however, was something different. Here was a walking-and-talking advocate of Armageddon theology declaiming his fantasy within sight of the Temple Mount itself.

Suddenly I found myself speechless. I could not argue or even prolong the conversation. I just wanted to get away from my self-appointed eschatology instructor as soon as I could, so I made up an excuse and scurried away. But my brief encounter with him had taught me something: whether I liked it or not, a certain type of Jewish-Christian dialogue was already going on. And I desperately wished it were not. I quietly prayed that this charlatan might not meet or talk to too many Israelis or Jews, but I know there were many like him. The euphoria I had felt about being in the Holy City was dashed, so I decided to cheer myself up by purchasing a ticket for a three-day bus tour to the Galilee.

"Passing Through"

Next morning, I reported early to the bus terminal. Already things looked better. Having now savored the city where Jesus had confronted Pilate, I wanted next to see the area where he grew up and began his ministry. My fellow passengers on the minibus were a fascinating lot. There were nine of us altogether, and, as we introduced ourselves to each other, it turned out that my companions were all Jewish tourists from various parts of the world, including England, the United States, Brazil, and South Africa. I was relieved to know there were no independent evangelists with the Last Days on their minds. We all had a jolly time, especially during an overnight visit at a kibbutz, where we ate a tasty fish dinner and played a rough game of touch football with some of the kibbutzniks. The following day, one of our first stops was at the spot on the Jordan River where — as the guides tell gullible tourists — Jesus was baptized by John the Baptist.

I had been forewarned, of course, that, while no one has the least idea of the actual location where this event took place, each guide nevertheless has a favorite riverside parking area where he or she can tell the story of Jesus' immersion by John and the riders can stretch their legs and gawk at the river. So I knew it was probably not the exact spot where the gospels say the Spirit of God descended as a dove and blessed the work Jesus would soon begin. But I was taken in anyway. After all, it *might* be the spot. It did happen somewhere nearby. So I felt compelled to go beyond just the customary snapshot of the sluggish brown stream languidly flowing by. I wanted to wade in. As a thirteen-year-old boy, I had waded in once before. I had been baptized, following what our minister told us was the example of Jesus. He had referred to it then as "passing through Jordan." I simply could *not* look on motionless as the same water that Jesus was baptized in — albeit some nineteen hundred years later — splashed and gurgled by. So I took off my shoes and socks, rolled up my trousers, and strode in, first to my ankles, then to my knees, then up over the hems of my trousers to my thighs.

At first my fellow tourists smiled and made humorous comments. Then a kind of appalled silence fell over them. I had told two of them when the driver informed us we were going to stop at this baptismal location about my being baptized by immersion, and they probably wondered whether I was going to repeat the entire performance right before their eyes. I did not. After a few moments of standing in the Jordan, my toes caressing the sand and pebbles and the capillary action beginning to draw the dampness up toward my pockets, I turned and sloshed out. The other bus riders breathed a sigh of relief. They welcomed me ashore almost the way the aging deaconesses had helped me out of the baptismal pool at the little Baptist church in my hometown some forty-five years ago. As we climbed back in the bus and continued north, however, the subject of the conversation changed dramatically. We talked about Jesus.

It started when the English barrister asked me what it meant for me to "follow him." As I tried to answer, while putting my socks back on, everyone chimed in. Did I really believe he was God on earth? That he had walked on water and performed all those other miracles? Why had Christians for so many centuries blamed the Jews for what had happened to Jesus? As I rolled my slacks down and put my shoes back on, the conversation grew even more serious. Several of the passengers on the bus began to tell me what they thought about Jesus of Nazareth. Their comments were frank and wide-ranging. One man confessed there was no one in history he admired more. Another said Jesus' claim to be the Messiah was either fraudulent or had been invented by the early Christians. A young woman from the United States told me she had cried after seeing a performance of *Jesus Christ Superstar* because at fifteen she had found him so attractive but that when she told her parents they had warned her that her crush was inappropriate, so she had switched to Paul Newman. The visitor from South

Africa talked at length about his admiration for the Jewish painter
Marc Chagall and described in enthusiastic detail how Chagall
had tried to reappropriate the figure of Jesus into the long history
of Jewish suffering and persecution by picturing a figure clothed in
a prayer shawl and wearing phylacteries crucified amid pogroms
and expulsions. A tourist from the United States, a cheerful elderly
gentleman with very thick glasses, seemed pleased with himself
when he remembered a phrase a rabbi had taught him many years
ago, that "Jews can appreciate the faith *of* Jesus but not the faith
about Jesus."

It went on and on. As the bus careened into the Galilean twilight, its penetrating horn rasping at cars that did not give way
quickly enough, I marveled at the candor of the conversation. Here
in the homeland of Jesus, perhaps as could happen nowhere else,
Jews and Christians (at least one Christian) were talking about
the man who has for centuries been both a bridge and a barrier
between these two communities of faith, and for some reason it
seemed more real than the discussions I had heard in advanced
theology seminars.

Refresher Course

Christians have had to struggle for many centuries with the
fact that the founder of Christianity was Jewish and remained so
throughout his entire life. They must constantly recognize that he
had no Bible except what we call the Old Testament and that, if
he were to return to planet earth today and seek a familiar house
of worship in which to pray, he would no doubt seek out a synagogue, not a church. Jews, on the other hand, have had to watch
as their holy books were incorporated, without their permission,
into the Scriptures of another tradition and as one of their prophets was elevated to divine status, which naturally makes Jews
uncomfortable. For centuries Jews were reluctant to think of Jesus
as a prophet at all. Since the Holocaust and the birth of the state
of Israel in 1948, however, the conversation between Jews and
Christians has taken a wholly new turn: the figure of Jesus, rather
than functioning as a taboo subject or an impossible obstacle, has
begun to serve as one point of meeting. Just as they have in conversations with Hindus, Buddhists, and Muslims, Christians are
discovering that, in the dialogue with Jews, the well-intentioned
advice once given by so many cautious souls — that one should

soft-pedal the person of Jesus in conversations with members of other faiths — is proving to be ill-founded.

Jesus' name is Yeshua, a late form of the Hebrew Yehoshuah, which means "Yahweh is salvation." The title "Messiah" or "Christ" that Christians attribute to Jesus was of course not originally part of his given name but a Christian confession of faith. Christians are left with the "stubborn, irreducible fact" that our faith is centered on a Jew. The shortest way to describe Christians may be that we are those gentiles who try to serve and worship the God of the Jews. But the most uncomfortable fact for Christians to absorb is that, although we need Judaism, Judaism does not need Christianity. Christian theology is in large measure a series of interpretations of the events of Jewish history. But Jewish history was unfolding for centuries before Christianity appeared, and it has no particular need to interpret the events of Christian history. The relationship between the two faiths is nonreciprocal. Still, a new phase in the long and troubled relationship between Jews and Christians now seems to have begun, and the importance of the state of Israel in the emergence of this new dialogue cannot be exaggerated.

Since 1948, for the first time since the Great Diaspora and since Constantine made Christianity the religion of the empire, Jews have had a homeland where they can express their views — even about the most sensitive subjects — without fear of repercussions from Christian prelates and princes. This was not the case during the centuries that Jews lived under Christian rulers in what was often a hostile environment, when it would have been reckless indeed to talk about Jesus from a Jewish perspective. (It should be noted, of course, that many Jews lived in Muslim and other non-Christian countries, but they had less interest in the subject.) In the last forty years, however, since the founding of Israel, Jewish writing about Jesus, once a mere trickle, has become a torrent at both the scholarly and the lay level. After centuries of avoiding Jesus (with a few very notable exceptions), Jews now feel free to talk about him and, as my companions on the bus trip through Galilee so amply demonstrated, apparently *want* to.

Before such a dialogue can proceed, however, there is much bad history to be undone, or at least to be examined, carefully and pertinently, on the part of Christians. We as Christians have perpetrated so much poor religious education that we have become the victims of our own ignorance. We need to realize, for starters, that Jesus did not reject Judaism and that Christianity began as a tiny movement *within* Jesus' own ancestral faith. We need to be reminded that our Church first came into being as a Church of Jews, that it soon included both Jews and gentiles, and that only later — and gradually — did it become a Church mainly of gentiles.

We have also been misled by bad metaphors. Christianity has frequently been referred to as the "daughter" of Judaism. The problem with this analogy is that it conceals within itself the notion that the mother, having performed her birthing function, eventually grows old and dies while the daughter lives and grows into adulthood. Consequently, it reinforces the destructive idea that Christianity somehow "supersedes" Judaism and that therefore, as even the great Arnold Toynbee once wrote, the continued existence of Judaism after the coming of Christianity is something of an anomaly.

Recently, Alan Segal, in his excellent book *Rebecca's Children: Judaism and Christianity in the Roman World*, has suggested a much more fruitful metaphor. He demonstrates persuasively that the centuries immediately following the life of Jesus mark the beginning of not one but two great religious traditions in the West, Christianity and Rabbinic Judaism. He sensibly argues that the proper figure of speech is, therefore, that of siblings, hence "Rebecca's children." Christianity and Rabbinic Judaism spring from the same parent — Ancient Judaism. They are more like Jacob and Esau who struggled with each other in the womb, who were born together, and who had to learn to live together as children of the same parent. Segal also shows that both Rabbinic Judaism and Christianity took decisive steps toward a more universalistic understanding of the faith. Thus, the rabbinic movement, which traces its roots to before the destruction of the Temple in 70 C.E., imaginatively responded to that traumatic event by making Jewish faith more "portable." Because of the work of the rabbis, Judaism was no longer bound to a particular geographic location or to ritual sacrifice in the Temple but could go anywhere, which it did. Christianity, on the other hand, also moved toward a more universal vision during the same period by abolishing the distinction between Jews and gentiles and by claiming that, through Jesus as the Christ, the Covenant had been enlarged to include those gentiles who chose to enter. Before the destruction of the Temple, Christianity had been no more than an apocalyptic sect within Judaism. Judaism had been something like a "civil religion" based in the Temple and in the land itself. From the ruins of the Temple there emerged, however, according to Segal, two sibling faiths forever linked by their common parent, but with variant understandings of the nature of that universality.

I find Segal's metaphor particularly fruitful, although I realize it will not appeal to Christian fundamentalists — like my unsought acquaintance in Jerusalem — who insist that Jews must be converted to Jesus as the Christ if they are to be saved. I doubt it will appeal to those unlikely Jewish "fundamentalists" who are wondering how to rebuild the Temple and to reinstitute animal sacrifice. Ironically, these two factions have found some common ground. There are even indications that some American Christian fundamentalists have contributed financial and other support to the Jewish religious right in Israel. The Christians do so because in their scheme of things the rebuilding of the Temple will move us one step further along the path to the Last Days, the great battle of Armageddon, and the reappearance of the Messiah. Ironically, they also believe that, when the Messiah arrives to rescue the Jewish nation, the Jews will recognize that the Messiah is Christ and will be converted. The Jewish fundamentalists, of course, do not accept this final act in the apocalyptic script, but seem willing to receive support and encouragement for the initial phases. The two constitute an odd couple indeed, but their curious mutual parasitism suggests that the new dialogue between Christians and Jews can proceed at various levels, some of which are rather ominous.

The bad history we have learned, however, does not end with the formative period of Christian and Jewish rabbinical history. It goes on. Very early in the relationship between these two "children of Rebecca," a serious feud began. Christian anti-Judaism appeared so quickly that it has even found a place in the Christian Scriptures themselves. One has only to listen to the version of the Passion narrative in the Gospel of John, for example, to sense the anti-Judaistic polemical context in which it was written. Some of the characterizations of Judaism we find in the Gospel of Matthew are also inaccurate and invidious. There was, of course, an element of Jewish anti-Christianism as well. Jews were mainly concerned, however, not with gentile Christians, but with those Jews who believed that by becoming Christians they no longer had to observe the Law. It was to apprehend these Jews — and not Christians as such — that Saul was making his trip to Damas-

cus when he encountered his vision, changed his direction, and
became the Apostle Paul.

When Christians came into imperial power, the situation became worse. Jews then had to live, not alongside another persecuted sect, but under Christian rulers who may or may not have
been friendly to the Jewish community. During the first centuries
of the Christian empire, Jews did not fare so badly. The Christian emperors closed pagan temples but not synagogues. As for
the inner life of the Jewish community itself, this was one of its
strongest and most energetic eras. The Jewish sages created the
normative Judaism that gathered up all that had gone before and
furnished the basis of all that was to follow.

Then, in the seventh century C.E., came Islam, which swept
across Africa and up through the Iberian peninsula into southern
France. It is a clear proof of how spiritually strong Judaism had become to point out that, although Christianity disappeared almost
completely from many sections of the Muslim world, Judaism continued and in some places even thrived. In fact, Jews lived more
freely and with less harassment under Islamic rule than they did
under Christian princes. During the medieval period, the picture
is not completely bleak. In some places, there was a good deal
of collaboration and mutuality. For centuries, indeed, Christians,
Jews, and Muslims lived on the Iberian peninsula cheek by jowl,
sometimes in conflict, but often with a remarkable degree of mutual respect and reciprocity. Some scholars now believe that Saint
John of the Cross may have picked up his most trenchant ideas
from Muslim mystics.

The Crusades, however, poisoned the air in an ugly way. Would-
be Christian warriors often found that it was easier to march into
a nearby Jewish village to rape and pillage than it was to make
the arduous trip to the Palestine to cast out the infidels from the
holy places. This domestic redirection of the Crusades was often fired by excited preachers who told the Crusaders that the
Christ killers should not be allowed to escape the sword any more
than the infidels should. Toward the waning of the Middle Ages,
governments began expelling Jews from the countries of Western
Europe. England expelled them in 1290 and France in 1394. In
Russia and in Eastern Europe, Jews were restricted to particular
areas and were frequently victimized by expulsions and pogroms.
The Iberian peninsula, which has since acquired a bad reputation
for religious intolerance, was an exception, at least for a time, to the

general European anti-Judaism. Eventually, however, even those Jews were forced to convert or to leave, and Muslims were defeated by the force of arms. The last Islamic citadel, Granada, fell to Ferdinand and Isabella in 1492, the same year the Spanish Jews were expelled. Spain quickly became one of the least tolerant of the Christian kingdoms.

The baleful history of Christian contempt for Jews was unfortunately not corrected at the time of the Reformation. In *The Roots of Anti-Semitism in the Age of the Renaissance and Reformation,* Heiko Oberman documents the anti-Judaism of not just Luther, whose hateful attitude is widely known, but also of the allegedly more enlightened Erasmus. Luther lumped the Jews together with the Turks and the pope as the enemies of the gospel. In one of his more hysterical writings, entitled "Concerning the Jews," he goes so far as to suggest that, since Jews had become such a peril, their synagogues should be burned and their homes destroyed. He insists that Jews should be kept as captives in a stable and that their rabbis should be strictly forbidden to teach. It is chilling to recognize that, although Luther did not succeed in implementing his anti-Jewish program, almost everything he called for was eventually made official state policy by the German National Socialist regime in the 1930s and 1940s. Historians, of course, point out that the Nazis were also anti-Christian and that they advocated a reversion to Teutonic myths. But it is undeniable that they also drew on a long tradition of Christian anti-Semitism, of which Luther's fulminations are only a small sample.

This historical Christian contribution to a process that terminated in Auschwitz makes me very reluctant to theologize about the Holocaust or to read Christian meanings into it. Almost everything any Christian has said on this subject sounds sour and wrong. As Emil Fackenheim has so poignantly reminded us, "A good Christian suggests that perhaps Auschwitz was a divine reminder of the suffering of Christ. Should he not ask instead whether his Master himself, had He been present at Auschwitz, would have resisted degradation and dehumanization? What are the sufferings of the Cross compared to those of a mother whose child is slaughtered to the sound of laughter or the strains of a Viennese waltz? The question may sound sacrilegious to Christian ears. Yet we dare not shirk it, for we — Christians as well as Jews — must ask: At Auschwitz, did the grave win the victory after all, or, worse than the grave, did the devil himself win?" When it comes to the Holocaust, perhaps the most appropriate Christian response is penitent silence and a firm resolution to prevent its recurrence.

History Takes a Turn

But to dwell entirely on the bad history of the past is to do a disservice to the remarkable changes in Jewish-Christian relations that have occurred in recent years. As my lively bus ride to the Galilee showed me, the founding of the State of Israel produced an environment in which Jews could now feel free to deal with questions they had wisely avoided in more dangerous circumstances. But other things have happened too. In 1965, the Second Vatican Council officially removed negative mentions of Jews from the liturgy (although it is hard to foresee how such negative descriptions can be deleted from the scriptural texts themselves). In the scholarly world, there have been important developments as well. In Christian theology itself, tracing the origins of Christianity not just to the Old Testament but to first-century Judaism has become a larger subject of study, especially since the uncovering of the Dead Sea Scrolls. There is also a vastly increased interest among Christians in the tradition of Rabbinic Judaism from the biblical period to the present. It must also be said, however, that the growing attention focused on this tradition has resulted largely from the efforts of (mainly Jewish) scholars of Judaism who have introduced the study of Judaica into universities and colleges all over the Western world.

One can reasonably hope that much of the ignorance that has kept Christians and Jews apart and perpetuated misunderstanding is beginning to decline. At the divinity school where I am a professor, for example, we have recently instituted a permanent and fully tenured professorship in Jewish religious thought — the Albert A. List Chair in Jewish Studies. The establishment of this chair clearly indicates that our faculty considers Judaism to be not a kind of leftover anomaly but a permanent and vigorous partner in a pluralistic religious world.

A Jesus for Jews

A parallel development has appeared among Jewish scholars as well. Jews are showing increased interest both in the New Testament period and in Jesus. Much of this interest springs from what Rabbi Alan Mittleman calls the Jews' "creative obsession with the richness of their own history." He puts it this way.

> In the writing of Jewish theologians, historians, Bible scholars and literary men and women, Jesus has been — tentatively at least — returning to his ancestral home. For 200 years, beginning with Moses Mendelssohn and his contemporaries, Jewish authors have been overturning the medieval Jewish caricature of Jesus and discovering in him a like-minded Jew. While not symmetrical with the Christian theological reappraisal of Judaism, there is a certain similarity. It is, simply, that the Jewish rediscovery of Jesus — like the Christian reappraisal of Judaism — is rooted in a new appreciation of Jewish history.... The "homecoming of Jesus," therefore, is an aspect of the modern Jew's act of historically oriented self-discovery, or of self-recovery. It is an aspect of the modern Jew's search for essence and definition.

My conversation with my fellow tourists in the little speeding bus echoed the "homecoming of Jesus" Rabbi Mittleman refers to, but it also reminded me that the recent reemergence of Jewish interest in Jesus builds on a scholarly tradition that has been developing for a long time.

The question about Jesus Jewish thinkers have pondered can be put very simply. Can Jesus have either a moral or even a religious significance for Jews? It has long been recognized that, for Jews, the prophet from Nazareth can have a *cultural* meaning, but the question I have mentioned places the issue of Jesus' significance for Jews at a much deeper level. It is an old discussion. Max Nordau, a collaborator with Theodore Herzl in founding the modern Zionist movement, wrote at the beginning of the century, "Jesus is the soul of our soul as he is the flesh of our·flesh. Who then would want to exclude him from the Jewish people?" The question, however, is not the exclusion of Jesus from the Jewish people. It is whether as a part of that people Jesus can be seen to have a positive rather than a negative religious significance. Schalom ben-Chorin answers the question as follows: "Jesus is a central figure in history and in the history of Jewish faith. He is a part not only of our past and present but also of our future, no less than are the prophets of the Hebrew Bible, whom we can also see not just in the light of the past."

The reader of this telling sentence is intrigued but also left wondering just what part Jesus is to play. Ben-Chorin opens the door for conversation but also sets one of the limits of the Jewish appreciation for the religious significance of Jesus: "I feel," he says, "his brotherly hand which grasps mine so I can follow him . . . but it is *not* the hand of the Messiah. This hand marked with scars. It is not a *divine* but a *human* hand in the lines of which is engraved the most profound suffering." Then ben-Chorin, pouring a lot into a few words, goes on to make the statement (which perhaps my fellow tourist's rabbi had once read) that "The faith *of* Jesus'" (emphasizing "of ") "unites us but faith *in* Jesus divides us."

In the conversation on the bus, I pointed out to the smiling gentleman with the thick glasses that some present-day Christian theologians, especially in Latin America, believe precisely that it is the faith *of* Jesus that is central. Jon Sobrino, for example, in his *Christology at the Crossroads*, argues that neither Jesus nor God but Jesus' own faith in the coming of the Reign of God should be the focus of Christian faith. We have faith *in* Jesus because he is the enactor and announcer of the coming of the Reign of God.

On the question of the significance of Jesus for his own people, it seems inappropriate for an outsider to say very much. It is a topic that Jews themselves must be left to deal with if and when they choose to. However, as one of those "outsiders" to whom Jesus also addressed his message, I have never found anyone who has written with quite the eloquence of Martin Buber. Buber, considering what the man from Nazareth might mean to his own kinsmen, affirms the spiritual significance of Jesus while at the same time insisting that Jews will always have their own way of understanding what this significance is. In a famous letter to Franz Werfel that he wrote in 1917, Buber responded to Werfel's inquiry about his view of Jesus by emphasizing the centrality of the human response to God rather than God's initiative. The letter is worth quoting at length:

> It is not I who wait for God, but God who waits for me. God waits so that He can say to you, to me, to every single person what according to the report in the Hebrew Gospel the Spirit said to Jesus when he raised him in baptism to sonship: My son I have awaited you in all the prophets, that you should come and that I should find peace in you. You are indeed my peace.
>
> No, dear friend, nothing is imposed on us by God, everything is expected. And you rightly say, it is up to us whether we want to live the true life in order to perfect it in our uniqueness. But according to the Christian teaching which has perverted the meaning and ground

of Jesus, it is not up to us but depends on whether we are chosen. But our teaching is: what counts is not whether God has chosen me but that I choose God. For it is really not God's affair to choose or reject. In so far as it refers the person to grace, that teaching, which calls itself Christian, hinders him from decision, the *metanoia* proclaimed by Jesus . . . therefore I shall fight for Jesus and against Christianity.

A few lines later, Buber continues with a description of the Reign of God that is similar to the one we find in liberation theology:

What Jesus calls the Kingdom — no matter how tinged with a sense of the world's end and of miraculous transformation it may be — is no other-world consolation, no vague heavenly bliss. Nor is it an ecclesiastical or cultic association, a church. It is the perfect life of man with man, true community, and as such God's immediate realm, God's basilea, God's earthly kingdom.

This remarkable reaching out by Jews toward the man whose name has for so many years been used as the pretense for their oppression obviously involves some enormous dangers. Christians must exercise great caution in responding to it. As Karl Plank has written (in *Night and White Crucifixion*) of the art of Marc Chagall, "To depict the Jew on the cross after the war was to confront a stronger taboo, for to do so required the victim to draw from the oppressor's cultural tradition. And the potential for being misunderstood would be enormous: by fellow victims who would perceive apostasy and betrayal instead of solidarity, by oppressors who would hear forgiving consolation instead of indictment." The new Jewish interest requires at least as energetic an effort on the part of Christians to redefine our understanding of Jews in such a way that they are no longer made the objects of the teaching of contempt or seen as historical curios from a previous period in history.

Engraftment

It has been rightly suggested that one route to this redefinition must begin with Saint Paul's passage in the eleventh chapter of Romans about the relations between Christians and Jews. A careful reading of that famous text makes it clear that, for Paul, the Covenant God made with Israel continues in force just as it did with Noah, Abraham, and Moses. Paul speaks plainly. He compares the gentiles to a "wild olive shoot which is grafted onto the tree, the olive tree of Israel." He goes on to point out that we who are so grafted should not boast since God is fully capable of choosing other shoots. Paul insists the gifts and the call of God are entirely irrevocable. The gospel of Jesus does not supersede God's call to the people of Israel or negate the Covenant made with them. It has the purpose of calling the gentiles so that they too may share in God's blessings.

A careful study of this central passage can teach us a number of things about the dialogue between Jews and Christians. First, the God about whom Paul is speaking is not some general God of the religious consciousness or of a vague monotheism. This God is the God of Abraham and Sarah, the God of the Covenant. Therefore, for Paul the question is *not* one of the relation between Jews and Christians at all. Rather, it is that of the relation between Israel (for the Jews continue to be God's people), on the one hand, and "the nations," on the other hand. Paul does not even use the word "Christian" in this discussion, although he undoubtedly knew the term, which was already in circulation at the time. It helps us today to understand the so-called Christian-Jewish dialogue to see that, for Paul, it had nothing to do with a conversation between two religious traditions but with the question of how all the other peoples of the earth were to enter the one Covenant of the one God.

Paul's experience on the road to Damascus was not a "conversion," and must not be understood as his "becoming a Christian." Paul did not become a member of another religious community. Rather, what came to him in that blinding light was a new conviction about the way he should fulfill his vocation as a Hebrew. He was not converted but "called" to a prophetic vocation both to his own people and to the gentiles. His vocation, he believed, was to proclaim the good news of the expansion of the Covenant both to those who were already inside (the Jews) and to those who had previously been outside (the rest of us). Paul's view of gentiles and Jews appears most graphically in the second chapter of the Epistle to the Ephesians, which, although some scholars believe it was not written by Paul himself, certainly expresses his perspective on this issue. The text reads, "Remember that at one time you gentiles in the flesh were . . . separated from Christ, alienated from the commonwealth of Israel, and strangers to the covenants of promise having no hope and without God in the world." "But now," the writer continues, "in Christ Jesus you who once were far off have been brought near."

For Paul, who calls himself a "Hebrew of the Hebrews," Jesus signifies that the God who created the world, who called Sarah and Abraham, who gave humankind the Law at Sinai, and who spoke through the prophets had now taken another decisive step. This time, the same God was inviting the gentiles into the Covenant, thus reconciling alienated peoples to each other. Again, it is important to emphasize that the people who are reconciled are not Christians and Jews but Israel and the nations.

In the light of this historic text about dialogue, Paul's often misunderstood criticisms of the Jews in the Epistle to the Romans must be read with great care. They are not the reproofs of an outsider who has now left his religious community to become the member of another one. They are rather the words of an insider who — like the earlier prophets — chides his fellow Jews *because* he is an insider. Paul speaks here like Isaiah and Amos and Jeremiah. He continues the tradition of the prophets who lovingly taught their own people. This is quite different from sniping at them from a position outside that community of faith.

Empowerment

As we neared the hotel where we were to spend our evening together, my fellow passengers on the little bus began to ask each other some very practical questions. What would it mean, they fantasized, if Christians and Jews could put away the suspicion and animosity that has distorted our relations over the centuries? The tourist from South Africa, who was very sympathetic to the efforts of the black freedom struggle, put it as well as anyone. If in fact, he said, both Jews and Christians are trying to do the will of the same God, then we should be trying to increase the realm of freedom, because God has always favored the poor and insisted that how we treat the stranger in our midst is the real test. I told him I saw nothing to disagree with in this statement. But no sooner had those words left my lips than the bus suddenly slowed to a crawl and — as if to underline what my friend had just said about the strangers in our midst — we found ourselves grinding slowly through a gang of workers who were repairing the road. Suddenly all the conversations stopped. Everyone looked out at this crowd of laughing, perspiring men, whom we all knew were Palestini-

ans. They stopped and stared back. No one — inside or outside —
waved or smiled. For two, maybe three minutes, the bus inched
along. Then it stopped while one of the workers directed two cars
coming from the opposite direction to drive through. The silence
in the bus continued. After a moment the man signaled to our
driver, who steered us slowly back onto the hard surface, slipped
into second and then high gear, and took off for our evening's
destination.

We had never been in danger. But even after the bus was clip-
ping along at fifty miles an hour again, for some reason no one
talked. Why? I wondered. Was it embarrassment? Awkwardness?
Or was it perhaps that we all shared an unspoken recognition
that the question of who is the stranger in whose land is not
at all clear when one is driving through what some Israelis call
the "occupied territories" and others refer to as "Greater Israel"?
Nothing is ever simple in the Middle East, but, as the decades-
long Israeli-Palestinian struggle has worsened in recent years,
what was already complex has now become downright convo-
luted. Do Christians have any right whatever, or any obligation,
to play a role?

Johann Baptist Metz, the German Catholic theologian, once
wrote an eloquent essay about the complicity of Christians in
the Jewish Holocaust. In the course of that article he said, "We
Christians can never go back behind Auschwitz: to go beyond
Auschwitz, if we see clearly, is impossible for us by ourselves. It is
possible only together with the victims of Auschwitz." This strikes
me as a wise and helpful comment. But like many such comments
it raises almost as many questions as it answers. What does it mean
for Christians and Jews to journey together when the strife within
Israel threatens not only the lives of those immediately involved
in it but has become the tinderbox of a conflagration that could
escalate into a much wider war?

One current Jewish writer, Marc Ellis, has responded to Metz
by paraphrasing him in these words: "We Jews can never go back
behind empowerment: to go beyond empowerment, if we see
clearly, is impossible for us by ourselves. It is possible only with
the victims of our empowerment." This is also an astute observa-
tion, but it still does not answer the question of *what* Christians
can or should do in light of the deteriorating situation in Israel.

When the conversation on the minibus finally started again it
was subdued and sporadic. And it was about something else: cam-

eras and film and how good it would feel to get to the inn. It was not about Palestinians or Israelis or Jews or Christians or Jesus. I sat quietly and gazed out the window at the twilight. It was not going to be easy, I realized, this journey of dialogue some Christians and some Jews have embarked on together. The fact that among the Christians most needed in the dialogue are the Palestinian ones makes it even harder, but even more urgent. The pain and anger and guilt that lurk along the way will tempt us at every step to allow the dialogue to deteriorate into something nicely "religious," a theological or historical conversation that steers away from potentially divisive issues. It could become a dialogue of the devout, so rarefied it doesn't ruffle anyone. It could melt away into yet another version of that endless "spiritual quest" that lures so many seekers so far into the elysium that they forget the nettlesome issues with which people of faith have to wrestle on *terra firma*. Yet it seemed clearer than ever to me during that instructive bus ride that a genuine Jewish-Christian dialogue cannot take place in a sealed vehicle while the others stare in the windows. It must be pursued in the ordinary rough-and-tumble world of suffering, hope, disappointment, and perseverance, not as the attempt to achieve unforgettable peak experiences or mystical rapture. Indeed, although Christians can drift easily into this kind of ecstatic euphoria, it is precisely our bond with the Jewish people that constantly brings us back to where God really is in the world, and that keeps us from soaring too high into the ether.

The Gift of Torah

Christians certainly need Jews. Without them in our past, we would have had no Bible, no Jesus, no knowledge of God. Without them in our present, we cannot understand God, the world, or ourselves. But we Christians must also recognize that although Jews are central to our faith, we are not central to theirs. As Christians we *must* talk about Jesus, and, as my fellow passengers on the tourist bus taught me, Jews are willing to talk about him too. But what divides Christians from Jews is not that we have different views of Jesus (which of course we do). What divides us is that Jews have something we do not. They have Torah. They have God's gift of both a written revelation in Scripture (which we can share up to a point) and an equally authoritative oral tradition codified by the rabbis into the Mishnah and the Talmud, which we do not have and never can. When the Temple was razed in 70 C.E., Christians came to believe that Jesus the Christ had taken its place. Jews believed its place was assumed by Torah, a living and breathing ongoing revelation. Jacob Neusner puts it this way:

> The symbol of Torah is multidimensional. It includes the striking detail that whatever the most recent rabbi is destined to discover through proper exegesis of the tradition is as much a part of the Torah revealed to Moses as is a sentence of Scripture itself. It is therefore possible to participate even in the giving of the law by appropriate, logical inquiry into the law. God himself, studying and living by Torah, is believed to subject himself to the same rules of logical inquiry. When an earthly court overruled the testimony, delivered through miracles, of the heavenly one, God rejoiced, crying out, "My sons have conquered me!" — so the sages believed. In a word, before us is a mythicoreligious system in which earth and heaven correspond to one another, with Torah — in place of Temple — the model of both.

The Gift of Otherness

A fundamental ground rule for any dialogue between Christians and Jews must be this: there can never be a question of Christians attempting to convert Jews to Christianity. The whole idea is a contradiction in terms. It is those of us who are called Christians who are, we believe, "adopted" into the Covenant God made with the Jews, not the other way around. We are the latecomers, the wild twig that is grafted onto the existing tree. When I told one of my fellow bus passengers that the New Testament scholar Krister Stendahl once called Christians "honorary Jews," he laughed. He said that he was fond of collecting the religious sentiments expressed on bumper stickers and that one he frequently sees is "I found it" (usually with an exclamation mark) on bumper stickers of enthusiastic Christians. He said that a Unitarian neighbor of his sports a sticker that adamantly insists, "I am still looking." Then he added that he had once thought of pasting a sticker on his own bumper that would read, "We never lost it."

I told him his theology deserved an A+ . It is we gentile Christians who, according to the Apostle Paul, were once the lost and wandering ones "outside the Covenant of Israel." It is we who have been "converted" and have entered as newcomers. I also reminded my friend that, although the other bumper stickers he mentioned started with "I," it was significant that his be-gan with "we." This says something important to us about the faith of Israel: it is not the faith of individuals but the faith of a people.

Christians are slowly learning to welcome "otherness," reli-gious, cultural, and otherwise, not as an inconvenience we must somehow put up with but as a gift of God, a reminder of our human finitude and of the unsearchable richness of the Holy One. However, it seems increasingly clear to me that, as urgent as con-versations with Buddhists or Hindus may be, we must come to terms first with those "others" who have lived in our very midst from the beginning. Dialogue is important wherever it occurs, but at times it seems that working so hard on conversations with other religious traditions while ignoring the otherness that is closest to us can be a kind of escape. Those who remain God's original cho-sen people continue to live as our neighbors and friends and even as our husbands and wives. In the past, Christians have dealt with this closeness in all the worst ways. Perhaps God is giving us another chance.

Beyond Otherness

We can neither deny nor minimize the differences between Christians and Jews. Jews do not accept the pivotal Christian claim that in Jesus the Covenant people has been enlarged to include Christians. This difference is not trivial and should not be over-looked. Nonetheless, recalcitrantly, stubbornly, and slowly, we Christians are coming to recognize that our former ways of relat-ing to Jews — conversion, expulsion, destruction — were always terribly wrong. Can we believe that now, after nearly two millen-nia of doing it badly, Christians are learning that the two children of Rebecca can live as siblings?

When I think of this question, I am enormously encouraged by the statement on Judaism recently adopted by the United Church of Christ. It is an eloquent affirmation of the continuing validity of God's Covenant with the Jewish people and a reminder of the deeds for which we as Christians hope to be forgiven. The text runs as follows:

> We in the United Church of Christ acknowledge that the Christian
> Church has, throughout much of its history, denied God's contin-
> uing covenantal relationship with the Jewish people expressed in
> the faith of Judaism. This denial has often led to outright rejection
> of the Jewish people and to theologically and humanly intolerable
> violence.
>
> Faced with this history from which we as Christians cannot,
> and must not, disassociate ourselves, we ask for God's forgiveness
> through our Lord Jesus Christ. We pray for divine grace that will
> enable us, more firmly than ever before, to turn from this path of
> rejection and persecution to affirm that Judaism has not been super-
> seded by Christianity; that Christianity is not to be understood as the
> successor religion to Judaism; God's covenant with the Jewish peo-
> ple has not been abrogated. God has not rejected the Jewish people;
> God is faithful in keeping covenant.

This says a lot. But it says it in words. And Jews have heard eloquent words on the subject before.

When our bus reached the hotel, most of the passengers raced
for the showers, but Alex, the English lawyer, and I went into the
bar for a cool drink. Apparently with the others out of earshot, he
now felt free to voice some misgivings. It was certainly fine that I
felt the way I did, he said, but was there any real hope that most
Christians would begin to change their attitude toward Jews? Or
was this dialogue business really just one more new strategy in
the old game, a slicker soft-sell gimmick to nudge Jews closer to
the baptismal font?

At first, I was a little hurt by his remark. But then I thought
about my eschatology teacher in the sunglasses, with his crazed
vision of cosmic battles and the mass conversion of Jews, and I
shook my head. My fellow tourist waited, but I knew I had little
basis on which to reassure him. It has been a long, sad story. One
of the first documents Christian theology students study comes
from the second century C.E.. It is by Justin Martyr and is called
A Dialogue with the Jew Trypho. But it is not a dialogue. It is a
trick polemic in which the Christian Justin tries to prove Trypho
wrong and to demonstrate that Christ had superseded Judaism.
That pseudo-dialogue, which began so early, has lasted too long.
Alex knew, and I know, that, since this phoniness has been perpetrated mainly by Christians, Christians will have to do most of
the work in restoring credibility to what is beyond any doubt the
most important dialogue of all.

II. Jesus and Dialogue

The Dialogue Dilemma

Has the great dialogue among the world religions stalled, the dialogue that so many of us welcomed so warmly and so recently? Why has the "wider ecumenism," which had offered hope of crossing not only denominational lines but faith lines as well, begun to sputter and stammer and, in many instances, simply to stop? Why have relations among the ancient spiritual traditions of the human family, which many of us believed were improving a few years back, turned rancorous and even violent as new outbreaks of separatism, xenophobia, and hostility erupt?

To make matters worse, these same faith communities are increasingly divided within themselves, and the rifts are often exacerbated by political tensions. Sunni and Shiite Muslims declare each other to be worse than infidels. Jews, both pious and secular, who want to find some way to live at peace with Palestinians, despair over the zealotry of the Gush Enumin, who believe God has given their people land on which Palestinians have dwelt for generations. Christians who work for interfaith understanding have been shocked and perplexed by the attacks of fundamentalists who condemn them as traitors to the gospel but who themselves seem willing to cooperate with "those heathen" if their politics are acceptable. Indeed, people in any religious tradition who are committed to dialogue often find themselves upbraided as turncoats by their own brothers and sisters.

The Horns of the Dilemma

Admittedly, the picture is not unrelievedly gloomy. Here and there, small circles of Muslims and Jews, Hindus and Sikhs, Buddhists and Christians, continue to meet and talk and even to work together, but they do so despite the currents that seem to be flowing against them. What has gone wrong?

I believe that the most nettlesome dilemma hindering interreligious dialogue is the very ancient one of how to balance the universal and the particular. Every world faith has both. Each nourishes in rite and saga its own unique and highly particular vision. Maybe it is the message of the one true God delivered without blemish to the Prophet. Or it is the fathomless Brahman from which all that is and all that is not come and return. Or the faithful Son of God dying on the cross. Or the supreme moment when enlightenment comes to the patient figure seated under the Bo tree. Or the bestowal of the life-giving gift of Torah on a chosen people. Whatever it is, the particular hub defines the center around which each world faith rotates, endowing it season after season and century after century with its characteristic ethos.

At the same time every world faith, if it is truly a world faith and not a local cultus, also generates a universal vision. Brahman embraces all ages, each drop of water, and every savior. The Koran names a God who created all people equal and who decrees that a unified human family should mirror his sublime unity. The crucified Christ is raised to life by a God who favors the outcasts and the heartbroken and who summons all tribes and tongues into an inclusive community of service and praise. The bodhisattva compassionately refuses to enter nirvana until every sentient being can enter with him.

Thus each world faith has both its axis and its spokes, its sharply etched focus and its ambient circumference. Further, it is the mark of a truly world faith that these two dimensions are not only held together: they strengthen and reinforce each other. Somewhere, somehow, all that now seems fragmented and contradictory, all that appears tragic or inexplicable, is gathered into a single mystery of meaning and value.

The crisis in the current state of interfaith dialogue can be stated simply: the universal and the particular poles have come unhinged. Faced with a world in which some form of encounter with other faiths can no longer be avoided, the ancient religious traditions are breaking into increasingly bitter wings. Those who glimpse the universal dimension advocate dialogue and mutuality. They search out what is common and that which unites. Those who emphasize the particular often shun dialogue and excoriate their fellow believers who engage in it more fiercely than they condemn outsiders. This ugly chasm, running through all religions, gives rise to a "worst-possible" scenario one might envision if the current trend persists. Imagine a time when tiny cadres of "dialoguers" would perch on the fringe of each faith community, endlessly refining the language and concepts in which they converse with those on the universalist wings of the other faiths. Meanwhile, on the opposite side of each religion, zealous cohorts of radical particularists would congregate, anathematizing their

backsliding co-religionists for compromising the truth by frater-
nizing with the reprobate. It is not an attractive prospect.

But we need both poles. I count myself as one of the universalists. Yet sometimes as I have sat in genteel — or even mildly acri-
monious — gatherings of urbane representatives of different faith
traditions, under the auspices of the World Council of Churches or
the Center for the Study of World Religions at Harvard, my mind
has strayed from the conference room out to those jagged corners
of the world where other confessors of these same faiths are killing
or proselytizing — or just frigidly ignoring — each other. I have
wondered at such moments whether the "dialogue" has not become a tedious exercise in preaching to the converted and I have
secretly wished to bring some of those enthusiasts in. Deprived
of the energy such particularists embody, a dialogue-among-the-
urbane can, and sometimes does, deteriorate into a repetitious
exchange of vacuities. It could end with a whimper.

At the same time I fully believe that without the large-hearted
vision of the universal that the interfaith conversation incarnates,
particularism can deteriorate into fanaticism. And in our present
overarmed world, zealotry can easily hasten the moment when
everything ends with a bang. So we are left with a paradox. Without the universal pole, there would be no dialogue at all. But
without the particular, the dialogue dissipates its source of primal
energy. Without the Cross or the Koran or the Bo tree, the religions
that were called into being by these sacred realities would atrophy
and, along with them, the inclusive visions they spawned would
fade away too. The paradox of the great world faiths is that they
both create a dream of a single human family and threaten that
dream at the same time. What can be done?

Closing the Gap

It seems too formulaic simply to say that the universalists and
the particularists need each other, especially since they seldom
think they do. Still, I believe they do, and as one who has participated in the dialogue for decades, I have drawn, in this essay,
on my own experience to show how the indispensable element of
particularity can be brought back in. Doing so, however, requires
me to point out the two most salient ways in which Christians
who engage in the dialogue have — often quite inadvertently —
neglected the hub in their commendable effort to enlarge the rim.

The Personal Voice

The first way the particular is diminished in interfaith dialogue is through the loss of the personal voice. Dialogue often climbs quickly to airy exchanges about "Christianity" and "Buddhism" or one of the other faiths. The dialoguers, who are frequently trained to think in abstract, conceptual terms, are sometimes reluctant to say much about "my" faith in Jesus Christ, or "my" devotion to Krishna, or "my" path toward enlightenment. Even the language of "our" faith or "our" path is often left behind as the talk soars into that realm of discourse (invaluable for its own purposes) one finds in an academic seminar on comparative religion. Soon people are yawning and glancing at their watches.

I believe a certain careful and modest restoration of personal narrative — call it "testimony" if you will — can help restore some of the life-giving particularity to the dialogue among religions. After all, it is never the religions themselves that converse but individual people who embody those religions. I have seen more than one interfaith colloquium that was drifting toward death by tedium restored to life when someone had the courage to speak personally rather than in general terms. For this reason, the essays in my book *Many Mansions*, from which the present essay is excerpted, grow almost entirely from my own encounters with actual people of other faiths — enriched and broadened, of course, by reading and reflection. They are unified by the lived experience of one person and thus represent not "the" Christian dialogue with other religions but rather one Christian's encounters with particular people of other faiths.

The Jesus Factor in Interfaith Dialogue

The second way Christian participation in the dialogue has sometimes lost sight of the particularity pole has been by soft-pedaling the figure of Jesus himself. There are many exceptions to this *sotto voce* treatment of Christ. Still, I have noticed — as will become evident later on — that when reference to Jesus is postponed or downplayed, conversations between Christians and people of other traditions tend to become arid, but when the figure of Jesus is brought to the fore, either by the Christians or — as sometimes happens — by the others, the dialogue comes alive.

One can of course understand why Christians who believe

in the dialogue do not want to push Jesus down other people's throats as soon as the opening gavel has been rapped. After all, Jesus is in some ways the *most* particularistic element of Christianity, and in an interreligious dialogue one is presumably trying — at least at first — to present the less divisive aspects of one's own tradition. The trouble is that, not only has this understandable reticence deprived the dialogue of the vigor it needs to survive, but it has also produced another unfortunate consequence. This secondary result is that Christians who think of Jesus as a model in other areas of their lives do not look to his example or teaching for direction in the dialogue itself. I think this twofold neglect of the figure of Jesus — both as a theme and as a source of guidance — has exacted a heavy toll.

I do not mean to suggest that those Christians who even now are working with great dedication in talks with Buddhists or Muslims or Jews never mention Christology (that branch of Christian theology that deals with the meaning of Jesus Christ). They do. Often they seek to find some bridge to the other faiths through a "cosmic Christ" such as the one portrayed in the Epistle to the Ephesians, a Christ who is said to be present throughout the universe and therefore presumably can be also found in the lived worlds of Hindus and Muslims. More frequently, however, the Christian participants have tried to base the dialogue on completely different facets of religious tradition. Sometimes, for example, they turn to the idea of God the Creator, the Mystery out of whom all that is emerges. At other times, they focus on the Divine Spirit, present in every person or even in every sentient being. In recent decades, they have preferred to explore the experience of faith itself as a universal human experience that exhibits common stages of development through the succeeding phases of human life. Most recently, they have sought to wrestle, together with people of other faiths, with the awful issues everyone must confront today — nuclear war, hunger, disease, the despoiling of the ecosphere — and to reach into the various traditions as possible sources of values and visions for facing such horrors. These paths to interfaith encounter differ markedly, but they all have one thing in common: they keep the historical Jesus of the gospels distinctly in the background.

Each of these approaches to the crafting of an adequate Christian grasp of the multiplicity of faiths has its value. Each has advanced the dialogue in some measure. We need to continue to try to work with all of them. Still, I confess that I find these approaches, all of which hold the Jesus-fact in abeyance, not wholly satisfactory. The problem with them is twofold. First, for the vast majority of Christians, including those most energetically engaged in dialogue, Jesus is not merely a background figure. He is central to Christian faith. Not only do the Christian dialoguers recognize this, but so do their Muslim, Buddhist, Shinto, Hindu, and Jewish conversation partners. Wherever one starts, whether with creation (which, incidentally, is not a particularly good place to begin a dialogue with Buddhists, who reject the whole notion), with the omnipresent enlivening Spirit, with the faith experience as such, or with something else, any honest dialogue between Christians and others will sooner or later — and in my experience it is usually sooner — have to deal with the figure of Jesus.

Yes, some might say, but is it not better to delay so potentially divisive a topic until some more inclusive groundwork has been laid? This may be the case in some instances, but I have never been persuaded that an interfaith dialogue is enhanced by designing it like one of those elementary collections for teaching the piano that begins with "Frère Jacques" and works up to Chopin preludes at the end. Everyone always knows that the question of who Jesus was and is, and what he means today, will inevitably appear. Until it does, it sometimes feels as though one is — at least to some degree — engaging in the necessary pleasantries that often precede a genuine conversation but are really not integral to it. When will the other shoe drop?

The second part of my problem with dialogue tactics that play down the Jesus factor is that — surprisingly — it is just this factor that the non-Christian participants often seem most interested in and most eager to get to. This is not something one is led to expect will happen in interfaith dialogue. But it does. Indeed, it happens so often that it raises serious questions about the other approaches, at least insofar as they try to proceed — ever so carefully and judiciously, they suppose — without this central point up front.

It took me a lot of time and many false starts to learn this. I too wanted to minimize the possibility of giving needless offense to the people of other faiths who had taken the venturesome step of entering into dialogue with me: to steer clear of unnecessary roadblocks or any suggestion of proselytizing. But I kept discovering that my tactics for nurturing the tender shoot of interfaith exchange did not connect with those of my partners across the

table. I too tried to avoid talking about Jesus too quickly, but I
soon discovered my interlocutors wanted me to, and their bearing sometimes suggested that they did not believe they were really
engaged in a brass-tacks conversation with a Christian until that
happened. Of course in this respect they were right.

The "others" want to hear what Christians think about Jesus.
When Chogyam Trungpa, a Tibetan lama, invited me to teach
summer school at the Naropa Institute in Boulder, Colorado, the
first Buddhist higher educational institution in the United States,
I accepted. I then suggested several alternative topics for my lectures and seminars, all leaning toward a comparative approach to
religion. Trungpa and his fellow Buddhists were not interested.
Instead, the course they encouraged me to offer was "The Life
and Teachings of Jesus." A few years later, when I had my first
serious conversation with a Muslim, he immediately wanted to
compare Jesus with the prophet Muhammad. Shortly afterward,
when I was asked to address a gathering of Vaishnava Hindu
scholars during a trip to India, I carefully chose a safe "universal" topic — I think it was something like "the role of religion in
the modern world." The Indian teachers sat patiently through my
presentation and the long translation that followed. But, when
the discussion period came, the first question they asked me was
what I believed about Jesus and the form of love he exhibited
(*agapē*). Soon we were all talking about Jesus, and then about
the love Krishna shows to a devotee and the devotee to Krishna.
My efforts at theological prudence, going slow, avoiding possibly
thorny issues — although I certainly meant well — had merely
succeeded in delaying the real exchange for two hours. I came
away convinced that, whatever might be said for the other modes
of dialogue, in my own future opportunities I would not assume
that my partners wanted me to hold the Jesus factor in abeyance.
More recently, other Christians who have engaged in difficult but
real dialogue have come to the same conclusion. The only person
I know who has ever met the Ayatollah Khomeini told me that
the first thing Khomeini wanted to talk about was Jesus.

Of course, merely suggesting that Jesus be made more central
to the dialogue does not solve anything at all. The questions of
what role Jesus plays and *how* he is introduced still persist. This
is why I have always been so intrigued by the "many mansions"
Jesus speaks of in John 14:2 ("In my father's house are many mansions") as well as by John 14:6: "I am the way, the truth, and the

life: no man cometh unto the Father, but by me." These verses stand only a few lines away from each other in the same chapter of the same gospel. But they have traditionally supplied both the dialogic universalists and the antidialogic particularists with their favorite proof texts. Those who look with appreciation on other faiths frequently cite John 14:2 and suggest that the "many mansions" may refer to the heavenly places in which Hindus and Buddhists will dwell — alongside Christians — in the hereafter. Those who insist that all others must accept Christ or be damned, however, prefer to cite John 14:6 and declare that Jesus alone is the one true way to salvation. What can we say about this curious juxtaposition of seemingly contradictory texts? Could it be telling us about the need to hold the universal and the particular together and about the central place Jesus must have for Christians even in the most expansive interfaith dialogue? The thoughts and experiences recounted in this essay document my continuing struggle with these questions. I present them, not as a formula for all future dialogue, but as an addition and a complement to approaches I have found only partially satisfying. Thus my first point has been that, placing the figure of Jesus on the agenda of interfaith dialogue, far from killing it, actually enlivens it. My second point is related but different. It is that Jesus does have something vital to teach us about how to participate in interfaith dialogue. At first this may sound quite improbable. So far as we know, the rabbi from Nazareth never met a Buddhist or a Hindu. Islam did not appear until 600 years after his crucifixion. Despite speculations that regularly appear about his "hidden years," probably Jesus' interreligious experience was confined to the different sects and movements within the Judaism of his day and to the people, mainly Romans, whom even he called "heathens." At first glance, it hardly seems we can learn much from him on this subject.

Jesus also had no direct experience with many of the other vast questions we deal with today: runaway technology, genocidal weapons, AIDS, and the ethical issues involved in corporate takeovers, disinvestment, advertising, and insider trading. He never had to cope with the temptations that arise in filling out an expense account or an IRS form. But this misses the point. To be a disciple of Jesus does not mean to emulate or mimic him. It means to follow his "way," to live in our era the same way he lived in his — as a sign and servant of the Reign of God. To "follow" Jesus does not require us to choose twelve apostles or to turn water into wine but to take his life project — making the coming of God's Reign of Shalom real and immediate — as our own. I believe that friendship among the peoples of the world faiths and the nurturing of a sense of "species consciousness" is an indispensable facet of the coming of God's Shalom. I also believe there are at least four ways in which the Jesus of the gospels, he who "came preaching the Reign of God," provides useful guidelines for building such an interfaith consciousness.

How Jesus Helps

The first is that a focus on Jesus moves the encounter from the theoretical level to the practical one. The Reign of God is not an abstract ideal. It is a reality actualizing itself in history. Consequently, as soon as this Kingdom becomes the focus, we see that religions do not exist apart from their local manifestations. Further, these concrete expressions of a tradition vary markedly from place to place. Except in the minds of textbook writers, there is no such thing as Buddhism or Hinduism, or Christianity for that matter. There are only *persons* who think of themselves as Buddhists, Hindus, or Christians. Comparing classical religious texts can be misleading unless one understands what these texts mean to the actual people who chant them, study them, and try to live by them. And these meanings change from time to time and from place to place. Genuine interreligious dialogue occurs only when we recognize how a tradition actually shapes people's lives. Those who ignore this insight soon find themselves touring a never-never-land of "religions" that do not exist except in comparative religion monographs. To follow Jesus means to deal with specifics, not generalities.

Such a down-to-earth approach to interreligious conversation is anything but easy. It makes what was already an arduous undertaking even more difficult. Christians committed to dialogue with the people who live according to other faiths can no longer be content with the "library" versions of those traditions. Nor will it help to complain that the actual Buddhist or Islamic movements we meet today are not the real thing but decadent or "politicized" corruptions (as though "pure" editions existed once upon a time). The example of Jesus' own life demonstrates that any dialogue must take place with actual people. A so-called interreligious dialogue with the Platonic ideals of what this or that religious tradition ought to be in its pure essence leads nowhere.

The second way the Jesus of the gospels facilitates interfaith dialogue is by reminding us that religion is always a mixed blessing. Jesus, after all, was fiercely opposed by many (not all) of the religious people of his day. His attacks on the misuse of religion remind us that, wherever religion exists, we can be sure that someone is trying to use the gods to dominate, frighten, or oppress someone else. Indeed, any honest attempt at interfaith dialogue must deal with the fact that our century has not only spawned hundreds of new religious movements but that some of those movements are destructive and some of the most demonic claim to be expressions of Christianity.

What are the limits of tolerance? Were the Christians of Japan being intolerant when they opposed the state Shinto that the military used during World War II to lead their nation to ruin? Was Bonhoeffer being narrow-minded when he refused to be cozily ecumenical with the *Deutsche Christen* who supported the Nazi effort to synthesize Christianity with the spirit of the German *Volk*? Should no one raise questions about human sacrifice, or consigning widows to their husbands' funeral pyre, or collecting Rolls Royces in the name of Christ? The more we think about it, the more obvious it becomes that a benign tolerance, which sees anything religious as good, will simply not do.

Intimidated by this need to "grade" religious practices, some gentle souls suggest that maybe we should simply declare a kind of moratorium both on proselytizing and on interreligious discussion. Why not just live and let live? The idea is not without its attractions.

But it is impossible. People travel today at the speed of sound, and ideas travel at the speed of light. It is idle to hope that various cultures and religions could simply leave each other alone. There will always be interaction. Some kind of encounter, even dialogue, is unavoidable. The hard question is how to enter into a genuinely open encounter without losing sight of the need to make judgments and, at times, even to take sides.

This is where the example of Jesus is most pertinent. Jesus was not a model of vacuous tolerance. He did make judgments about the faith of the people he met. In fact, he did so all the time. He argued with the Pharisees and excoriated the rulers of the Temple. But the key to Jesus' approach to any religious perspective was, "By their fruits shall ye know them." He seemed singularly uninterested in the doctrinal content or ritual correctness of the different religions he encountered. He was, however, terribly concerned about the practical outcome of people's spiritual commitments. He once told a pagan Roman he had not found such a faith as his anywhere in Israel.

Third, Jesus' example also reminds us that the search for human oneness-in-diversity in interreligious dialogue is not *only* a matter of making judgments. It also sometimes requires refraining from judgment. This has its rewarding and even its lighter side. When I was living among Tibetan Buddhists, for example, it took me some time to appreciate the frolicsome way they approach even the deepest tenets of their faith. They sometimes called it the "crazy wisdom." I found that, as a Christian, I eventually had to lay aside the notion that dialogue must always be serious. The same is true with the so-called primal religions. At a conference in Japan, a pioneer of Christian dialogue with tribal peoples once observed that Western Christians tend to be at ease only with those adherents of other faiths who are as precise and sober as they are. Perhaps we need to place the "theology of play" at the service of interfaith encounter, especially with Buddhists and those who used to be called "primitive" peoples. Jesus often responded to people's serious questions by rattling off a story, and some of his stories — like the one about the speck in my neighbor's eye and the two-by-four in my own — are downright hyperbolic. I am sure people laughed when he told them. To insist that dialogue must always be about clear and distinct ideas is to impose a narrowly Western verbal-doctrinal style. What occurs, then, is nothing but a more subtle form of religious imperialism. Exchanging jokes and anecdotes is also a form of dialogue.

Can Christians allow themselves to enter into this friskier and more "ludic" expression of interfaith exchange? There's reason to believe that the tragic schism between the Byzantine and Latin churches deprived Western Christians of a tradition that preserved this roguish element. There was for many years in the Orthodox world the tradition of the holy fool. Harking back to Saint Paul's words in the Epistle to the Corinthians about being "fools for Christ," the holy fools were not only accepted but venerated. Alexander Syrkin describes, for example, one Symen, a contemporary of the Emperor Justinian I (527–65). Symen is said to have dragged a dead dog through the streets and then gone to the church and thrown nuts at the worshipers. Sometimes he would creep through the village on all fours, get himself beaten by a town ruffian, trip people as they walked, and stroll through the market with no clothes on. Apparently, the theological tactic behind all this tomfoolery was to awaken his surprised audiences from their lethargy, lampoon conventional values, and bring people to religious insight without accruing any praise or credit to himself.

When we look for an analogous tradition in Western Christianity, the closest we come is to Saint Francis and his earliest friars. Clearly, the behavior of the saint himself was viewed as mad by many of his contemporaries, beginning with his parents. Legend says that Francis, like Symen, stripped himself of the finery his well-to-do family had provided and stood naked in the town square, and that the citizens inveighed against him until the local bishop protected him. Francis said he wanted to "become naked" so he could "follow the naked Christ." But Francis also had a comic streak. As a boy, he had admired traveling troubadours. Later he called himself and his followers *joculatores Domini* (jesters of the Lord). Many of the stories about them handed down in *The Little Flowers* are strongly reminiscent of the capers attributed to the Russian holy fools. Once, for example, Francis is said to have sent Rufinus through the streets to the church to preach clad only in his underwear. On another occasion, the inimitable Brother Juniper cut the adornments and decorations from a church and gave them to poor people so they could get money to buy food. The famous pilgrimage Francis himself took through the battle lines of the crusading armies to visit the caliph was a classic fool's errand. The reason the Muslims did not kill him is that they also had a certain respect for holy madness.

In an interreligious dialogue, this crazy wisdom has an important theological meaning. It implies that the participants realize — as mystics also do — that even their best words fall far short of the divine reality, so far short as to be somewhat ridiculous. This insight undercuts distinctions that are very precious to the West: correct/incorrect, secular/sacred, wisdom/folly, purity/dirtiness. It thus points toward what mystical theology calls the *coincidentia oppositorum*, the ultimate union of what appear to be opposites.

The fourth way the Jesus of the gospels helps facilitate interreligious encounter is that he teaches us to expect to find God already present in the "other," including the one with whom we are in dialogue, no matter how strange or unfamiliar that other's ideas or religious practices may seem. Christ meets us in and through the stranger. I have always known that this is true "in principle," but by participating in the dialogue I have learned it is also true in reality. To step into real dialogue, as Martin Buber knew, is to step onto holy ground. It invites both blessedness and pain. No one who enters — really enters — remains unaffected. If they do, there is room for doubt whether they have entered at all. Dialogue changes those who risk it. It upsets more than stereotypes and preconceptions about the "other"; it works an even more subtle transformation of the way I understand and live my own faith. To enter honestly into dialogue is to embark on a perilous personal voyage with no clear destination in view. Unforeseen things can happen. One of the risks is running the possibility of being viewed by one's co-religionists with suspicion or distrust — "Why do you want to bother with *them*?" Another is to find oneself asking questions, perhaps only inwardly, about what one's own faith really means, questions that would never have come up without the provocation of the other. The fearful gatekeepers who have insisted throughout the ages that "pure religion" can be maintained only in a ghetto or compound have not been entirely wrong. To expose one's tradition to dialogue is willy-nilly to open it to change, ferment, and internal debate. I believe God can and does speak to us through people of other faiths. And as people of faith have always known, when God speaks, mountains melt and the seas roar.

Balancing the Scales

Christians have entered into serious dialogue with people of other faiths only very recently. As we have seen, one of the questions this conversation has sparked *within* Christianity itself concerns what Jesus means for the dialogue. But the question of what Christ means for our encounter with the other inevitably raises the even more basic one of what Christ means for us as Christians. It never fails. I invariably return from a conversation with a genuine believer in one of the other faiths with Christ's famous question to Peter ringing in my mind: "Who do you say that I am?" But, as I listen, I find I am not putting the question to the other. I am putting it to myself.

Perhaps the most unexpected thing I have learned in the dialogue with people of other religions is how important it is for me to keep in touch with those of my own faith community who remain suspicious and fearful of that dialogue. This has sometimes proven difficult, and I have often found it easier to converse with universally minded Buddhists or Hindus than with fellow Christians who not only dismiss such people as pagans but also want to dismiss me for not recognizing it. Still, I believe the critically important conversation among people of diverse faiths could founder and fail if we — the dialoguers — lose touch with our fellow believers who cluster on the particularistic side. We may not admit it, but we do need each other. They remind us that without the radical particularity of the original revelation, we would have no faith to share. We remind them that without the universal dream they falsify the message and diminish the scope of the original vision.

Multiple specters stalk the human enterprise today. We have reached a point where strife between nations and religions could lead to the final apocalypse. We need more than ever to doxologize the fragile oneness of the whole earth and all her inhabitants. Yet for men and women of faith, the sacred stories by which we hymn the unity of our species and its animal and cosmic neighbors need not be invented. Paradoxically, those stories and symbols are already embedded in the same traditions that sometimes threaten to tear us asunder. Our task is to claim these reminders of our common destiny from within the desperate sources that first gave them voice.

I invite my readers to echo, in their own experience, the discoveries and disappointments that have marked my attempts to cultivate the conversation with people of other faiths while trying to nurture the vital sources of the faith that motivates the conversation. From Jesus I have learned both that he is the Way and that in God's house there are many mansions. I do not believe these two sayings are contradictory. In fact I have come to see that only by understanding one can we come to understand the other.

CHAPTER TWO

The Foreground of Christian Origins and the Commencement of Jesus Research

James H. Charlesworth

Introduction: The Background Becomes Foreground

In the study of Christian Origins what was considered only the background has now sometimes become recognized as part of the foreground. What was perceived as only the prelude to New Testament work has become the continuing agenda for reflection and reexamination.

Redaction criticism,[1] which has proved to be a most valuable methodology, removed gospel research ever farther away from the time of Jesus and focused our attention upon the last decades of the first century. New Testament scholars worked less on the Eighteen Benedictions and more on the alteration of the twelfth, which was interpreted (incorrectly) as denoting a permanent separation of Jews from Christians.

At the same time another area of research in Christian Origins was receiving our attention and turning us to the first decades of "Christianity," when it was a *group within* Early Judaism. The study of Jewish documents from Jesus' own time and the exploding international interest in them are beginning to cause a shift from the 90s to the 40s. There are reasons

---

[1]Redaction criticism is the method used by scholars to study the editorial (redactional) activity of ancient authors, especially the evangelists. This method has shown that the evangelists were not mere compilers of tradition, but sometimes gifted thinkers who revealed their theological position and sociological situation.

to posit the claim — once considered incredible by more than the Bultmannians — that the greatest achievements in Christian thinking, especially in Christology, occurred in the very first decades and deep within a Jewish movement, the *Palestinian Jesus Movement (PJM).*

The shift in the tide is occasioned by a commitment to the study of Jewish writings contemporaneous with Jesus, and the recognition that Early Judaism by Jesus' time was incredibly sophisticated, cosmopolitan, and brilliantly developed. Many theological, symbolical, and linguistic terms and ideas associated with Paul, John, and Christianity, and thus once labeled "Pauline," "Johannine," and "Christian," are now clearly seen to be pre-Christian and sometimes even Jewish.

This trend is receiving endorsements by specialists in the major universities and seminaries throughout the world, and along with it comes a myriad of new questions. For example, note the following: Since we now know that the PJM is only one of the many groups within Early Judaism, we must ask what does "conversion" to such a group mean sociologically and theologically? What real and significant or observable changes occurred for (and in) the person who crossed the boundaries and into the PJM? How is entering the PJM indicative of something quite different from the usual cliché "conversion to Christianity" or the informed older paradigm of conversion suggested by A. D. Nock?[2] What is it that we are beginning to see more clearly?

What are the ramifications of the recognition that many of the earliest Christians were highly trained, brilliant, and ingenious individuals? How does this insight shift our perception of the sociology of Early Christianity? If many members of the PJM were erudite and brilliant Jews — and possessed outstanding knowledge and skills before they entered the PJM — then much of the so-called genius of Christianity is now found to be within Judaism. Wherein, therefore, lies the genius of Jesus' earliest followers? Wherein lies the unique theological perspective of Jesus himself?

The "uniqueness" of Jesus has become less clear in light of the discovery deep within Early Judaism of many creative ideas once perceived as uniquely his. What then are the implications of this

---

[2] A. D. Nock, *Conversion: The Old and the New in Religion from Alexander the Great to Augustine of Hippo* (Oxford, 1933). See now the impressive study by A. Segal, "Messianism and Conversion: Outline for a New Approach," in *The Messiah*, ed. J. H. Charlesworth, with J. Brownson, S. Kraftchick, and A. Segal (in press).

discovery for Jesus' place in Early Judaism and as the "founder" of Christianity? Above this intriguing set of questions one perception is lucid: we are not forced back to Bultmann's position that Jesus is only the presupposition of the theology of the New Testament.[3] Such questions, while inviting, are far too many and problematic to be treated, except improperly, in one paper.

In the following chapter, I shall simply try to suggest the road to be traveled in searching for answers to such questions. In delineating this path my focus now will be primarily on the literary evidence of Early Judaism, especially on the sixty-five documents in the new English edition of the Old Testament Pseudepigrapha.[4]

Since we cannot work without precise and refined methodological terms, let us first see to what extent old terms are now inappropriate, or need discarding or redefining, and what new terms are appropriate.

Choosing and Defining the Appropriate Terms

Unfortunately, our work as New Testament historians and exegetes has been sometimes inaccurate because of imprecise nomenclature. In my judgment some major terms should be defined as follows: **"Early Judaism"** should be used to describe the varieties of Judaisms dating from around the third century B.C.E. until the end of the second century C.E. Unlike such terms as "Late Judaism," Early Judaism has the connotation, *inter alia*, of being alive, with refreshing new insights into the relationships between time and history, highly developed and sophisticated metaphysical speculations on the cosmos, and introspective perceptions into the psychological complexities of being human.

Early Jews were brilliantly creative, with penetrating speculations into almost every facet of our world and universe. For this and many other reasons, I prefer to use the term "Early Judaism," and not others that reflect a distorting bias against Jewish phenomena.

Further, when describing Judaism the term **"hellenistic"** should no longer be used in a geographical sense to separate a putative "Hellenistic Judaism" from "Palestinian Judaism," but should be

[3]R. Bultmann, *Theology of the New Testament*, 2 vols., trans. K. Grobel (New York, 1951); see vol. 1, p. 3.
[4]See the discussion in my "Jesus, Early Jewish Literature, and Archaeology," pp. 177–98 in the present volume.

used to denote only a chronological time. The Hellenistic Period, which has different chronological limits at divergent archaeological sites in Palestine, should denote the time period when hellenistic (Greek and then Roman) influences penetrated into Palestinian culture. In the Diaspora it should specify the time following Alexander the Great's mastery over successive geographical areas.

By this definition, "hellenistic" can still be used in a cultural sense when not referring to Judaism, so that hellenistic influence is possible before a hellenistic period. This flexibility allows us, for example, to speak about the hellenistic influence on the Samaritan papyri before Alexander's conquest of Palestine.

Obviously, this will spawn discussion on the beginning and ending of the Hellenistic Period. If so, then we will have moved away from the confusion that now reigns. Some scholars use this term correctly, others cause unfortunate confusion by equating Diasporic Jews with hellenistic Jews.

Using "hellenistic" as an adjective for a chronological period clarifies our comparative analyses. For example, we can lucidly compare the post-exilic Jews with hellenistic Jews, and these two with early Byzantine Jews. Since we shall now need an adjective to refer to Jews living outside Palestine, I propose that we refer to them as *Diasporic Jews*, or more precisely as *Roman Jews*, *Egyptian Jews*, or other clearly meaningful and precise terms.

Some terms, while inappropriate etymologically or in a strict sense, probably will — at least for a while — be retained in many public forums because of their popular coinage. We scholars must not retreat into a nomenclature that smacks of opaque scholarly jargon. Hence, while **"Old Testament"** is often not as appropriate as "Hebrew Scriptures," or *Biblia Hebraica*, or *Tanach*, some Jewish and Christian scholars retain it because it is not offensive to modern Jews. "Old Testament" is a meaningful term and is well recognized by the public. It is a sacred corpus of Scriptures cherished by Jews and Christians. Should not one name be given to the corpus so that a future may open up in which Jews and Christians in colloquial language may recognize more commonality as attention is drawn to a shared collection of sacred writings?

The term **"New Testament"** is even more problematic than the term "Old Testament." Christians will probably draw a line, refusing to rename the twenty-seven books so important for their faith. This term may be retained with two caveats: First, it should never be used to indicate that the "Old Testament" is old, archaic, and out of date. Fortunately, the New Testament documents themselves can be cited against such preposterous thoughts, and happily (or providentially) the Church that bequeathed us the canon denounced Marcion who espoused such anti-Jewish notions.

Second, we must comprehend that New Testament scholars do not work on "the New Testament"; that is the domain of the Church historian of the late fourth and subsequent centuries. New Testament scholars devote their lives to the study of the first and contiguous centuries, and to the *documents in* the New Testament, and usually passages *in* these writings. Furthermore, we must recognize that it is very difficult to decide whether the New Testament documents should be studied within the history of Early Judaism or within the history of the Church.

Many terms, however, should now be discarded as no longer appropriate. The first such term to be replaced or redefined is **"intertestamental."** It is misrepresentative and offensive. The expression "intertestamental period" has become more and more inappropriate to denote the period from 250 B.C.E. to 200 C.E. It is simply inaccurate. The youngest book in the Old Testament is Daniel, which dates from around 165 B.C.E. The oldest writing in the New Testament is 1 or 2 Thessalonians, which dates from near 50 C.E. Hence, "intertestamental" has been used inappropriately to denote both the decades before 165 B.C.E. when some of the Old Testament writings were not yet finally edited or composed and the century after 50 C.E. when the New Testament writings were composed. The period covered by Early Judaism is also much broader than the time between the testaments. We now know, because of the Qumran Aramaic fragments, that the oldest apocalypse is not Daniel, but portions of so-called 1 Enoch and these date from the third century B.C.E.[5]

Moreover, the term "intertestamental" is demeaning. It implies that the Jewish literature of these centuries is inferior to those in the canon, and only important because of their relationships to other writings, namely those that were eventually claimed to be scriptural. This position may be acceptable to theologians, but it is intolerable for historians. Finally, the term "intertestamental" belies a Christian bias and confessional belief in two testaments.

---

[5]See the text, discussion, and photographs in J. T. Milik, with the collaboration of M. Black, *The Books of Enoch: Aramaic Fragments of Qumrân Cave 4* (Oxford, 1976).

If we continue to use the term "intertestamental," we should employ it to describe the *religious thoughts* that the early Christians inherited from Early Judaism. It is, therefore, a *theological* term that helps Christians to understand the many issues involved in seeking to comprehend the relation between their two testaments. Hence, G. von Rad's and W. Eichrodt's insights into the possible relation of the testaments need to be enriched by reflections on "intertestamental theology."

A term to be banished is **"normative Judaism."** Scholars incorrectly read back into Early Judaism the normativeness of Rabbinic Judaism. The rich diversity within Early Judaism all too frequently is either not perceived or is branded as exotic and insignificant.

"Heresy" and **"orthodoxy,"** thanks especially to W. Bauer,[6] are now seen to be inappropriate terms. If there was no monolithic Judaism, then there was no universally accepted individual or group to rule on behalf of all Jews that an idea, belief, or practice was not acceptable. In pre-70 Judaism the Essenes enjoyed the freedom to tell Pharisees and Sadducees that they were faithless to sacred tradition — and according to the Dead Sea Scrolls the Essene community at and near Qumran often exercised this right. It is abundantly clear that Judaism was not — indeed, is not — doctrinally based. Debates over the meaning of Torah reflect a *living* tradition and a *tolerance* of informed but divergent opinions.

"Sectarian Judaism" is a dangerous term and must not be utilized without careful qualification. If there is no normative, orthodox, and monolithic Judaism, then sects cannot be seen as hostile to and outside of a nonexistent core. A "sect" means a social or ideological unit distinct from and rejected by a normative majority. There were many different types of Jews; there were far more than four so-called sects. We should rather think about *groups* in which there were subgroups.

We know far too little about these so-called four "sects." The only sources for the Pharisees, for example, are the New Testament documents, Josephus, and a few paragraphs in the Mishnah. Certainly each of these is tendentious and heavily edited. The Pharisees were very latitudinarious. A legalistically oriented Pharisee, for example, may have been closer in many ways to a Sadducee than to a fellow, apocalyptically inspired Phar-

---

[6]W. Bauer, *Orthodoxy and Heresy in Earliest Christianity*, eds. R. Kraft and G. Krodel (Philadelphia, 1971).

isee. These insights and refined nomenclature may be illustrated by comparing the two English editions of the Old Testament Pseudepigrapha.

In R. H. Charles' collection, *The Apocrypha and Pseudepigrapha of the Old Testament*, Jubilees was attributed to the Pharisees.[7] In the same volume (p. 630), G. B. Gray assigned the Psalms of Solomon to the Pharisees. He advocated, "We need not hesitate to see in the 'righteous' of the Psalms the Pharisees, and in the 'sinners' the Sadducees (cf. iv. 2ff.); and in the Psalms themselves the work of one or more of the Pharisees." Similarly, Charles argued that the author of the Testament (or Assumption) of Moses "was a Pharisee of a fast-disappearing type...."[8] In the new English version of the Old Testament Pseudepigrapha *not one* document is assigned to the Pharisees, or to any other so-called sect.[9]

Another inappropriate term is **"primitive Christianity."** Christianity developed out of a highly sophisticated and phenomenologically complex Jewish "religion" and culture. Jesus' followers inherited more than one thousand years of tradition; many of the traditions were oral, others written. The latter traditions had been edited, expanded, and debated upon over many centuries as we know so well thanks to at least one hundred years of research and study on the Old Testament, especially on the composition of the Pentateuch and Isaiah.

To talk about "primitiveness" in earliest Christianity implies a negative (perhaps anti-Jewish) judgment on Early Judaism. We should now recognize that much of the genius and sophistication of earliest Christianity derives from Early Judaism, which was not so much a religion as a cosmopolitan culture impregnated with influences from Persia, Syria, Greece, Rome, and Egypt.

As historians, we must also ask whether **"Judaism"** should be understood in exclusively religious categories. Since many influences came through wars and economic relationships, especially

---

[7]R. H. Charles (ed.), *The Apocrypha and Pseudepigrapha of the Old Testament in English*, 2 vols. (Oxford, 1913) vol. 2, p. 8: "The author of Jubilees is a true Pharisee in that he combines belief in Divine omnipotence and providence with the belief in human freedom and responsibility."

[8]Ibid., vol. 2, p. 411: "From the preceding facts it follows that our author was neither Sadducee, Zealot, nor Essene, but a Pharisaic Quietist. He was a Pharisee of a fast-disappearing type, recalling in all respects the Chasid of the early Maccabean times, and upholding the old tradition of quietude and resignation."

[9]J. H. Charlesworth, ed., *The Old Testament Pseudepigrapha*, 2 vols. (Garden City, New York, 1983–85).

the caravan routes, we dare not assume that a Jew is a "religious" Jew. Many Jews were religious only for convenience, social respectability, or because of the perennial need for an efficacious "god." It is easy inadvertently to think about Jews as "religious" people because we work almost always with religious texts. Some rare exceptions are the Zenon papyri, the Samaritan papyri, and the Bar Kokhba letters. The Apocrypha, Pseudepigrapha, and Dead Sea Scrolls are collections of religious texts; Philo's writings and Josephus' books are religious documents. Yet, that does not entitle us to portray all pre-70 Jews as religious people. This fallacy is operative in informed discussions of the Zealots. Revolutionaries should not be defined only by religious categories. The last days in Jerusalem were characterized by some horrifying actions that were an utter betrayal of Torah and God. Unfortunately, many publications are not carefully attuned to the sociological dimensions of Early Judaism.

It is also imperative that we find some means for considering the incipient Christologies and beliefs of those who knew and followed Jesus, before Easter. Perhaps the term *Pre-cross Christology* is helpful. Even if we do not have archaeological and literary evidence of the lives and beliefs of the first Galilean followers of Jesus, we must — if our study and research are to be historically valid — reflect on and include in our surveys of earliest Christianity the perspectives of Jesus' followers who antedate Jesus' crucifixion and resurrection around 30 C.E. The prior understanding of the Galileans (and perhaps Judeans) may have been shaped by or altered by the events of 30, but such an alteration is not necessarily demanded, and the prior ground for understanding and allegiance may well have (and probably did) define the subsequent claims or experiences.

The Palestinian Jesus Movement (PJM) was obviously geographically based in Palestine, centered on Jesus, and was a recognizable social group developing at times in ways disturbing to other Jews. With these perceptions we can improve our penetration into Early Judaism, out of which "Christianity" developed.

Methodology and Sensitivity

What I have been attempting to communicate is that we must improve the methodologies by which we approach the phenomena in Early Judaism, and by which we assess their value and importance for the PJM. We must beware of trends that produce a circuitous approach to Jesus and his time.

It is easy to slip into finding data that confirm a position we wish to defend. It is a beautiful idea to see in the New Testament a call to human liberation, but it is idiosyncratic and self-serving to conclude with Jane Schaberg of the University of Detroit (in her *The Illegitimacy of Jesus: A Feminist Theological Interpretation*) that Mary had an illegitimate pregnancy and that this fact reveals the good news that God sides with the socially outcast woman and child. The well documented evidence of Jesus' socializing with the disenfranchised, the poor, and the impure sufficiently substantiates the theological truth that Jesus claimed in action and speech that God accepted as faithful Jews many who had been rejected as impure by some Pharisees and other Jews.

Matthew's account of the virgin birth may indeed reflect the Jewish polemic that Joseph wished to put Mary aside quietly because she had had sexual intercourse with another man and became pregnant. But to use polemics, in which the father is even sometimes identified as "Pandera," to argue for a feminist apologetic is to falsify the historical base for interpretation. The proper exegesis must be followed, and it must be disinterested in the sense that the desired conclusion must not dictate the selecting and interpreting of data.

Four positive factors are necessary in exegesis. First, we should let the authors of the documents speak on their own terms and with their own concepts, fears, and dreams. Second, we must be humble, sympathetic and non-apologetic in our approach. Not only Christians but also Jews have repeatedly failed to listen with sympathy. Third, we should focus upon a coherently whole document, or portion of a composite work, to see terms, motifs, and possible parallels in their *context* and with their given *functions*. Then, we may step back and attempt to perceive possible additions to the document, and the document's relationships with other writings of Early Judaism.

Canon

It is disheartening to note that out of an anachronistic and confessional, canonical stance some scholars continue to disparage those who focus their research on the so-called extracanonical works as if they are second-class citizens in the academy. Far too frequently, the importance of these other collections of documents is recognized by Christians only because they are perceived to be relevant to the Bible, in particular to the New Testament, or by Christians and Jews only because they help explain Christian Origins or Rabbinic Judaism.

It is significant for the concept of the New Testament canon that the librarians in the Vatican have been wise and perceptive. Charles' *Apocrypha and Pseudepigrapha of the Old Testament*, James' *Apocryphal New Testament*, Kautzsch's *Die Apokryphen und Pseudepigraphen des Alten Testaments*, the texts of 1 Enoch, 2 Enoch, 3 Enoch, the Testaments of the Twelve Patriarchs, and other so-called apocryphal documents, and studies upon them, are shelved in the Biblioteca Apostolica Vaticanna under *"Sacra scriptura."* It is imperative that Jews and Christians recognize the rich literary heritage they share, thanks to the fruitfulness of interconfessional contemporary research.

Portraying Early Judaism

We have not yet been able to reconstruct a portrait of Early Judaism. Yet, it is safe to say that the old picture of a normative Judaism has been shattered by the vast amount of new literary evidence from Early Judaism, especially the documents gathered together in the *Old Testament Pseudepigrapha* and under the popular title, the "Dead Sea Scrolls."[10] Against the whole idea of a normative Judaism many insights have been brought forward by many specialists to demonstrate that the concept of a normative Judaism results primarily from a tendency to read back into the first century C.E. and earlier much later, heavily edited rabbinic texts, and secondarily from the impression that Paul somewhat accurately portrayed Judaism as a normative system. Most scholars have come to discard the concept of "normative Judaism" for pre-70 phenomena, but a few indiscriminately perpetuate this and other anachronistic models.

One factor, perhaps the major one, has not yet been emphasized in order to illustrate the total impossibility of any type of closed, systematic, normative Judaism; and, correlative to that model, an esoteric, insignificant aberrant phenomenon that would

---

[10]See the discussion in my "Jesus, Early Jewish Literature, and Archaeology," pp. 177–98 in the present collection.

eventually be labeled "Christian." This factor is the complex, divergent, and cosmopolitan nature of *Jewish apocalypsology*,[11] which demarcates early Jewish theology not only from earlier biblical theology but also from subsequent rabbinic theology.

During the post-exilic period, as G. von Rad so brilliantly pointed out, there was a major and unparalleled shift in the perception of history and of God's action on behalf of his chosen nation Israel.[12] The old model of history as the only arena in which God is moving his nation toward a perfect future has collapsed. Now, after Ezra and in the great apocalyptic literature, this model has been replaced; there is an alteration in the way of perceiving history. History is no longer the primary arena in which the Jew can confront God. Contemporary events — namely, the subjection of the sons of Israel to enslavement not to Yahweh but to foreign idolatrous nations — tended to falsify and to disprove the faithful recitation of confessions, recitals of history, and the Deuteronomic optimism in history. Many Jews claimed that the salvation of Israel — usually seen, after about 197 B.C.E., as reduced to only a faithful remnant — must come from a cataclysmic event from the beyond, anticipated only through divine revelations obtained through apocalyptic trips to the heavens above, the world ahead, or in apocalyptic visions and dreams. The present is perceived as devoid of salvific movements; only the other world and eschaton provide meaning, salvation, and

---

[11] I have created this neologism in order to specify literary and social phenomena related to the disclosure of paradigmatically important heavenly, often protological and eschatological secrets (*protological* denotes anything that is "proto," that is, at the beginning of creation; *eschatological* refers to anything that is at the end [*eschatos*] of the linear flow of history and time). This term, "apocalypsology," is deemed necessary because "apocalyptic" is now rightly restricted to its use as an adjective; it should not be used as a noun (in German it is a noun). The term "apocalypticism" describes social phenomena; "apocalypses" signify literary works.

[12] G. von Rad, *Old Testament Theology*, 2 vols., trans. D. M. G. Stalker (New York, 1962–65). G. von Rad overemphasized the contrast between the theology of the prophetic books and the theology of the apocalypses. A contrast is obvious, but von Rad incorrectly overstressed it; the alteration is not so "thorough-going" (vol. 1, p. 407) as he claimed. Also, a significant link between prophecy and apocalypsology is not "completely out of the question" (vol. 2, p. 303). I doubt that "the accounts of the history of God's people as we meet them throughout apocalyptic literature . . . are really devoid of theology!" (vol. 2, p. 303). Finally, the following statement is simply inaccurate: "Apocalyptic literature's view of history is therefore pessimistic in the extreme . . ." (vol. 2, p. 305). How can this statement allow for the fact that the prayers in the apocalypses are always heard by God, and that the end (*eschatos*) is always described as devoid of all the pains suffered by humans and is indeed a blessed time (see esp. 1 En, 2 En, 2 Bar, 3 Bar, HistRech)? It should appear obvious why I wish to acknowledge my indebtedness to von Rad — as there *is* a shift in the perception of history from prophecy to apocalypsology — but feel compelled to modify his view.

the threefold unification of humanity with itself, humans with nature and animals, and created beings with the Creator. These characteristics helped shape all the religious writings of Early Judaism, whether they be apocalypses, testaments, wisdom tracts, or hymns and prayers.

The apocalyptic fervor in Early Judaism was pervasive; it tore apart the nation and eventually contributed to the two massive revolts against Rome. When the Jews thought about God visiting the earth, it was in terms of a time long ago, as before the Fall in the Garden of Eden, or when he was with the patriarchs, or guiding the monarchy (especially during the time of David), or speaking again through the prophets. To talk about God visiting the earth would be to talk either about the distant past or the longed-for, rapidly approaching future, the endtime.

What is so impressively clear is that the explosive atmosphere in Early Judaism is precisely what is also absent in later Rabbinic Judaism. Rabbinic *Halakah* is designed for a people settled down in history, not living with one foot on the earth and the other in the eschaton. In polishing these rules of conduct for daily life the rabbis used much older traditions (originally preserved in oral form), deriving, sometimes with little modification, from pre-70 Judaism. What had been passed on through the centuries to the Mishnah, Tosephta, and Talmudim had been transposed from a non-normative framework — in which apocalyptic speculations and apocalypsology itself flourished — into a more systematized, organized, so-called normative structure of Judaism in which *Halakoth* were pervasively paradigmatic for this life here and now.

What is missing in Rabbinics, and what is so pervasively characteristic of Early Judaism, is the thoroughgoing, categorically eschatological and apocalyptic form and function of thought and life. Granted, the belief in the bodily resurrection of the individual after death and the yearning for the sending of God's Messiah lingered on and were influential.[13] But the *function* and *setting* of these ideas and beliefs were totally different from what they had been, at least in many segments of Palestinian pre-70 Judaism. Jacob Neusner is entirely correct, therefore, in his magisterial work titled *Judaism: The Evidence of the Mishnah*, to argue forcefully against the classical treatment of Judaism so definitive for many

---

[13] See the discussions on this point in *The Messiah*, especially the contributions by S. Talmon and B. Bokser.

New Testament scholars, namely, Moore's *Judaism in the First Century of the Christian Era: The Age of the Tannaim*. Neusner is certainly right in his judgment: "Moore describes many kinds of Judaism as if they formed a single, fully symmetrical construct. The claim of 'normativity' for this Judaism is not merely wrong. It is confusing, for it specifies one 'Judaism' where there are many."[14] The new translations of the Pseudepigrapha and Dead Sea Scrolls amply illustrate the wide divergences — each "normative" in its own way and for its own group or circle — that were alive in Early Judaism.

Liturgical Order

During the time of Hillel and Jesus, and for the first time in the history of the Jews, prayers in the synagogue began to move from spontaneous expression to a set statutory form. It is wise to remember that the movement toward canonization of Scripture was accompanied by the development of set liturgies. Some of the daily and synagogal prayers still uttered today throughout the world when Jews gather for prayer or worship reached a form somewhat recognizably similar to their present form before the destruction of Jerusalem in 70 C.E.[15]

Other prayers are equally important for a better understanding of Early Judaism and the origins of Christianity. Only two examples will be brought forward for examination. Each of them is taken from my translations in the *Old Testament Pseudepigrapha*.[16] The first is the Prayer of Manasseh. Note these eloquent and beautiful penitential thoughts:

> You, therefore, O Lord, God of the righteous,
>   did not appoint grace for the righteous,
>   such as Abraham, Isaac, and Jacob,
>   those who did not sin against you;
>   but you appointed grace for me, (I) who am a sinner.

---

[14]J. Neusner, *Judaism: The Evidence of the Mishnah* (Chicago, London, 1981) p. 7.

[15]Here I am indebted to the pioneering work of J. Heinemann, *Prayer in the Talmud: Forms and Patterns*, trans. R. S. Sarason (SJ 9; Berlin/New York, 1977). Also, see Charlesworth, "A Prolegomenon to a New Study of the Jewish Background of the Hymns and Prayers in the New Testament," in *Essays in Honour of Yigael Yadin*, ed. G. Vermes and J. Neusner (JSJ 23:1–2; Oxford, 1982) pp. 265–85. Consult also the articles (especially that by S. C. Reif) in the proceedings of the Jewish-Christian liturgy conference at Notre Dame University, June 1988.

[16]Charlesworth (ed.), *The Old Testament Pseudepigrapha*, vol. 2, ad loc. cit.

> . . .
> And now behold I am bending the knees of my heart before you;
> and I am beseeching your kindness.
> I have sinned, O Lord, I have sinned;
> and I certainly know my sins.
> I beseech you;
>   forgive me, O Lord, forgive me!
> Do not destroy me with my transgressions;
> do not be angry against me forever;
> do not remember my evils;
> and do not condemn me and banish me to the depths of earth!
> For you are the God of those who repent.
>   (The Prayer of Manasseh, verses 8, 11–13)

Here we find an emphasis upon God's unmerited grace, and a suggestion that forgiveness is not possible through works but only through God's gracious love. In fact, the very beginning of verse 14 is as follows: "In me you will manifest all your grace . . . ," and that is not because the individual is worthy, but as the righteous Jew acknowledges in the very next line: "I am not worthy, you will save me according to your manifold mercies." Here in these few verses we find adumbrations of Paul's ideas. Obviously Paul's soteriology was also influenced by Jesus' creative thoughts which were themselves shaped by early Jewish traditions. From a rich storehouse of traditions Paul concluded that the individual is saved only by faith and not by works. Of course, Paul brought a totally new slant to this concept, because he grounded it in the life, crucifixion, and resurrection of an unparalleled, important individual whom he called "Jesus Christ."

Another prayer, certainly not as well known as the Prayer of Manasseh, yet exceedingly important for understanding the foreground and background of early Christianity, is the Prayer of Jacob. In this prayer we observe how a Jew calls upon God and acknowledges that all gifts, including wisdom, derive solely from God. The individual cannot earn God's favor; but unlike the Prayer of Manasseh it is assumed possible to manipulate and improve the possibility of receiving his favor. In this prayer we find apocalyptic elements well known from early Jewish and Christian writings, and the emphasis upon the reception of eschatological gifts in the present, a thought well known from some passages in the Hodayoth, in the Gospel of John, and in the Odes of Solomon. Note the following passage from the Prayer of Jacob:

Make straight the one who has [th]e prayer [fr]om the rac[e]
    of Israel [a]nd those who have received favor from you,
    God of gods.

He who has the secret name *Sabaoth* . . .
    God of gods; amen, amen.

[He] who is upon (the) stars abo[ve] (the) ages,
    who brings forth snow,
    a[nd] who always passes throu[g]h the stars and pla[n]ets,
    [and makes] (them) run in every way by your creating
    (power).

Fill me with wisdom,
Empow[e]r me, Lord;

Fill my heart with good things, Lord;

As an ear[th]ly angel,
as [hav]ing become immortal,
as having recei[ved] the gift which (is) from [yo]u, [a]men,
amen.

                                (The Prayer of Jacob, verses 14–19)

Summary

All of these insights are possible because of the unexpected
discovery of many documents that predate 70 C.E. The new and
effulgent understanding of time, history, the cosmos, and humanity — the *Zeitgeist* of Early Judaism — is perhaps the singularly most important contribution the early Jewish documents can
make to our research as New Testament scholars. When these documents are read empathetically and reflectively for hours without interruption and with a concerted attempt to understand the
Jews' own need and time, we come the closest we possibly can
to the spirit and the vibrating pulse of Early Judaism, and to
the world in which the early Jews, like Hillel and Jesus, lived.
When we *add* to this understanding the insights and feelings obtained from reading the *Halakoth*, especially the daily customs for
prayer and piety, preserved in the Tannaitic literature, we come
even closer to the lively spirit that characterized the first-century
Jew.

We can grasp some of the life of the early Jews not only because
of the tortured words, struggles for survival, and intra-Jewish
polemic in many of their documents, but also because we know

the early Jews tended to share a common presupposition, namely that all of us are chiseled out of the rock of a shared earthiness. They also shared a common confession: the *Shema*.

But when we seek to understand what might in fact have been the common elements that tended to unify the early Jews, we move far beyond the confines of this chapter and into other areas that need exploration. Suffice to say for the present that Early Judaism was not anarchistic and totally torn apart. Neither was it so unified and systematic as scholars have tended to portray it. We should not think about Judaism as a uniform "religion"; rather, we should think about *Judaisms* and the various dimensions and freedom of expression and reflection before 70. From this perspective, we come much closer to a refined view of Jesus and earliest Christianity.

In this sense, the background of Early Christianity is the foreground of Jesus and his earliest followers: Early Judaism. Moreover, the gospels are not simply post-Easter confessionals; they are post-Easter confessionals full of and shaped by pre-Easter traditions (see Illus. 12, 13). These insights have enabled Jewish and Christian scholars, in the past decade, to make some startling and unprecedented advances in the historical study of Jesus of Nazareth.

The Commencement of Jesus Research

The new perception of the foreground of Christian Origins is the main reason Jesus research commenced around 1980. Before that time New Testament scholars, focusing almost myopically on the canonical New Testament, were involved periodically in the so-called old quest and subsequently the new quest for the historical Jesus.

The old quest was the product of the European Enlightenment and began in the period 1774–78, when Reimarus' fragments (the Wolfenbüttel Fragments) were published posthumously by Lessing.[17] The first real attempt to write a biography of Jesus was D. F. Strauss's massive *Das Leben Jesu*, which was published in 1835 and 1836.[18] It is a monumental publication, demonstrating the complexity of "myth" (especially in the first century), and

---

[17]See C. H. Talbert (ed.), *Reimarus: Fragments*, trans. R. S. Fraser (Chico, Calif., 1985).
[18]See the convenient English version: D. F. Strauss, *The Life of Jesus Critically Examined*, ed. P. C. Hodgson, trans. G. Eliot (Philadelphia, 1972).

illustrating the need to pursue unbiased historical research. No other book on Jesus during the "old quest" can match the brilliance and serious methodology of Strauss's *Life of Jesus*. The later *Vie de Jésus* by E. Renan,[19] published in the early 1860s, is more a work of art than a product of historical research.

The nineteenth century closed with M. Kähler's claims that "Christian faith and a history of Jesus repel each other like oil and water" and that the gospels are post-Easter confessionals.[20] His brilliant theological insights were highly influential, notably on Barth, Bultmann, and Tillich. The old quest itself ended decisively in 1906 with A. Schweitzer's demonstration that the nineteenth-century lives of Jesus only mirrored the Victorians' presumed portrait of Jesus.[21] Their Jesus had been created in the likeness of an admired sophisticated contemporary man. The barrenness of the quest for the Jesus of history by nineteenth-century scholars is reminiscent of a judgment by Herman Melville in *Moby Dick* (1851):

> In pursuit of those far mysteries we dream of, or in tormented chase of that demon phantom that, some time or other, swims before all humans hearts; while chasing such over his round globe, they either lead us on in *barren mazes* or midway leave us whelmed [italics mine].

From approximately 1906 to 1953 a moratorium on the quest seemed to prevail at many centers for New Testament research. R. Bultmann, certainly the most influential New Testament scholar during that period, did write a book titled *Jesus*, but in that book he stressed the following point:

> I do indeed think that we can now know almost nothing concerning the life and personality of Jesus, since the early Christian sources show no interest in either, are moreover fragmentary and often legendary; and other sources about Jesus do not exist.[22]

To me this judgment is remarkable. While Bultmann was the most brilliant New Testament scholar who lived during the first half of

---

[19] E. Renan, *The Life of Jesus* [trans. is anonymous, see the Preface] introduction by J. H. Holmes (New York, 1927; reprinted 1955).

[20] M. Kähler, *The So-called Historical Jesus and the Historic Biblical Christ*, trans. C. E. Braaten, with a foreword by P. J. Tillich (Philadelphia, 1964); see p. 74 for comments cited.

[21] A. Schweitzer, *The Quest of the Historical Jesus: A Critical Study of its Progress from Reimarus to Wrede*, trans. W. Montgomery, with a preface by F. C. Burkitt (New York, 1910, 1964).

[22] R. Bultmann, *Jesus and the Word*, trans. L. P. Smith and E. H. Lantero (London, 1934; reprinted 1958) p. 14. The passage quoted is in tension with many wise and illuminating comments about Jesus by Bultmann in other publications.

this century, his real genius was in theology and not in history. He was a powerful and influential critic in pre- and postwar Germany; but — as are we all — he was a product of his times, and also (far too) heavily influenced by Harnack, Schweitzer, Kähler, and Heidegger.

The statement that "other sources about Jesus do not exist" discloses the focus of Bultmann's vision: He showed no interest in archaeology and the land of Israel. He did not attempt to master the vast literary deposits of Early Judaism that are contemporaneous with Jesus. His gaze did not include the important references to Jesus by Josephus,[23] or the less important accounts by Tacitus and Suetonius. He did not examine the agrapha or extracanonical gospels, as did Resch and Jeremias. He tended to see only the point (no longer universally accepted without qualification)[24] that the intracanonical gospels are the only sources for a study of the historical Jesus.

The judgment that the "early Christian sources" are fragmentary is not fully representative of their complex nature. The false impression is also given to at least some readers that we are working with fragments, like the thousands of broken and decayed scrolls from Qumran Cave IV.

Most importantly, the claim that "the early Christian sources show no interest" in "the life and personality of Jesus" is simply inaccurate. One of the interests of the earliest Christians was in Jesus' life and self-understanding; otherwise the production of the gospels themselves is unthinkable. Such points were driven home by P. Benoit,[25] N. Dahl,[26] and especially Bultmann's most articu-

---

[23]See Charlesworth, *Jesus within Judaism* (Anchor Bible Reference Library 1; Garden City, N.Y., 1988).

[24]See, for example, J. D. Crossan's argument that the Gospel of Peter preserves an account of Jesus' passion that was used by each of the intracanonical evangelists. Crossan, *Four Other Gospels: Shadows on the Contours of Canon* (Minneapolis, N.Y., 1985).

[25]P. Benoit: "The feeling for history is perhaps not the dominant motive in the formation of the gospel tradition, but it is at least one of the motives, and merits consideration along with the others, apologetics, polemics, and the rest." See Benoit, "Réflexions sur la *Formgeschichtliche Methode*," republished in *Exégèse et Théologie* (Paris, 1961) pp. 25–61 (p. 48 for above quotation).

[26]In his inaugural lecture at the University of Oslo in November of 1946, eventually published as *Jesus in the Memory of the Early Church* (Minneapolis, 1976), Dahl stated that "above all it must have been in the assembly of the faithful that one recounted how Jesus traversed the countryside healing the sick and casting out demons, how he had been opposed and unrecognized, and how he had come to the aid of his disciples. These events were not recounted because of a detached historical interest; nevertheless, the stories betray a concern to remember past events" (p. 29). Unfortunately, most New Testament scholars did not grasp the final point Dahl was making. Dahl told me that his inaugural

late, creative, and forceful student, E. Käsemann. In 1953, before a gathering of Bultmann's former students (by that time many were influential professors), Käsemann lectured on "The Problem of the Historical Jesus." He clearly disclosed the complex nature of the intracanonical traditions and, among numerous brilliant insights, articulated this most important principle: "History is only accessible to us through tradition and only comprehensible to us through interpretation."[27] This statement, which is worth memorizing, discloses that because the gospels are interpreted traditions, they do preserve the continuing efficaciousness of tradition for faith. At the same time, they provide a way back to the Jesus of history.

Kähler's often misunderstood dictum — the gospels are post-Easter confessionals — is abandoned. The gospels record *pre-Easter* traditions, and they preserve them in a meaningful way. Of course, the interpretation of tradition alters and shapes it; and it is not easy to distinguish between tradition and addition.

During the 1950s, 1960s, and 1970s, many scholars who had shunned the quest for the historical Jesus resumed the task. The period is usually labeled "the new quest."[28] The "new" indicates, *inter alia*, that no one who is a scholar, or informed about scholarly research, is going to attempt to write a biography of Jesus. Even so, we know more about Jesus than about almost any other first-century Jew.[29]

The most significant attempt at something like a life of Jesus produced during the period of the new quest is G. Bornkamm's *Jesus of Nazareth*, which was published in German in 1956.[30] In some ways it is still the best book on Jesus, but it is now significantly dated.

During the late 1960s and early 1970s the new quest began to wane. Since about 1980 an explosion of interest in the historical Jesus can be perceived. No certain date or particular event can be said to have heralded its appearance. Rather it began almost un-

---

lecture was an appeal to recognize the possibility and importance of discerning reliable information about the Jesus of history.

[27] E. Käsemann, "The Problem of the Historical Jesus," in *Essays on New Testament Themes*, trans. W. J. Montague (SBT 41; London, 1964) p. 18 (= 190).

[28] See J. M. Robinson, *A New Quest of the Historical Jesus* (SBT 25; London, 1959; republished frequently).

[29] I am grateful to David Flusser and Geza Vermes for pointing out this fact to me during private discussions. An exception to the statement, and the need for the adverb "almost" in the sentence above, is the knowledge we have of Paul the Apostle. We know relatively very little about Honi, Hanina, Hillel, Shammai, Gamaliel, and Johanan ben Zakkai.

[30] G. Bornkamm, *Jesus of Nazareth*, trans. I. and F. McLuskey, with J. M. Robinson (New York, London, 1960).

noticed; even today some New Testament scholars are oblivious that it is in full swing.

It began about 1980 because of the convergence of numerous events: the publication of the Temple Scroll (the largest of the Dead Sea Scrolls), the completion of the new edition of the Old Testament Pseudepigrapha, the growing recognition that first-century synagogues had been identified in what was ancient Palestine (including Galilee), the discovery of an apparently un-edited version of Josephus' reference to Jesus, a renewed interest in ancient documents (thanks to the discovery of hundreds of early manuscripts, especially near Qumran and Nag Hammadi), and the growing awareness that first-century Palestinian life is now amazingly visible and palpable, thanks to the indefatigable ar-chaeological labors of many, especially the Israelis (see Illus. 16).[31] Moreover, many fine New Testament scholars, here and abroad, have moved appreciably away from the liberal disdain for his-tory and the hyper-preoccupation with strictly ideological agen-das. The one impression most powerfully forced upon me after lecturing in universities in England, Scotland, Ireland, Norway, Sweden, West Germany, France, Austria, and Switzerland, dur-ing 1983 and 1984, was this resounding thought: the Bultmannian School is dead.

The singular most important difference between the quest and Jesus research, which began about 1980, is that during the former periods, both the old and the new quest, scholars were *search-ing* for Jesus. Now, scholars find themselves *bumping into* pre-70 Palestinian phenomena: some Old Testament Pseudepigrapha, all the Dead Sea Scrolls, houses in Capernaum (one that may well have belonged to Peter and in which Jesus would have spo-ken), streets and the remains of massive houses, stairways, gates, and thousands of artifacts — especially stone jars — from pre-70 Jerusalem.

Reading a first-century, pre-70 script on leather and walking on Herodian stone-paved streets just south of the Temple walls raises in me questions about life in Palestine before the Roman de-struction. Along with many other scholars, I find myself jolted by reflections on life back then (see Illus. 9, 12). In doing research on historical (but not historic) documents and stones, we are deeply involved in history and are attempting to reinterpret the life of pre-

---

[31] For pertinent bibliography and further discussion see Charlesworth, *Jesus within Judaism.*

70 Jews. We find ourselves eventually engaged in Jesus research, which may be defined simply as the attempt to understand the man of history in light of all the evidence that is now pouring our way. The New Testament traditions about the pre-Easter Jesus are subsequently read in appreciably different ways.

To search for Jesus, motivated by theological concerns, is categorically different from being led to ponder about the Jesus of first-century Palestine, prompted by *realia* of history. Reflecting on the disparity between the quest and Jesus research reminds me of the following passage from Edgar Allan Poe's *The Raven* (Stanza 1):

> Once upon a midnight dreary,
>   while I pondered, weak and weary,
> Over many a quaint and curious
>   volume of forgotten lore —
> While I nodded, nearly napping,
>   suddenly there came a tapping,
> As of some one *gently rapping* ...
>   [Italics mine. —J. H. C.].

Jesus research is not a search for the historical Jesus. It is a response to many stimuli, some deriving from the intracanonical writings, including Paul's letters, others from the extracanonical documents, still others from amazingly unexpected archaeological discoveries, which are both literary and non-literary.

The explosion of interest in the Jesus of history since 1980 is unprecedented. Never since the appearance of Reimarus' work (1774–78) — and certainly no comparison can be made before his time — have so many scholars published so many notable books on the historical Jesus (see the Annotated Bibliography at the end of the present volume). Well over thirty of these are significant and distinguished publications. The range of religious perspectives is impressive, from conservative Christians, like F. F. Bruce, to so-called liberal, secular Christians, like E. P. Sanders. Not only Christians, but also Jews are deeply engaged in Jesus research; the most distinguished among the Jewish authors are D. Flusser, G. Vermes, A. Segal, and E. Rivkin. All of the latter now join me in the attempt to clarify certain dimensions in the life and teaching of Jesus of Nazareth. It is impressive — and encouraging — to see how polemics and confessionalisms are replaced by careful and sensitive historical and scientific research.

CHAPTER THREE

Reflections on Jesus-of-History Research Today

John P. Meier

Introduction

In a recent novel, *Roger's Version,* John Updike pits a Barthian theologian toying with skepticism against a conservative and naive computer student in a fierce debate over whether the existence of God can be proved. As I sit at my desk, looking at a slender volume titled *Jesus and the Word* (1926) by the skeptical and sometimes Barthian Rudolf Bultmann,[1] and the much larger and more confident *Jesus and Judaism* (1985) by E. P. Sanders,[2] I wonder whether the twentieth century has not witnessed a similar debate on the historical Jesus. The comparison, though, is not quite apt. Sanders, neither conservative nor naive, does not represent the antithesis to Bultmann; that role belongs to the exegetical acrobats of an earlier generation, the conservative Protestants and Catholics who wrote "lives of Jesus" that desperately sought to harmonize the discordant testimony of the four gospels at any price. The breathtaking intellectual gymnastics of the Catholic "lives" seem especially poignant today, since often they were the result of official pressure rather than personal narrowness. Scholars like Ferdinand Prat[3] and Marie-Joseph Lagrange[4] knew better, but they were subject to censorship and silencing by the Vatican.

---

[1]R. Bultmann, *Jesus* (Berlin, 1926); E.T. *Jesus and the Word* (New York, 1958).
[2]E. P. Sanders, *Jesus and Judaism* (Philadelphia, 1985).
[3]F. Prat, *Jesus Christ: His Life, His Teaching, and His Work* (translated from the 16th French ed.; Milwaukee, 1950).
[4]M.-J. Lagrange, *L'évangile de Jesus Christ* (Paris, 1928, 1954).

Sanders' book, by contrast, represents more of a centrist approach, an honest attempt to avoid both the minimalism of an existentialist like Bultmann and the uncritical acceptance of the gospel narratives by fundamentalists who think they are watching videotape replays. Whether one prefers the Baptist Norman Perrin or the German Catholic Anton Vögtle, the post–liberal-Protestant Sanders or the Jewish Dead Sea Scrolls expert Geza Vermes, one senses that the last forty years have produced a rough consensus on valid sources, method, and criteria in that most enduring of modern treasure hunts, the quest for the historical Jesus. Although decisions still vary greatly on the authenticity of individual sayings of Jesus, and one expert will feel more confident than the next on whether Jesus used this or that title, a surprising amount of convergence has emerged since World War II. It is symptomatic that, in a 1974 work, *Jesus in Contemporary Historical Research*, Gustaf Aulén, a Swedish bishop, was able to draw up a sketch of Jesus' message and ministry based not on his own original research but simply on basic agreements he found among a wide range of exegetes.[5]

It is in this sense that Sanders represents the culmination of the post–World War II period in the quest for the Jesus of history. It is not that Sanders does not present new and debatable views; he does, from claiming that Jesus did not demand repentance to playing down the sayings of Jesus and totally ignoring the titles attributed to him. These challenges to the received wisdom will make his book must reading, even in Updike's mythical divinity school on the Charles. Yet the greatest value of *Jesus and Judaism* is that it acts as a summation and a watershed. It is a classic because it brilliantly embodies a whole generation's desire to avoid exaggerations from right or left, to stop portraying Jesus as a predecessor of Heidegger or Ortega or Luther or Aquinas, and to try to understand what this Jew meant to say and accomplish in first-century Palestine.

That all this should have happened since 1945 is not totally accidental. Granted, popularizers have exaggerated the importance for Jesus-of-history research of the Jewish scrolls discovered at Qumran and the gnostic codices recovered at Nag Hammadi. One easily forgets that nothing in either discovery tells us anything directly about the historical Jesus. Still, these finds have joined

---

[5]G. Aulén, *Jesus i nutida historisk forskning* (Stockholm, 1973); E.T. *Jesus in Contemporary Historical Research* (Philadelphia, 1976).

forces with Greco-Roman studies, rabbinic research, and the sociology of the New Testament to tie down our picture of Jesus of Nazareth to a concrete time and place. While Qumran is actually more useful in showing us how variegated pre-70 C.E. Judaism was, and while Nag Hammadi is more relevant to Church history from the second to the fourth centuries, these discoveries have helped keep professorial flights of fancy within certain limits. As the quest in the eighteenth and nineteenth centuries shows, the historical Jesus readily becomes the clear crystal pool into which scholars gaze to see themselves. The archaeological finds since World War II have fended off this academic narcissism just at a time when New Testament researchers might have been tempted to cave in to the lotus-eating of structuralism and semiotics.

Nevertheless, no amount of archaeology guarantees objectivity in interpretation of the data. The personal pilgrimages of Sanders or Vermes have left their own lineaments on the portraits of Jesus they paint. And so it must be. Not that this inevitable influence of personal stance justifies junking objectivity in favor of a new-journalism approach to historicity — far from it. Objectivity in the quest for the historical Jesus is, to borrow a phrase from Karl Rahner, an "asymptotic goal": we have to keep pressing toward it, even though we never fully arrive. Pressing toward the goal of objectivity is what keeps us on target — along with an honest admission of one's own point of view. Without that admission, archaeology and sociology can still become mere tools of more sophisticated apologetics.

For instance, as a Roman Catholic, I must constantly be on guard against anachronistically reading back the expanded universe of Church dogma into the "big-bang" moment of Jesus' earthly life. Yet I would maintain (more apologetics?) that a Catholic is paradoxically freer than, say, a fundamentalist in pursuing the quest. For one thing, Catholics distinguish carefully between what they know by reason and what they know by faith. The question of the Jesus of history automatically brackets — *not* betrays — what is known by faith and restricts all affirmations to what is verifiable or at least arguable by historical reasoning. One can best picture the process by imagining a gathering of Catholic, Protestant, Jewish, and agnostic scholars trying to hammer out a consensus document on what they could say about Jesus from purely historical sources and arguments. A Catholic could accept the consensus without imagining that it captured the full reality of

Jesus. Moreover, Catholics have traditionally rejected a Bible-only approach to faith in favor of a Scripture-plus-tradition view. For a Catholic, the full reality of Jesus Christ is mediated through multiple channels: Scripture, sacraments, Church Fathers, medieval and modern theologians, the teaching of popes and bishops, and contemporary experience. My faith in Christ does not rise or fall with my attempt to state what I can or cannot know about Jesus of Nazareth by means of modern historical research. The Jesus of history I sketch is at best a fragmentary, hypothetical, changeable reconstruction; it is not — and could hardly be — the object of the Church's faith and preaching. Thus, the very restrictive nature of the enterprise is at the same time liberating. Since I am not trying to argue myself or anyone else into faith (a hopeless task anyway), I can let the historical chips fall where they may. This does not mean that there is a total dichotomy between reason and history on the one hand and faith and theology on the other. After all the historical research has been done, there remains the work of correlating the images of Jesus formed in historical reconstructions and in statements of faith. But such a project would take us far beyond the scope of this essay, which is a modest one. Some forty years after Qumran, I am simply trying to frame my own answer to the question first posed during the Enlightenment and debated ever since: What can "all reasonable people" (that Platonic will o' the wisp) say with fair probability about the historical Jesus?

Birth and Early Years

To begin with, the very notion that Jesus was born exactly 1,991 years ago on December 25 is hopelessly wrong. A sixth-century monk named Dionysius Exiguus (Denny the Dwarf) is responsible for our present B.C./A.D. (= B.C.E./C.E.) system of dating, and unfortunately his math was not as good as his piety. Jesus (Hebrew *Yeshu* or *Yeshua'*, a commonly used name that was a contraction of the Hebrew form of Joshua; see Illus. 1) was born toward the end of the reign of King Herod the Great, hence somewhere around 6–4 B.C.E. His mother was Miriam (Mary), his putative father Joseph. That is all we can say for certain about his birth. The worldwide census under Caesar Augustus while Quirinius was governor of Syria is the result of Luke's garbling and compressing of later events. Only one chapter apiece from Matthew and Luke speaks of a birth at Bethlehem (see Illus. 2). The rest of the New Testament knows only of Nazareth as Jesus' place of origin. Thus, Bethlehem may simply be symbolic of Jesus' status as the new David. I would not, however, be so quick to jettison some kind of Davidic descent for Jesus, as does John L. McKenzie;[6] many different and early streams of New Testament tradition affirm it. In any event, Davidic sonship is traced through Joseph, not Miriam.

Jesus spent about the first thirty years of his life in Nazareth, an obscure hilltown in southern Galilee (see Illus. 3–5). We know almost nothing about this period, perhaps because nothing significant happened. Apparently there was little if anything in Jesus' background or education (if any existed) to prepare his neighbors for the shock of his later ministry. Out of the whole New Testament, only one verse (Mk 6:3) tells us that Jesus was a *tektōn*, most likely a carpenter, though the word can mean stonemason or smith. In this, Jesus probably followed the trade of Joseph, though the matter is by no means as clear as most people think. Presumably, Joseph died before Jesus began his ministry. At least, Joseph is not mentioned during it, in contrast to Miriam, Jesus' mother, and his brothers Jacob (James), Joseph, Judah (Judas), and Simon. Sisters are also alluded to, but not named. Since the Enlightenment, controversy has raged between Protestants and Catholics over these brothers and sisters, Protestants generally taking them to be true siblings, while Catholics usually see them as cousins. Recently, the German Catholic scholar Rudolf Pesch has favored the sibling interpretation,[7] and the dean of German Catholic exegetes, Rudolf Schnackenburg, has written diplomatically that the question needs to be discussed further.[8] Actually, the most disconcerting aspect of Jesus' family life is that his relatives did not believe in him during his public ministry.

The New Testament never speaks of Jesus' marital status. The idea that he remained celibate rests mostly on an argument from silence; but in the face of all the references to his father, mother, brothers, and sisters, the silence may be significant. Some scholars suggest that Jesus' reference to eunuchs who make themselves such for the sake of the Kingdom (Mt 19:12) is a reply to critics who sneered at his single status. Others propose that Jesus was consciously imitating the celibate life of Jeremiah, another

---

[6]J. L. McKenzie, *The New Testament without Illusion* (New York, 1980) p. 20.

[7]R. Pesch, *Das Markusevangelium. I. Teil* (Freiburg, 1976) pp. 322–25.

[8]R. Schnackenburg, in a review of R. E. Brown et al., *Mary in the New Testament*, in *BZ* 11 (1967) 305–7.

prophet who called Israel to repentance at a critical juncture in its history. The influence of the "monks" at Qumran is likewise invoked, but whether celibacy was ever practiced there is still debated (see Illus. 21).

What *is* certain about Jesus' status is that he was a layman. Christian rhetoric about "Christ the high priest" has obscured the fact that Jesus the layman consorted almost entirely with other Jewish laypeople, his few encounters with priests being invariably hostile — including the final one that precipitated his death. We miss the sharp barb in the parable of the Good Samaritan if we forget it is an anticlerical joke, told by Jesus the layman to other Galilean laypeople who disliked the priestly aristocracy in Jerusalem as much as he did (see Illus. 7 and 8). Since Jesus plied his ministry for the most part among the common people of Galilee and Judea, he presumably taught in Aramaic, the ordinary language of the lower classes. His reading of Scripture in the synagogue points to a knowledge of Hebrew, and commercial transactions in Galilee may have introduced him to Greek (used perhaps with Pilate during his trial?). But there is no indication of higher education or rabbinic training (see Jn 7:15). Jesus, like John the Baptist, was addressed as "Rabbi," but in the early first century the title was used widely and loosely.

Baptism and Ministry to Israel

Sometime around 28–29 C.E. (see Lk 3:1), during the reign of the Emperor Tiberius (14–37 C.E.), Jesus journeyed to the Jordan River to receive a "baptism of repentance for the forgiveness of sins" from John the Baptist, a Jewish prophet known as well from the Jewish historian Josephus. (Josephus also seems to mention Jesus in two passages, but their authenticity is debated among scholars.) The embarrassing nature of Jesus' submission to a baptism of repentance conferred by John, a point increasingly played down by the four gospels, argues for the event's historicity and its pivotal place in the life of Jesus. By accepting John's baptism, Jesus indicated he accepted John's message of the imminent disaster that was threatening Israel in the last days of its history, a disaster to be avoided only by national repentance. When Jesus struck out on his own, he continued the Baptist's warning about divine judgment soon to come. It is no accident, then, that some of Jesus' closest disciples had been followers of the Baptist. Sanders rightly takes to task recent literary critics who have sought to make Jesus relevant by ignoring his emphasis on an imminent and definitive intervention of God, bringing salvation or doom. To remove this future thrust from Jesus' preaching about the coming Kingdom of God is to isolate him from his first-century Jewish Palestinian matrix.

Although Jesus followed in the Baptist's footsteps, perhaps even baptizing for a while (see Jn 3:22, 26; 4:1), there was a major shift in his message. While John emphasized judgment and punishment, Jesus proclaimed the good news that God, like a loving father, was seeking out and gathering in the lost, the poor, the marginalized, yes, even the irreligious. Gathering is indeed the word; for Jesus was not concerned — as nineteenth-century liberal piety often portrayed him — simply with touching individual souls. The audience Jesus sought to address was none other than all Israel. Seeing himself as the final prophet sent to a sinful nation in its last hour, Jesus sought to gather the scattered people of God back into one, holy community. In this sense, at the beginning of his ministry, Jesus could not have intended to *found* a Church because he *did find* a Church already existing — the *qāhāl*, the *'ēdâ*, that Yahweh had once called together in the wilderness and was now calling together again. How the gentiles fit into this vision is not clear. Perhaps Jesus thought that in "the last days" the "gentiles" would come on pilgrimage to a restored Mount Zion to be taught by Israel, as Isaiah had prophesied. In any case, Jesus saw himself as a prophet sent only to his own people. Positive encounters with individual gentiles occurred, but they were the exceptions that proved the rule.

Jesus concretely embodied his vision of an Israel restored in the last days by selecting from his followers an inner circle of twelve men, representing the twelve patriarchs of the regathered twelve tribes. Scholars like Günter Klein[9] and Walter Schmithals[10] have claimed that the Twelve are a retrojection of the early Church's organization into the life of Jesus. As a matter of fact, though, the group of the Twelve soon lost their prominence in the early Church, which indeed had trouble even remembering all twelve names! Moreover, the gospels' embarrassed acknowledgment that

[9]G. Klein, *Die zwölf Apostel: Ursprung und Gehalt einer Idee* (FRLANT N.F. 59; Göttingen, 1961).

[10]W. Schmithals, *Das kirchliche Apostelamt: Eine historische Untersuchung* (FRLANT N.F. 61; Göttingen, 1961); E.T. *The Office of Apostle in the Early Church* (Nashville, 1969).

Judas the betrayer was one of the Twelve hardly sounds like an invention of Church propaganda. That Jesus should choose *twelve* men to symbolize the restored Israel and not *eleven*, with himself as the twelfth, indicates that Jesus saw himself standing over against and above the nucleus he was creating. The choice of the Twelve makes clear that Jesus was not intending to found a new sect separated from Israel. His twelve "patriarchs" were rather to be the exemplars and center of a renewed people of God in the endtime. Some modern scholars, ignoring the lesson of Qumran, continue to suppose that Jesus' announcement of the end necessarily involved a lack of concern about organization and order among his disciples. That was not the case in the highly structured community at Qumran, and the appointment of the Twelve shows it was not the case among Jesus' followers.

The followers of the Nazarene extended far beyond the Twelve. Perhaps we can best imagine the situation in terms of concentric circles: the Twelve, other committed disciples who left family and employment to follow Jesus literally, and people who accepted Jesus' teaching but maintained their homes and jobs. No doubt some people passed back and forth between the outer two circles; the borders were hardly fixed. Jesus' relation to his disciples differed from that of the later rabbis in a number of ways. Jesus often took the initiative in calling people — including some not very promising candidates — to discipleship, even ordering them to forsake sacred duties to follow him: "Let the dead bury their dead." At least in his inner group, he expected commitment to himself to be a permanent affair; his disciples were not studying to be rabbis who would then leave him and set up schools of their own. Especially striking was Jesus' inclusion of women in his traveling entourage and his willingness to teach them. With both personal and financial support they stood by him — quite literally at the cross, when all the male disciples fled.

If we had only the Gospels of Mark, Matthew, and Luke (the "synoptic gospels"), we would get the impression that almost all of Jesus' followers came from the countryside and towns of Galilee; indeed, some scholars have referred to his supporters as "an agrarian reform movement." It is John's Gospel that reminds us that Jesus was also frequently active in and around Jerusalem — which helps explain how this supposedly agrarian movement suddenly became an urban phenomenon. John's Gospel is also correct, I think, in spreading Jesus' ministry over a number of Passovers and therefore over a number of years. Left with the synoptic gospels, we might easily compress Jesus' ministry into a couple of months. Fortunately, exegetes like C. H. Dodd[11] and R. E. Brown[12] have crusaded effectively against the Schweitzer-Bultmann dogma that John's Gospel may be safely ignored in reconstructing the historical Jesus, although the keepers of the Bultmannian flame still reject John's statements en masse.

Teaching in Parables and in Actions

Prophet and wisdom teacher that he was, Jesus used the rich rhetorical traditions of Israel to hammer home his message. Oracles, woes, aphorisms, proverbs, but above all parables ($m^e sh\bar{a}l\hat{\imath}m$) served to tease the minds of his audience, throw them off balance, and challenge them to decide for or against his claim on their lives. The parables are not pretty Sunday-school stories. They are troubling riddles, meant to destroy any false sense of security and create a fierce feeling of urgency. Any moment may be too late: the hearer must stake all on Jesus' message *now*, no matter what the cost. For God is about to work his own kind of revolution: the poor will be exalted and the powerful dispossessed. This startling and disturbing program is at the heart of the parables as well as the beatitudes. It is a promise of radical reversal, usually reduced by sermonizers to a spiritual bonbon. For Jesus, though, the revolution would be God's doing, not humanity's. This may be unpalatable to some liberation theologians, who are especially fond of the historical Jesus, as opposed to the Christ of dogma. Sad to say, their uncritical use of such gospel texts as Jesus' inaugural sermon at Nazareth would make the Holy Office look like Rudolf Bultmann by comparison. Indeed, in this, Bultmann's *Jesus and the Word* may have been correct: the historical Jesus seems to have had no interest in the great political and social questions of his day.[13] He was not interested in the reform of the world because he was prophesying its end. Whether this makes Jesus irrelevant to the academicians of the 1990s is itself irrelevant to our historical quest.

---

[11]C. H. Dodd, *Historical Tradition in the Fourth Gospel* (Cambridge, 1963); see also the same author's *The Interpretation of the Fourth Gospel* (Cambridge, 1953), especially pp. 444–53.

[12]R. E. Brown, *The Gospel according to John* (AB 29–29A; Garden City, N.Y., 1966–70).

[13]Bultmann, *Jesus and the Word*, pp. 25, 40–42.

Jesus' impact did not come simply from powerful rhetoric. As with the Old Testament prophets, word (*dābār*) was also deed. Jesus consciously willed his public activity to be a dramatic acting out of his message of God's welcome and forgiveness extended to the prodigal son. He insisted on associating and eating with the religious low-life of his day, "the toll collectors and sinners," Jews who in the eyes of the pious had apostatized and were no better than gentiles. This practice of sharing meals (for Orientals, a most serious and intimate form of social intercourse) with the religiously "lost" put Jesus in a continual state of ritual impurity, as far as the stringently law-observant were concerned. As Sanders emphasizes, Jesus no doubt shocked the pious by offering salvation to these outcasts without demanding the usual Jewish mechanism of repentance.[14] What Sanders does not sufficiently note is that, in effect, Jesus was making acceptance of himself and his message the touchstone of true repentance. No doubt this upset the pious even more. Instead of grim works of penitence, Jesus proclaimed the joy of the heavenly banquet soon to come and already anticipated in his table fellowship with those outside the pale. In keeping with this festive mood, Jesus and his disciples did not undertake the voluntary fasts practiced by the Pharisees and the followers of the Baptist. Indeed, so blatant was Jesus' merry-making that the devout contemptuously dismissed him as a bon vivant, "a glutton and a drunkard" (Mt 11:19).

There was, then, on Jesus' part a conscious coherence between his words and his deeds. Of great discomfort to some of us moderns is his claim to perform healings and exorcisms. At this point, many treatments of Jesus get hopelessly bogged down in a discussion of the possibility or the impossibility of miracles — which, properly speaking, is a philosophical rather than historical or even theological problem. But from the perspective of religious history, it is simply a fact that faith healers and miracle workers are common phenomena in both ancient and modern religions, from Honi the Circle Drawer and Apollonius of Tyana to the grotto of Lourdes and the televised epiphanies of Oral Roberts. How one explains such phenomena varies with both the subject studied and the observer commenting. Autosuggestion, psychosomatic diseases, mass hysteria are all possibilities, although the medical records at Lourdes do not always allow for such convenient es-

---

[14]Sanders, *Jesus and Judaism*, pp. 200–11.

cape hatches. In the case of Jesus, all that need be noted is that ancient Christian, Jewish, and pagan sources *all agreed* that Jesus did extraordinary things not easily explained by human means. While Jesus' disciples pointed to the Spirit of God as the source of his power, some Jewish and pagan adversaries spoke of demonic or magical powers. It never occurred to any of the ancient polemicists to claim that nothing had happened.

For the modern interpreter, the key point is to situate Jesus' healings within the overall context of his message and acts (something Morton Smith does not do in his *Jesus the Magician*).[15] Jesus saw his healing not simply as kind deeds done to help unfortunate individuals; rather, like his table fellowship, they were concrete ways of dramatizing and effecting God's victory over the powers of evil in the final hour of human history. The miracles were signs and partial realizations of what was about to come fully in the Kingdom. An already/not-yet tension lay at the heart of Jesus' vision. Yet, despite his stress on the imminent future of salvation, Jesus was not, strictly speaking, an apocalypticist; he had no interest in detailed time tables or cosmic journeys. Indeed, to the great chagrin of Christian theologians, he even affirmed his own ignorance of the day and hour of the final judgment (Mk 13:32).

Jesus and the Mosaic Law

We must keep this proclamation of the present-yet-coming Kingdom of God in mind when we try to understand Jesus' moral teaching. To put it in a laconic paradox: Jesus exhorts his followers to live even now by the power of a future event that has already touched and transformed their lives. Now, this is not quite the same thing as Albert Schweitzer's "interim ethic";[16] for Jesus gives neither a precise calendar nor any indication that his basic ethic is meant for only a short interval. The unrestricted love of God and neighbor that stands at the heart of Jesus' moral imperative is hardly a stop-gap measure for the time being. Actually, for the sake of accuracy, it should be noted that the word "love" does not appear all that frequently in the authentic sayings of Jesus. But if we gather together all of his pronouncements and parables that deal with compassion and forgiveness, the picture that results is a

[15]M. Smith, *Jesus the Magician* (San Francisco, 1978).
[16]A. Schweitzer, *The Quest of the Historical Jesus: A Critical Study of Its Progress from Reimarus to Wrede* (New York, 1910, 1968) pp. 365–66.

Jesus who stressed mercy without measure, love without limits — even love of one's enemies. To many of us, such ideals, however beautiful, seem simply un-doable. To Jesus, they were doable, but only for those who had experienced through him God's incredible love in their own lives. Radical demand flowed from radical grace. If religion becomes grace, then ethics becomes gratitude — and not just for the interim.

Trying to formulate Jesus' moral teaching into some codified, rational system is futile, especially since it is in his attitude to morality and law that Jesus proves himself the true charismatic in the classic sense. Faced with a crisis of traditional authority, the charismatic claims direct authority and intuitive knowledge that are not mediated through the traditional channels of law, custom, or established institutions. That is a perfect description of Jesus' approach; and it led to a basic tension in his treatment of the Mosaic Law. Jesus the Jew fundamentally affirmed the Law as God's will, though with a radicalizing thrust seen also at Qumran. At times, Jesus would engage in rabbinic-style debate to solve concrete problems. Yet on certain specific issues (divorce, oaths, unclean foods), he claimed to know intuitively and directly that Jewish Law or custom was contrary to God's will. In such cases, the Law had to give way to or be reinterpreted by the command of Jesus, simply because Jesus said so ("but *I* say to you"). He made no attempt to ground or authenticate such teaching in the manner of the Old Testament prophets ("the word of the Lord came to me, saying . . . ") or the later rabbis ("Rabbi X said in the name of Rabbi Y"). His peculiar and solemn introduction to various pronouncements, "*Amen*, I say to you," emphasized that he knew and taught God's will with absolute certitude. Hence, as people accepted or rejected his instruction, so they would be saved or condemned on the last day. It was perhaps this unheard-of claim to authority over the Mosaic Law and over people's lives, more than any title Jesus may or may not have used of himself, that disturbed pious Jews and the Jewish authorities. Along with the Temple, the Torah was *the* central symbol of Jewish religion, around which warring parties could rally. By assuming unlimited power over the Torah and by rescinding a key boundary marker between Jews and gentiles, Jesus inevitably put himself on a collision course not only with the Temple priests but also with sincere Jews in general.

Jesus and the Jewish Parties

Jesus' exact relation to the various Jewish parties of the day is extremely difficult to fix, all the more so because most of the rabbinic material comes from a later date. If it is naive to cite indiscriminately gospel texts written down one or two generations after Jesus' death, it is more than naive to quote rabbinic texts written down hundreds of years after Jesus died, as though Judaism had not undergone tremendous changes during the interval. To make vague claims about the Mishna and Talmud enshrining older traditions does not answer the pivotal question: how much older? The relation of Jesus to the various Jewish groups of the first century C.E. is thus vastly more complicated than most popular presentations of "Jesus the Jew" acknowledge. The question is: What kind of Jew? Different scholars have identified Jesus with almost every Jewish party known to exist. The favorite designation is "Jesus the Pharisee"; but that simply shifts the question to: What kind of Pharisee? Jesus has been painted as a nonconforming Pharisee because of his freedom *vis-à-vis* the Law and tradition, a Pharisee of the Shammai school because of his strict views on divorce, and a Pharisee of the Hillel school because of his humane emphasis on love of neighbor as central to the Law. Others have seen his critique of the Pharisees' oral tradition as indicating a preference for the Sadducees. Still others suggest that, since Jesus radicalized the obligations of the Law and proclaimed the imminent end of the present age, he had ties with the sectarians at Qumran. Despite the popularity of the last suggestion since the discovery of the Dead Sea Scrolls, Jesus' free-wheeling approach to written Law, his critique of purity rules, his distance from minute priestly concerns, and his openness to Jewish sinners make the identification improbable.

Then, too, there is the ever-popular attempt to present Jesus as sympathetic to armed revolt against the Romans. S. G. F. Brandon was an indefatigable proponent of such a view, but much of his argument rests on seeing Jesus' nonviolent ethic as a coverup contrived by the later Church.[17] To supply the real Jesus, Brandon reads between the lines of the gospels with more than a dollop of novelistic imagination. Naturally, if one is free to reject large portions of the gospel tradition and rewrite the rest to

---

[17]S. G. F. Brandon, *Jesus and the Zealots: A Study of the Political Factor in Primitive Christianity* (Manchester, 1967).

suit a given thesis, any interpretation of Jesus is possible. Recent essays by Ernst Bammel, C. F. D. Moule, and a host of colleagues investigating Brandon's method and individual arguments have rendered the whole Jesus-as-Zealot (or Zealot-sympathizer) approach highly dubious.[18]

If truth be told, Jesus did not fit any of these pigeonholes, which may be one reason he wound up deserted and crucified. The gospels may not be entirely wrong, though, in presenting the Pharisees as the group with which Jesus was most often in dialogue and debate. It is a commonplace in New Testament research today to affirm that the negative, polemical picture of the Pharisees in the gospels largely reflects later debates between Church and synagogue and do not go back to Jesus himself. Though this is largely true, the claim presupposes that we know the exact social status and religious views of the Pharisees in the pre-70 C.E. period. Actually, both Jewish and Christian scholars still debate such questions; the ground-breaking work of Jacob Neusner on the Pharisees[19] remains a focal point of contention, with the writings of Ellis Rivkin providing an alternative view.[20]

On any reading, however, there were certainly points of contact between the Pharisees and the Nazarene. Like Jesus, the Pharisees were religiously committed lay people who, disgusted with the corrupt rulers and high priests of Israel, sought personal and national reform through a fierce commitment to doing God's will in ordinary daily life. Unlike the Sadducees, their outlook was not restricted to this world; they hoped to share in a future resurrection and eternal life. The tragedy is that, while Jesus and the Pharisees could agree on the basic goal of personal reform and national restoration along spiritual lines, they were diametrically opposed on the way to achieve such renewal. As far as we can tell — and the evidence is by no means clear — the Pharisees of the pre-70 period emphasized the voluntary acceptance by lay people of the same rules of ritual purity that bound the Temple priests. Detailed regulations concerning tithing, washing, eating, and observance of the Sabbath were meant to sanctify everyday life, turning the nation into a spiritual temple by obedience to both

---

[18]E. Bammel and C. F. D. Moule (eds.), *Jesus and the Politics of His Day* (Cambridge, New York, 1984).

[19]J. Neusner, *The Rabbinic Traditions about the Pharisees before 70* (Leiden, 1971).

[20]E. Rivkin, *A Hidden Revolution* (Nashville, 1978); *What Crucified Jesus?* (Nashville, 1984).

the written Law and oral tradition. The charismatic freedom Jesus displayed toward the Law, his announcement of the imminent coming of the Kingdom, and the personal claim all this implied naturally put him at odds with the Pharisees. Yet in many ways they remained the Jewish group closest to his own views, and as a party they were not directly involved in his death.

The Identity of Jesus

Looking at all Jesus said and did, we are confronted by one central question: Who did Jesus think he was? Or to put the question in terms more open to verification: Who did he claim to be? Jesus himself — at least in sayings that seem to be authentic — gave no clear and detailed answer. Totally absorbed in proclaiming and realizing the Kingdom of God, he showed no indication of suffering an identity crisis, no need to engage in the tiresome modern hobby of finding oneself. He apparently was quite sure of who he was, though no one since has been. The crux of the problem lies in the paradox that, although Jesus rarely spoke directly about his own status, he implicitly made himself *the* pivotal figure in the final drama he was announcing and inaugurating. The Kingdom was somehow already present in his person and ministry, and on the last day he would be the criterion by which people would be judged.

Jesus seems to have based such monumental claims, at least in part, on his special relationship with God. Following J. Jeremias,[21] E. Schillebeeckx has focused on Jesus' use of the Aramaic word *Abba* — "(my own dear) Father" — in his prayer to God and the whole relationship that lies behind such prayer.[22] The intimate address of *Abba*, foreign to the liturgies of Temple and of synagogue, expresses an extremely close, confident relation to God, says Schillebeeckx; it betokens the wellspring of Jesus' ministry. There is a danger here, however, of basing a great deal on very little. *Abba* occurs only once in the four gospels and could be a retrojection of early Jewish-Christian prayer, reflecting a popular Aramaic practice not recorded in formal liturgical documents. On balance, though, Schillebeeckx is probably correct: Jesus' experi-

---

[21] J. Jeremias, *Abba: Studien zur neutestamentlichen Theologie und Zeitgeschichte* (Göttingen, 1966); E.T. *The Prayers of Jesus* (SBT 2/6; London, 1967).
[22] E. Schillebeeckx, *Jesus: An Experiment in Christology* (New York, 1979) pp. 256–71.

ence of intimate relationship with God as *Abba* was one — if not the only — basis of his mission.

Did Jesus go beyond this and actually apply any titles or categories to himself? Many a volume has been written over the past few decades cataloguing the titles given Jesus in the New Testament and weighing the possibility that some of them derive from Jesus himself. The results range from the optimistic (O. Cullmann)[23] to the skeptical (G. Bornkamm and E. P. Sanders, who both waive any detailed investigation). Among Jewish authors, G. Vermes is surprisingly accepting of titles, provided they are purged of Christian ideas.[24] At the very least, I think it safe to say that Jesus saw himself as a prophet, indeed the final prophet sent to Israel in its last days; a similar figure appears in the Dead Sea Scrolls. Jesus' reputation for performing miracles may have conjured up hopes that the wonder-working Elijah had returned to prepare Israel for the end. Vermes even suggests that we see Jesus as standing in the tradition of the *ḥasid*, the charismatic holy man of Galilee, a product of popular folk religion rather than of academic theology. Be that as it may, the title "prophet" was not without its dangers. In Jewish thought of the time, the image of prophet was often connected with rejection and martyrdom; and so the title was much more ominous than might at first appear.

The title "Messiah" ("the Christ") is often presumed to be central to Jesus' identity, but that is to read later Christian concepts and definitions back into a much more confused situation. In the early first century C.E., there was no one clear doctrine on *a* or *the* Messiah, and some Jewish groups that looked for the imminent coming of God dispensed completely with any such intermediary figure. The authors or editors of the Dead Sea Scrolls expected two Messiahs, one Davidic and royal, the other — who took precedence — Levitical and priestly. Since the word "Messiah" simply meant "anointed one," it could be applied to various sacred agents of God in the endtime, including a prophet "anointed" by the Holy Spirit. The expectation of the common people and of the Pharisees did apparently center on a king like David. If Jesus was in fact of Davidic descent, it would not be surprising if some of his followers identified him with the Davidic type of Messiah. There is really no other reason why the disciples' belief in his

---

[23] O. Cullmann, *The Christology of the New Testament* (rev. ed.; Philadelphia, 1963).
[24] G. Vermes, *Jesus and the World of Judaism* (Philadelphia, 1983); *Jesus the Jew: A Historian's Reading of the Gospels* (Philadelphia, 1981).

resurrection at Easter should have in turn triggered their proclamation that he had been enthroned in heaven as the royal son of David (see Illus. 18). In themselves, the two ideas of resurrection and a new King David had no intrinsic connection. That speculation about Jesus as the Davidic Messiah was well-known, even to Jesus' enemies, is supported by the charge under which he was tried by Pilate and crucified: King of the Jews. There is no proof, though, that Jesus himself ever directly claimed to be the Messiah in the royal sense; he was perhaps all too aware of the dangers of a political interpretation.

As for the title "Son" or "Son of God," it is conceivable that a person who addressed God as *Abba* might understand himself in some sense or other as God's Son. As a matter of fact, the titles "Son of God" and "Son of the Most High" are applied to a mysterious royal figure of the endtime in a fragmentary Dead Sea Scroll text. Still, very few gospel sayings in which Jesus calls himself "the Son" have much chance of being authentic. The best candidate is Mark 13:32, which affirms that "the Son" (*ho huios*; = Jesus) does not know the time of the final judgment. It seems improbable that the early Church went out of its way to make up sayings emphasizing the ignorance of its risen Lord. In any event, one must beware of reading into the title the meaning it acquired in later trinitarian controversies.

Of all the titles, the most confusing is "Son of man." As it now stands in the gospels, it refers to the earthly ministry of Jesus, his death and resurrection, and his coming as judge (alluding to Dan 7:13–14). The question of whether Jesus ever used the title, and if so in what sense, has received every answer imaginable. Bultmann held that Jesus used "Son of man" not of himself but of some other figure still to come.[25] Perrin argued that the title as applied to Jesus was totally a creation of the early Church.[26] Lindars suggests that Jesus originally used "Son of man" not as a title but simply as a modest circumlocution, "a man like myself"; it was the Church that turned it into a title.[27] Personally, I think it arguable that Jesus the parable-maker did use "Son of man" as an enigmatic designation of himself during his ministry as the lowly yet powerful servant of God's Kingdom. Faced with increasing

---

[25] Bultmann, *Jesus and the Word*, pp. 38–39.

[26] N. Perrin, *A Modern Pilgrimage in New Testament Christology* (Philadelphia, 1974).

[27] B. Lindars, *Jesus, Son of Man: A Fresh Examination of the Son of Man Sayings in the Gospels in the Light of Recent Researches* (Grand Rapids, Mich., 1983).

rejection, he may also have used the title to affirm his assurance of final triumph and vindication by God. On the other hand, the use of "Son of man" in the explicit predictions of Jesus' death and resurrection may well stem from the Church.

As for other title "Lord," there is really no problem in its being applied to Jesus during his earthly life. As we now know from the Dead Sea Scrolls, the Aramaic *mārēh* or *mārē'* could mean anything from a polite "sir" to a divine "Lord." No doubt different people addressed the title to Jesus with varying degrees of reverence, and the early Church simply continued the address, in a new transcendent sense, when praying to its exalted Lord.

Going to Jerusalem to Die

It is apparent that Jesus was much less interested in titles than we are. He was not primarily a theologian but a man of action. In the spring of 30 C.E. (or possibly 33), he took the decisive action of going on pilgrimage to Jerusalem for Passover, apparently determined to engage the leadership of Israel in a once-and-for-all confrontation. Two symbolic acts performed by Jesus were meant to press home the issue with the authorities: the "triumphal entry" into Jerusalem and the "cleansing" of the Temple (see Illus. 13, 16). The historicity of both events has been called into question; but if we think of limited symbolic gestures rather than Hollywood-style riots, both acts fit in with the tradition of prophecy-by-action practiced by the Old Testament prophets. The entry into Jerusalem implied but did not define some sort of messianic claim over the ancient Davidic capital. More crucial was the "cleansing" of the Temple, which was probably not a call for reform but a prophecy that the present Temple would be destroyed. Various sayings of Jesus point in that direction and cohere with Jewish apocalyptic thought of the time. The "cleansing" had much more ominous implications than the "entry." An attack on the Temple, however figurative, would have alienated not only the priests but also many pious Jews, even those opposed to the Jerusalem hierarchy.

As Schillebeeckx notes, given the challenge he put to the hostile authorities on their home ground, Jesus would have had to have been a simpleton not to have realized the mortal danger in which he was placing himself.[28] He did not have to be a very farsighted

---

[28]Schillebeeckx, *Jesus*, p. 299.

prophet to appreciate that a violent death in Jerusalem had become a real possibility. Bultmann claims that we cannot know anything about how Jesus understood and confronted his death, indeed whether he broke down when faced with it.[29] In recent years, H. Schürmann has vigorously challenged that position.[30] Admittedly, most critics would agree that the explicit predictions of death and resurrection reflect the theology of the early Church. Still, I think that some sayings which speak of his death in general terms, often with no mention of resurrection or ultimate triumph, may come from the historical Jesus.

In a number of sayings (e.g., Mt 23:37–39; Lk 13:31–33), Jesus speaks of his possible death as that of a prophet martyred in Jerusalem, in the long line of Old Testament prophets. The lack of titles beyond the generic "prophet," the placing of Jesus on the same level as the Old Testament prophets, and the absence of any mention of resurrection or vindication make it unlikely that these sayings were created by the Church. In the core parable of the evil tenants of the vineyard (Mk 12:1–8), the parable ends in unmitigated tragedy: "the son" (= Jesus) is killed, with no hint of reprieve or reversal. In Mk 10:35–40, James and John ask Jesus to grant them seats of honor next to him in the Kingdom. In reply, Jesus uses Old Testament images to tell them that all he can promise is a share in his death. The anecdote reflects badly on the glory-hungry sons of Zebedee. When one considers that, a few years after Jesus' death, James became the first martyr among the Twelve, it seems improbable that the early Church would have created such a slur on his memory. Moreover, Jesus' prophecy that John would suffer the same fate remained, as far as we know, unfulfilled. Finally, in the anecdote Jesus affirms his inability to assure seats at his right and left in the Kingdom; all in all, the story does not sound like later Christian propaganda. What is especially noteworthy in all these passages is that there is no saving significance attributed to Jesus' death, no idea of vicarious sacrifice. The death of Jesus is simply predicted; it has no positive value.

If Jesus ever did give a clearer explanation of how he viewed his approaching death, the most likely occasion would have been the last opportunity he had: the Last Supper. The historicity of this last

---

[29]Bultmann, "The Primitive Christian Kerygma and the Historical Jesus," in C. Braaten and R. Harrisville (eds.), *The Historical Jesus and the Kerygmatic Christ* (Nashville, 1964) pp. 15–42.
[30]H. Schürmann, *Jesu ureigener Tod* (Freiburg, 1975).

meal with his disciples is supported independently by Mark and John, special traditions in Luke, and an early formula preserved by Paul in 1 Cor 11. The meal took place on a Thursday evening, but the exact date differs in the synoptic gospels and John. John is probably correct in dating the supper on the Day of Preparation (for Passover), the 14th of Nisan. The Synoptics' presentation of the Last Supper as a Passover meal is later Christian theology. At the beginning and end of the meal, respectively, Jesus used bread and wine to represent graphically his coming death, which he accepted as part of God's will for bringing in the Kingdom. Jesus' interpretive words over the bread and wine are recorded in four different versions, all influenced by Christian liturgy; hence many scholars consider the original form irrecoverable. I would hazard the guess that the most likely reconstruction is: "This is my body [or flesh]. . . . This is the Covenant [sealed] by my blood." If these words adequately reflect what Jesus said, then he interpreted his death as the (sacrificial?) means by which God would restore his Covenant made with Israel at Sinai (cf. Ex 24:8) and bring it to fulfillment. This *last* supper — the last in a whole series of meals of salvation celebrated with sinners — was a pledge that, despite the apparent failure of Jesus' mission to Israel, God would vindicate him even beyond death and bring him and his followers to the final banquet in the Kingdom. Jesus insists that his disciples all drink from the *one* cup, *his* cup, to emphasize that they must hold fast to their fellowship with him even as he dies, if they are to share that fellowship again in the Kingdom (see Illus. 17).

Trial and Death

After the supper, Jesus led his disciples outside the city to a country estate on or at the foot of the Mount of Olives (Gethsemane means "oil press"; see Illus. 13). There he was arrested by an armed band guided by Judas. The arresting police were in all likelihood controlled by the high priest, though John's Gospel gives indication of some Roman presence as well. The disciples abandoned Jesus and fled. From this point until the trial before Pilate, the succession of events is highly controverted, for three reasons: contradictions among the four gospels, our uncertainty about Jewish and Roman law in pre-70 Palestine, and religious apologetics that plague us still.

Sifting through the vast literature, I find three major scenarios proposed, each of which is possible. (1) A night trial was held before the Sanhedrin, presided over by Caiaphas the high priest (18–36 C.E.); this session either lasted until dawn or was followed by a brief session at dawn. This is the picture given in Mark and Matthew and is supported by J. Blinzler[31] and O. Betz.[32] (2) The Sanhedrin held only an early morning session. This is Luke's presentation and is supported by D. Catchpole.[33] (3) An informal hearing was held by some Jewish official, perhaps Annas, the father-in-law of Caiaphas, who had been high priest from 6 to 15 C.E.; but no formal trial took place before the Sanhedrin. This scenario can be reconstructed from John's Gospel and is defended by P. Winter.[34]

Winter in particular appeals to the many prescriptions of the Mishna tractate Sanhedrin that are flouted in the Synoptic versions. The problem, though, is that we cannot be sure that the rabbinic rules in Sanhedrin (written down around 200 C.E.) accurately reflect how the Sanhedrin conducted trials under a Roman prefect in the pre-70 period. Although all sides want certitude on this neuralgic issue, the truth is that the historian must remain uncertain. Whether a trial or an informal hearing took place before Jewish authorities, some accusation against Jesus would have been considered. His threats against the Temple, his teaching that rescinded commandments in the Law, his claim to be a prophet and perhaps something more might all have been considered; but once again we are in the dark. The ringing affirmations by Jesus that he was indeed the Messiah, Son of God, and Son of man look like portions of a christological catechism drawn up by post-Easter Christians.

What was certainly not invented by Christians is Peter's cowardly denial of being Jesus' disciple, a denial which occurred sometime during the Jewish process. This event, however embarrassing, is important, since it does place an eyewitness near the first stage of Jesus' passion. At the end of the process, the officials decided to charge Jesus before Pilate. Historians debate whether the Jewish authorities needed recourse to Pilate for a death sentence to be executed. Though the evidence is ambiguous,

---

[31]J. Blinzler, *The Trial of Jesus: The Jewish and Roman Proceedings against Jesus Christ Described and Assessed from the Oldest Accounts* (Westminster, Md., 1959).

[32]O. Betz, *What Do We Know About Jesus?* (Philadelphia, 1968).

[33]D. R. Catchpole, *The Trial of Jesus: A Study in the Gospels and Jewish Historiography from 1770 to the Present Day* (SPB 16; Leiden, 1971).

[34]P. Winter, *On the Trial of Jesus* (SJ 1, 2nd. ed; Berlin, New York, 1974).

it seems more plausible that Jn 18:31 is correct: at this period, the Sanhedrin no longer had the power to execute a death sentence.

From 26 to 36 C.E., Pontius Pilate was *prefect* of Judea (*not* procurator, as Tacitus thinks; an inscription discovered at Caesarea Maritima in 1961 confirms that Pilate held the lower title of prefect [see Illus. 11]). Scarcely interested in theological disputes, Pilate would have been concerned only with accusations involving threats to Roman rule. Hence Jesus was brought before him charged with claiming to be King of the Jews — which may indicate that the Jewish process had touched on Jesus' messiahship. It was on this charge of kingship, understood no doubt in terms of being a revolutionary, that Jesus was tried and condemned by Pilate. A placard bearing the charge may have been affixed to the cross. The whole Barabbas incident, however, may be a later theological dramatization of what was at stake in the trial.

Roman crucifixion was usually preceded by scourging, which apparently so weakened Jesus that he could not carry the crossbeam (the upright stake probably remained in place at the site of execution). To aid Jesus, the soldiers pressed into service one Simon from Cyrene in Africa; his sons, Alexander and Rufus, must have been well-known members of Mark's church (cf. Mk 15:21). Once again, an eyewitness is present, this time for the whole process of carrying the cross and the crucifixion. Besides Simon, sympathetic witnesses included only a handful of female followers from Galilee. The placing of the mother of Jesus and the "beloved disciple" at the cross — present only in the Fourth Gospel — may reflect the symbolic mentality of John the Evangelist.

The crucifixion naturally took place outside the walls of the holy city, at a spot called Golgotha ("Skull Place"), possibly an abandoned quarry by the side of a road. Despite our traditional references to "Mt. Calvary," the gospels say nothing about a hill. The best archaeological candidate for the site is the Church of the Holy Sepulchre in Jerusalem; despite continuing debates over the path of Jerusalem's walls in the first century, it seems that the site of the present church lay outside the walls in 30 C.E. (see Illus. 14, 15).

No Passion narrative specifies whether Jesus was tied or nailed to the cross, though nail marks are mentioned in accounts of resurrection appearances. The use of nails does fit in with recent archaeological discoveries of crucified bodies around Jerusalem (see Charlesworth's *Jesus within Judaism*). With regard to what Jesus may or may not have said from the cross, the historian can reach no certain conclusion. All of the "seven last words" (a later conflation, in any case) may come from post-Easter Christian tradition. This includes the famous cry of abandonment, "My God, my God, why have you forsaken me?" (Mk 15:34; Ps 22:2), a favorite among psychiatrists and spiritual writers who show no knowledge of its place in Jewish prayer.

Jesus died relatively quickly, and Jewish law (Deut 21:22–23) required that the body not be left hanging overnight — all the more so when Passover Day (the 15th of Nisan) coincided that year with the Sabbath. Joseph of Arimathea, an influential Jew, interceded with Pilate in order to provide (temporary?) burial in a tomb he owned nearby (see Illus. 12). The actual tomb, long since destroyed, probably lay in a spot now enclosed by the Church of the Holy Sepulchre (see Illus. 14, 15). The so-called Garden Tomb of General Gordon, beloved of tourists, is a product of nineteenth-century romanticism. The Galilean women at the cross also witnessed the preparations for burial, though the only name constant in all the traditions is Mary Magdalene. The story of setting a guard at the sealed tomb to prevent a grave robbery stems from later Jewish-Christian debates; it is intriguing, though, that neither side in later polemics thought to deny that the tomb was soon empty.

As for the Shroud of Turin, scholars are still divided in their judgments, especially since the relic is first documented in the fourteenth century, when many dubious "relics" were flooding the West. Even if the shroud does go back to the time of Jesus, thousands of Jews were crucified in Palestine from around 198 B.C.E. to 200 C.E. with barbaric tortures similar to those suffered by Jesus. Even if the shroud could be shown to be that of a first-century Palestinian Jew, a multitude of unfortunate candidates could qualify. Hence it is wise not to base any conclusions on the shroud. Recent carbon-14 tests simply reinforce this caution.

Since the "Jesus of history" is by definition the Jesus open to empirical investigation by any and all observers, the resurrection of Jesus, of its very nature, lies outside the scope of this chapter. This does not mean that the resurrection is not real, but simply that it is not an ordinary event of our time and space, verifiable in principle by believer and nonbeliever alike. All that history can say is that, starting in the early 30s of the first century, people who had known Jesus during his earthly life and who had deserted him out of fear did a remarkable about-face after his disgraceful death and affirmed that Jesus had risen and appeared to them. That these people were not raving lunatics is shown by their skillful organization and propagation of the new movement. That they were sincere is demonstrated by their willingness to die for what they claimed. How any of us reacts to all this is a question not only of historical investigation but also of existential decision. In the end, there are the hermeneutics of belief and the hermeneutics of unbelief. What is beyond dispute is that Jesus of Nazareth is one of those perennial question marks in history with which humankind is never quite done. With a ministry of two or three years he attracted and infuriated his contemporaries, mesmerized and alienated the ancient world, unleashed a movement that has done the same ever since, and thus changed the course of history forever.

CHAPTER FOUR

Jesus the Jew

Geza Vermes

"Jesus the Jew" — which is also the title of a book[1] I have
written — is an emotionally charged synonym for the Jesus of
history (as opposed to the divine Christ of the Christian faith)
that simply restates the obvious fact, still hard for many Christians and even some Jews to accept, that Jesus was a Jew and not
a Christian. It implies a renewed quest for the historical figure
reputed to be the founder of Christianity.

In one respect this search is surprising — namely, that it has
been undertaken at all. In another, it is unusual — that it has
been made without (so far as I am consciously aware) any ul-
terior motive. My intention has been to reach for the historical
truth, for the sake, at the most, of putting the record straight;
but definitely not in order to demonstrate some theological preconception.

Let me develop these two points.

If, in continuity with medieval Jewish tradition, I had set out
to prove that Yeshu was not only a false Messiah, but also a
heretic, a seducer, and a sorcerer, my research would have been
prejudiced from the start. Even if I had chosen as my target the
more trendy effort of yesterday, the "repatriation of Jesus into
the Jewish people" (*Heimholung Jesu in das jüdische Volk*), it is
unlikely to have led to an untendentious enquiry, to an analysis
of the available evidence without fear or favor, *sin ira et studio*.

By the same token, when a committed Christian embarks on
such a task with a mind already persuaded by the dogmatic
suppositions of his Church, which postulate that Jesus was not
only the true Messiah, but the only begotten Son of God — that

---

[1]G. Vermes, *Jesus the Jew: A Historian's Reading of the Gospels* (London, 1973 and
New York, 1974, 1976 [2nd ed.], 1981, 1983).

is to say, God himself — he is bound to read the gospels in a particular manner and to attribute the maximum possible Christian traditional significance even to the most neutral sentence, one that in any other context he would not even be tempted to interpret that way.

My purpose, both in the written and the verbal examination of "Jesus the Jew," has been to look into the past for some trace of the features of the first-century Galilean, before he had been proclaimed either the apostate and bogey man of Jewish popular thought or the second Person of the Christian Holy Trinity.

Strangely enough, because of the special nature of the gospels, a large group of Christians, including such opposing factions as the out-and-out fundamentalists and some highly sophisticated New Testament critics, would consider a historical enquiry of this sort *ipso facto* doomed to failure. Our knowledge of Jesus, they would claim, depends one hundred percent on the New Testament — on writings that were never intended as history, but as a record of the faith of Jesus' first followers. The fundamentalists deduce from these premises that the pure truth embedded in the gospels is accessible only to those who share the evangelists' outlook. Those who do not do so are — to quote a letter[2] published in *The Guardian* — "still in the night... and so (have) no title to write about things which are only known to (initiates)."

At the other extreme stands the leading spokesman of the weightiest contemporary school of New Testament scholarship, Rudolf Bultmann. Instead of asserting with the fundamentalists that no quest for the historical Jesus *should* be attempted, Bultmann was firmly convinced that no such quest *can* be initiated. "I do indeed think," he wrote, "that we can know now almost nothing concerning the life and personality of Jesus, since the early Christian sources show no interest in either."[3]

Against both these viewpoints, and against Christian and Jewish denominational bias, I seek to reassert in my whole approach to this problem the inalienable right of the historian to pursue a course independent of beliefs. Yet I will at the same time try to indicate that, despite widespread academic skepticism, our considerably increased knowledge of the Palestinian-Jewish realities

---

[2] *The Guardian*, October 10, 1969.

[3] R. Bultmann, *Jesus and the Word*, trans. L. P. Smith and E. H. Lantero (London, 1934; New York, 1962) p. 14. (He died in 1976.)

of the time of Jesus enables us to extract historically reliable information even from nonhistorical sources such as the gospels.

In fact, with the discovery and study of the Dead Sea Scrolls and other archaeological treasures (see Illus. 1, 11, 19, and 21), and the corresponding improvement in our understanding of the ideas, doctrines, methods of teaching, languages, and culture of the Jews of New Testament times, it is now possible not simply to place Jesus in relief against this setting (as students of the Jewish background of Christianity pride themselves on doing) but to insert him foursquare within first-century Jewish life itself. The questions then to be asked are where he fits into it, and whether the added substance and clarity gained from immersing him in historical reality confer credibility on the patchy gospel picture.

Let us begin then by selecting a few noncontroversial facts concerning Jesus' life and activity and endeavor to build on these foundations.

Jesus lived in Galilee, a province governed during his lifetime not by the Romans, but by a son of Herod the Great (see Illus. 3–6, 9, 22, and 23). His hometown was Nazareth, an insignificant place not referred to by Josephus, the Mishnah, or the Talmud, and first mentioned outside the New Testament in an inscription from Caesarea, dating to the third or fourth century C.E. Whether he was born there or somewhere else is uncertain. The Bethlehem legend is in any case highly suspect (see Illus. 2).

As for the date of his birth, this "is not truly a historical problem," writes one of the greatest living experts on antiquity, Sir Ronald Syme.[4] The year of Jesus' death is also absent from the sources. Nevertheless the general chronological context is clearly defined. He was crucified under Pontius Pilate, the prefect of Judea from 26 to 36 C.E. His public ministry is said to have taken place shortly after the fifteenth year of Tiberius (28/29 C.E.), when John the Baptist inaugurated his crusade of repentance. Whether Jesus taught for one, two, or three years, his execution in Jerusalem must have occurred in the early 30s of the first century.

He was fairly young when he died. Luke reports that he was approximately thirty years old when he joined John the Baptist (Lk 3:23). Also, one of the few points on which Matthew and Luke — the only two evangelists to elaborate on the events preceding and

---

[4]R. Syme, "The Titulus Tiburtinus," *Vestigia* 17 (1973) 600.

following Jesus' birth — agree is in dating those events to the days of King Herod of Judea (Mt 2:1–16; Lk 1:15), who died in the Spring of 4 B.C.E.

Let me try to sketch the world of Jesus' youth and early manhood in the second and third decades of the first century. In distant Rome, Tiberius reigned supreme. First, Valerius Gratus and then Pontius Pilate governed Judea. Joseph Caiaphas was high priest of the Jews, the president of the Jerusalem Sanhedrin, and the head of the Sadducees. Hillel and Shammai, the leaders of the most influential Pharisaic schools, were possibly still alive, and during Jesus' lifetime, Gamaliel the Elder became Hillel's successor. Not far from Jerusalem, a few miles south of Jericho, on the western shore of the Dead Sea, the ascetic Essenes were worshiping God in holy withdrawal and planning the conversion of the rest of Jewry to the true Judaism known only to them, the followers of "the Teacher of Righteousness." And in neighboring Egypt, in Alexandria, the philosopher Philo was busy harmonizing the Jewish life-style with the wisdom of Greece, a dream cherished by the civilized Jews of the Diaspora.

In Galilee, the tetrarch Herod Antipas remained lord of life and death and continued to hope (in vain) that one day the emperor might end his humiliation by granting him the title of king. At the same time, following the upheaval that accompanied the tax registration or census ordered in 6 C.E. by the legate of Syria, Publius Sulpicius Quirinius, Judas the Galilean and his sons were stimulating the revolutionary tendencies of the uncouth Northerners, tendencies that resulted in the foundation of the Zealot movement.

Such was the general ambience in which the personality and character of Jesus the Jew were formed. We know nothing concrete, however, about his education and training, his contacts, or the influences to which he may have been subjected. Quite apart from the unhistorical nature of the stories relating to his infancy and childhood, the interval between his twelfth year and the start of his public ministry is wrapped in total silence by the four evangelists.

Jesus spent not only his early years, but also the greatest part of his public life in Galilee. If we adopt the chronology of the synoptic gospels (Mt, Mk, and Lk), with their one-year ministry, apart from brief excursions to Phoenicia (now Lebanon) and Perea (now present-day northern Transjordan), he left his province only once — for the fateful journey to Jerusalem at Passover. But even if the longer time-table of the Fourth Gospel is followed, the Judean sojourns of Jesus correspond to the mandatory pilgrimages to the Temple, and as such were of short duration. Therefore, if we are to understand him, it is into the Galilean world that we must look.

The Galilee of Jesus, especially his own part of it — Lower Galilee around the Lake of Gennesaret (= "Sea of Galilee") — was a rich and mostly agricultural country (see Illus. 3–5). The inhabitants were proud of their independence and jealous of their Jewishness, in which respect — despite doubts often expressed by Judeans — they considered themselves second to none. They were also brave and tough. Josephus, the commander-in-chief of the region during the first Jewish War, praises their courage and describes them as people "from infancy inured to war" (*War* 3.41).

In effect, in the mountains of Upper Galilee, rebellion against the government — any government, whether Hasmonean, Herodian, or Roman — was endemic between the middle of the first century B.C.E. and 70 C.E., from Ezekias, the *archilēstēs* (the chief brigand or revolutionary) whose uprising was put down by the young Herod, to the arch-Zealot Judas the Galilean and his rebellious sons, to John the son of Levi from Gush Halav and his "Galilean contingent," notorious in besieged Jerusalem for their "mischievous ingenuity and audacity" (*War* 4.558) at the time of the 66–70 C.E. war. In short, the Galileans were admired as staunch fighters by those who sympathized with their rebellious aims; those who did not thought of them as dangerous hot-heads.

In Jerusalem, and in Judean circles, Galileans also had the reputation of being an unsophisticated people. In rabbinic parlance, a Galilean is usually referred to as *Gelili shoteh*, "stupid Galilean." He is presented as a typical "peasant," a "boor," an *'am hā'āreṣ*, a religiously uneducated person. Cut off from the Temple and the study centers of Jerusalem, Galilean popular religion appears to have depended — until the arrival at Usha, in the late 130s C.E., of the rabbinic academy expelled from Yavneh — not so much on the authority of the priests or on the scholarship of scribes, as on the personal magnetism of their local saints, such as Jesus' young contemporary, Ḥanina ben Dosa, the celebrated miracle-worker.

Moving from these lengthy preliminaries, we now turn to the gospels to make our acquaintance with Jesus the Jew, or more exactly, Jesus the *Galilean* Jew. I intend to leave to one side the speculations of the early Christians concerning the various divinely contrived roles of Messiah, Lord, Son of God, etc., that their Master was believed to have fulfilled before or after his death. Instead, I will rely on the accounts of the first three gospels, which suggest that Jesus impressed his countrymen, and acquired fame among them, chiefly as a charismatic teacher, healer, and exorcist. I should specify at once, however, that my purpose is not to discuss his teachings. Few, in any case, will contest that his message was essentially Jewish, or that on certain controversial issues (for example whether the dead would rise again) he voiced the opinion of the Pharisees.

His renown, the evangelists proclaim, had spread throughout Galilee. According to Mark, when Jesus and his disciples disembarked from their boat on Lake Kinneret (see Illus. 3),

> he was immediately recognized; and the people scoured the whole country-side and brought the sick on stretchers to any place where he was reported to be. Wherever he went, to farmsteads, villages or towns, they laid out the sick in the market places and begged him to let them simply touch the edge of his cloak; and all who touched him were cured (Mk 6:54–56).

Similarly, Mark, referring to events in Capernaum, writes:

> They brought to him all who were ill and possessed by devils. . . . He healed many who suffered from various diseases, and drove out many devils (Mk 1:33–34).

And both Luke and Mark report Jesus himself as saying:

> "Today and tomorrow, I shall be casting out devils and working cures" (Lk 13:32).

And:

> "It is not the healthy that need a doctor but the sick; I did not come to invite virtuous people but sinners" (Mk 2:17).

Twentieth-century readers may wonder whether such a person should not properly be classified as a crank. We must, however, bear in mind, firstly, that it is anachronistic and, consequently, wrong to judge the first century by twentieth-century criteria; and, secondly, that even in modern times, faith-healers and *Wunderrebbe* and their secular counterparts in the field of medicine, can and do obtain parallel therapeutic results when the individuals who ask for their help are animated by sufficient faith.

To assess correctly Jesus' healing and exorcistic activities, it is necessary to know that in bygone ages the Jews understood that a relationship existed between sickness, the devil, and sin. As a logical counterpart to such a concept of ill health, it was consequently believed until as late as the third century B.C.E. that recourse to the services of a physician demonstrated a lack of faith since healing was a monopoly of God. The only intermediaries thought licit between God and the sick were men of God, such as the prophets Elijah and Elisha. By the beginning of the second pre-Christian century, however, the physician's office was made more or less respectable by the requirement that he, too, should be personally holy. The Wisdom writer, Jesus ben Sira (Sirach), advised the devout when sick to pray, repent, and send gifts to the Temple, and subsequently to call in the physician, who would ask God for insight into the cause of the sickness and for the treatment needed to remedy it. As Sirach words it:

> The Lord has imparted knowledge to men that by the use of His marvels He may win praise; by employing them, the doctor relieves pain (Sir 38:6–7).

Jesus' healing gifts are never attributed to the study of physical or mental disease, or to any acquired knowledge of cures, but to some mysterious power that emanated from him and was transmitted to the sick by contact with his person, or even with his clothes. In the episode of the crippled woman who was bent double and unable to hold herself upright, we read that

> He laid his hand on her, and at once, she straightened up and began to praise God (Lk 13:13).

Sometimes touch and command went together. A deaf-mute was cured when Jesus placed his own saliva on the sufferer's tongue and ordered his ears to unblock, saying:

> "Ephphetha [*'eppatah*]: Be opened!" (Mk 7:33–34).

There is nevertheless one story in which Jesus performs a cure *in absentia*, that is to say without being anywhere within sight, let alone within touching distance, of the sick man. Matthew's account of the episode reads:

When (Jesus) had entered Capernaum a centurion came up to ask his help. "Sir — he said — a boy of mine lies at home paralysed...." Jesus said, "I will come and cure him." "Sir," — replied the centurion — "who am I to have you under my roof? You need only say a word and the boy will be cured. I know, for I am myself under orders, with soldiers under me. I say to one, Go! and he goes; to another, Come here! and he comes; and to my servant, Do this! and he does it." Jesus heard him with astonishment, and said to the people following him, "I tell you this: nowhere, even in Israel, have I found such a faith." Then he said to the centurion, "Go home now. Because of your faith, so let it be." At that moment the boy recovered (Mt 8:5–13).

I quote this in full not only because of its intrinsic interest, but also in order to compare it with a Talmudic report concerning one of the famous deeds of Jesus' compatriot, Ḥanina ben Dosa. It will be seen from the second story how closely the two tales coincide.

It happened that when Rabban Gamaliel's son fell ill, he sent two of his pupils to R. Ḥanina ben Dosa that he might pray for him. When he saw them, he went to the upper room and prayed. When he came down, he said to them, "Go, for the fever has left him." They said to him, "Are you a prophet?" He said to them, "I am no prophet, neither am I a prophet's son, but this is how I am blessed: if my prayer is fluent in my mouth, I know that the sick man is favored; if not, I know that the disease is fatal." They sat down, and wrote and noted the hour. When they came to Rabban Gamaliel, he said to them, "By heaven! You have neither detracted from it, nor added to it, but this is how it happened. It was at that hour that the fever left him and he asked us for water to drink" (b.Ber 34b).

Instead of ascribing physical and mental illness to natural causes, Jesus' contemporaries saw the former as a divine punishment for sin instigated by the devil, and the latter as resulting from a direct demonic possession. Therefore, by expelling and controlling these evil spirits, the exorcist was believed to be acting as God's agent in the work of liberation, healing, and pardon.

Jesus was an exorcist, but not a professional one: he did not use incantations such as those apparently composed by King Solomon,[5] or foul-smelling substances intolerable even to the most firmly ensconced of demons. He did not go in for producing smoke, as young Tobit did, by burning the heart and the liver of

---

[5] *Ant* 8.45.

a fish (Tob 8:2), or for holding under the noses of the possessed the Solomonic *baaras* root, the stink of which, so Josephus assures us, drew the demon out through the nostrils.[6] Instead, Jesus confronted with great authority and dignity the demoniacs (lunatics, epileptics, and the like) and commanded the devil to depart. This act is usually said to have been followed by relief, and at least a temporary remission of the symptoms. (Even in the gospels, the demons seem to have had an uncanny facility for finding their way back to their former habitats [Mt 12:34–44].)

> So (Jesus and his disciples) came to the other side of the lake, into the country of the Gerasenes. As he stepped ashore, a man possessed by an unclean spirit came up to him from among the tombs where he had his dwelling. He could no longer be controlled; even chains were useless; he had often been fettered and chained up, but he had snapped his chains and broken the fetters. No one was strong enough to master him. And so, unceasingly, night and day, he would cry aloud among the tombs and on the hillsides and cut himself with stones. When he saw Jesus in the distance, he ran and flung himself down before him, shouting loudly, . . . "In God's name, do not torment me!"
>
> For Jesus was already saying to him, "Out, unclean spirit, come out of this man!" . . . The people . . . came to Jesus and saw the madman who had been possessed . . . sitting there clothed and in his right mind; and they were afraid (Mk 5:1–15).

Once more I must parallel the gospel narrative with one concerning Ḥanina ben Dosa, in this case detailing his encounter with the queen of the demons.

> Let no man go out alone at night . . . for Agrath daughter of Mahlath and eighteen myriads of destroying angels are on the prowl, and each of them is empowered to strike. . . . Once she met R. Ḥanina ben Dosa and said to him, "Had there been no commendation from heaven, 'Take heed of R. Ḥanina ben Dosa . . . ,' I would have harmed you." He said to her, "Since I am so highly esteemed in heaven, I decree that you shall never again pass through an inhabited place" (b.Pes 112b).

Jesus, curing the sick and overpowering the forces of evil with the immediacy of the Galilean holy man, was seen as a dispenser of health, one of the greatest blessings expected at the endtime, when "the blind man's eyes shall be opened and the ears of the

---

[6]*Ant* 8.46–47.

deaf unstopped"; when "the lame man shall leap like a deer, and the tongue of the dumb shout aloud" (Isa 35:5–6).

But in this chain of cause and effect, linking, in the mind of the ancients, sickness to the devil, one more element remains, namely sin. Besides healing the flesh and exorcizing the mind, the holy man had one other task to perform: the forgiveness of sin. Here is the famous story of the paralytic brought to Jesus in Capernaum.

> Four men were carrying him, but because of the crowd they could not get him near. So they opened up the roof over the place where Jesus was ... and they lowered the stretcher on which the paralyzed man was lying. When Jesus saw their faith, he said to the paralyzed man, "My son, your sins are forgiven." Now there were some lawyers sitting there and they thought to themselves. "Why does the fellow talk like this? This is blasphemy! Who but God alone can forgive sins?" Jesus knew in his own mind that this is what they were thinking, and said to them, "Why do you harbor thoughts like these? Is it easier to say to this paralyzed man, 'Your sins are forgiven,' or to say, 'Stand up, take your bed and walk'? But to convince you that the Son of man has right on earth to forgive sins" — he turned to the paralyzed man — "I say to you, stand up, take your bed and go home!" And he got up, and at once took his stretcher and went out in full view of them all (Mk 2:3–12).

"My son, your sins are forgiven" is of course not the language of experts in the Law; but neither is it blasphemy. On the contrary, absolution from the guilt of wrong-doing appears to have been part and parcel of the charismatic style. This is well illustrated in an important Dead Sea Scrolls fragment, the Prayer of Nabonidus, which depicts a Jewish exorcist as having pardoned the Babylonian king's sins, thus curing him of his seven years' illness. In the somewhat elastic but extraordinarily perceptive religious terminology of Jesus and the spiritual men of his age, "to heal," "to expel demons," and "to forgive sins" were interchangeable synonyms. Indeed, the language and behavior of Jesus is reminiscent of holy men of ages even earlier than his own, and it need cause little surprise to read in Matthew that he was known as "the prophet Jesus from Nazareth in Galilee" (Mt 21:11), and that his Galilean admirers believed he might be one of the biblical prophets, or Jeremiah, or Elijah *redivivus* (Mt 16:14). In fact, it could be advanced that, if he modeled himself on anyone at all, it was precisely on Elijah and Elisha, as the following argu-

ment with the people of his home town, Nazareth, would seem
to bear out:

> Jesus said, "No doubt you will quote the proverb to me, 'Physician,
> heal yourself!' and say, 'We have heard of all your doings in Caper-
> naum; do the same here, in your own home town.' I tell you this —
> he went on — no prophet is recognized in his own country. There
> were many widows in Israel, you may be sure, in Elijah's time . . . yet
> it was to none of these that Elijah was sent, but to a widow at Sarepta
> in the territory of Sidon. Again in the time of the prophet Elisha there
> were many lepers in Israel, and not one of them was healed, but only
> Naaman, the Syrian" (Lk 4:23–26).

Jesus was a Galilean *ḥasid:* there, as I see it, lies his greatness
and also the germ of his tragedy. That he had his share of the
notorious Galilean chauvinism would seem clear from the xeno-
phobic statements attributed to him. As one review of *Jesus the
Jew* puts it — a review written, interestingly enough, by the Gar-
dening correspondent of the *Financial Times!* — "Once he called
us 'dogs' and 'swine' and he forbade the Twelve to proclaim the
gospel to . . . Gentiles."[7] But Jesus was also, and above all, an ex-
emplary representative of the fresh and simple religiousness for
which the Palestinian North was noted.

And it was in this respect that he cannot have been greatly
loved by the Pharisees: in his lack of expertise — and perhaps
even interest — in halakhic matters, common to Galileans in
general; in his tolerance of deliberate neglect of certain traditional — though not, it should be emphasized, biblical — customs by his followers; in his table-fellowship with publicans and
whores; and last, but not least, in the spiritual authority explicitly or implicitly presumed to underpin his charismatic activities,
an authority impossible to check, as can be done when teachings are handed down from master to disciple. Not that there
appears to have been any fundamental disagreement between
Jesus and the Pharisees on any basic issue, but whereas Jesus,
the preacher of *teshuvah*, of repentance, felt free rhetorically to
overemphasize the ethical as compared with the ritual — like certain of the prophets before him — he perhaps could be criticized
for not paying enough attention to those needs of society that
are met by organized religion. As a matter of fact, this Pharisaic

---

[7] *Financial Times*, February 7, 1974.

insistence on the necessity of faithfulness toward religious obser-
vances as well as of a high standard of ethics, has, as it were, been
vindicated by a Christian *halakhah*, evolved over the centuries,
that is scarcely less detailed and casuistical than our Talmudic
legislation!

Nevertheless, the conflict between Jesus of Galilee and the
Pharisees of his time would, in normal circumstances, merely be
attributed to the in-fighting of factions belonging to the same religious body, like that between Karaites and Rabbanites in the
Middle Ages, or between the orthodox and progressive branches
of Judaism in modern times.[8]

But in the first century, circumstances were not normal. An eschatological and politico-religious fever was always close to the
point of eruption, if it had not already exploded, and Galilee was
a hotbed of nationalist ferment. Incidentally, there is no evidence,
in my reading of the gospels, that would point to any particular
involvement by Jesus in the revolutionary affairs of the Zealots,
though it is likely that some of his followers may have been committed to them and may have longed to proclaim him as King
Messiah, destined to liberate his oppressed nation.

But for the representatives of the establishment — Herod Antipas in Galilee, and the chief priests and their council in Jerusalem — the prime unenviable task was to maintain law and order
and thus avert a major catastrophe. In their eyes, revolutionary
propaganda was not only against the law of the Roman provin-
cial administration, but also murderously foolish, contrary to the
national interest, and liable to expose to the vengeance of the in-
vincible emperor not only those actively implicated, but countless
thousands of their innocent compatriots. They had to be silenced
one way or another, by persuasion or by force, before it was too
late. As the high priest is reported to have said of Jesus — and it
is immaterial whether he did so or not — "It is more to your interest that one man should die for the people, than that the whole
nation should be destroyed" (Jn 11:50). Such indeed must have
been the attitude and thinking of the establishment. Not only actual but even potential leadership of a revolutionary movement

---

[8]It may come as a surprise to many that at the time of the birth of Jesus, the Pharisaic
confraternity numbered, according to Josephus (*Ant* 17.42), only a little over six thousand members, as against four thousand Essenes (*Ant* 18.20), whereas the total Jewish
population of Palestine is estimated to have amounted to from two to two-and-a-half
million.

called for alertness and vigilance. John the Baptist, who according to Josephus was "a good man" and "exhorted the Jews to live righteous lives," became suspect in Herod's eyes because of an "eloquence" that might "lead to some form of sedition.... Herod decided therefore that it would be much better to strike first and be rid of him before his work led to an uprising."[9] Jesus, I am convinced, was the victim of a similar preventative measure devised by the Sadducean rulers in the "general interest."

As Jesus hung dying on a Roman cross, under a *titulus* that read, "Jesus of Nazareth, king of the Jews," he cried out with a loud voice:

> *"Elōi elōi lema sabachthani?* My God, my God, why hast thou forsaken me?"* (Mk 15:34).

Nothing, to my mind, epitomizes more sharply the tragedy of Jesus the Jew, misunderstood by friend and foe alike, than this despairing cry from the cross. Nor was this cry the end of it. For throughout the centuries, as age followed age, Christians and Jews allowed it to continue and worsen. His adherents transformed this lover and worshipper of his Father in heaven into an object of worship himself, a god; and his own people, under the pressures of persecution at the hands of those adherents, mistakenly attributed to Jesus himself Christian beliefs and dogmas, many of which — I am certain — would have filled this Galilean *ḥasid* with stupefaction, anger, and deepest grief.

I recognize that this sketchy portrait, and even the fuller picture given in my book, *Jesus the Jew,* does him — and the reader — less than justice. In particular, no biographical approach to a teacher of the past can come alive without a discussion of his essential message. As a former Dean of Christ Church told me one day:

> My dear fellow, you are like an examination candidate who must answer several connected questions. So far you've only dealt with the first one: "What kind of a Jew was Jesus?" You have advanced a theory. But I won't know whether it's true or not until you reveal your solution to the remaining parts of the puzzle.

Henry Chadwick was, of course, correct; *Jesus the Jew,* whether printed or spoken, is but the first part of a trilogy. The preliminary version of the second part formed the three Riddell Memorial Lectures delivered in 1981 in the University of Newcastle, and

---

[9]*Ant* 18.117–18.

subsequently included in *Jesus and the World of Judaism* under the title, *The Gospel of Jesus the Jew*.[10] A more detailed treatment of the teaching of Jesus, and an exploration of the metamorphosis of Jesus the Jew into the Christ of Christianity in the works of Paul, John, and the rest of the New Testament writers, are still to be presented in a forthcoming volume, *The Religion of Jesus and Christianity*. In the meanwhile I must accept that some listeners or readers will prefer to suspend judgment on my assessment of this remarkable man.

As has already been said, I began my search for the Jesus of history for its own sake, to prove that, by employing the right methods, something of the authentic image of the Master from Galilee can be recovered from the dark historical past. How did reviewers and critics, Jewish and Christian, respond to *Jesus the Jew*?

Jewish reactions, with one or two atypical exceptions, have been generally positive. Thus David Daube concludes his review of *Jesus the Jew:* "Whether it will do much toward removing ill will and distrust may be doubted. These attitudes are largely independent of scholarly data. Still, with luck, it may do a little. The present climate gives some ground for hope."[11] Likewise David Flusser sees in both *Jesus the Jew* and its sequel, *Jesus and the World of Judaism*, a valuable contribution to both "the progress of Judaic studies" and an improved understanding of "the Jewish roots of Christianity."[12] Again, not long ago, Magen Broshi, director of the Shrine of the Book, home of the Dead Sea Scrolls in Jerusalem, described *Jesus the Jew* in the *Jerusalem Post* as the ideal book for Jews who know little or nothing about Jesus, and when told that he was a Jew, wonder whether their leg is being pulled. "Actually," Broshi writes, "Jesus was so Jewish that a modern (Jewish-Israeli) reader of the Gospels might even find some of his anti-Gentile utterances somewhat embarrassing."[13]

Among Christians, there have been occasional public outbursts. (What happened behind closed doors is less clear, although rumor has it that the Catholic publishers of the French version, *Jésus le Juif*, were severely reprimanded in private by angry episco-

---

[10](Newcastle, 1981.) Reissued in *Jesus and the World of Judaism* (London, 1983; Philadelphia, 1984) pp. 15–57, 144–69.

[11]*JJS* 25 (1974) 336.

[12]*Judaism* 35 (1986) 361–64.

[13]*Jerusalem Post*, December 7, 1984.

pal voices.) An outraged lady, reviewing the book in the extreme right-wing *La pensée catholique,* has termed it "scandalous and blasphemous."[14] Now and then, even scholars have allowed free expression to their annoyance, with remarks such as "Jesus the Jew deserves better than this,"[15] or "I am always immediately put off by those who claim to write about the Gospels as 'historians'; that immediately means that an axe is being ground."[16]

By contrast, the editor of a French Protestant periodical declared himself totally persuaded.[17] Nevertheless, the majority of comments have been sympathetic, but not altogether convinced. Canon Anthony Harvey, of Westminster Abbey, a former Oxford colleague, notes: "The more you stress the Jewishness of Jesus, the harder you make it to understand that extraordinary un-Jewish ability of his to cut a figure, and propound a message, which has had a profound influence on so many nations throughout the world — except the Jews."[18] Finally, in a characteristically British manner, and in Oxford's own *Journal of Theological Studies,* A. R. C. Leaney writes: "The result is a valuable contribution to scholarship, but it is hard to assess exactly how successful it is."[19]

[14] D(enise) J(udant), *La pensée catholique* 176 (1978) 88.
[15] L. E. Keck, *JBL* 95 (1975) 509.
[16] J. A. Fitzmyer, *JSNT* 4 (1979) 67, n. 33.
[17] M. Bouttier, *ETR* 54 (1979) 299.
[18] *The Times Literary Supplement,* February 24, 1984.
[19] *JTS* 25 (1974) 489.

CHAPTER FIVE

The Jewishness of Jesus: Facing Some Problems

Daniel J. Harrington, S.J.

Introduction

Any assessment of the positive results of the Second Vatican Council would have to include progress in Christian-Jewish relations. The Council's *Declaration on the Relationship of the Church to Non-Christian Religions (Nostra Aetate)* contains the following statement: "Since the spiritual patrimony common to Christians and Jews is thus so great, this sacred Synod wishes to foster and recommend that mutual understanding which is the fruit above all of biblical and theological studies, and of brotherly dialogues."[1] These words of Vatican II have led many Catholics, especially in the United States (where the largest Jewish community in the world lives and where Judaism is the most prominent non-Christian religion) to explore the relationship between Christianity and Judaism. This movement within Catholicism in turn has given renewed vigor to already existing Protestant-Jewish efforts at mutual understanding.

The agenda for the Christian-Jewish dialogue is quite full. Starting from our own day, it includes the State of Israel, the Holocaust, Christian persecution of Jews, the parting of the ways, and so on back to the beginnings of ancient Israel. A major topic on this agenda has been the Jewishness of Jesus.

There is a basic level on which most Christians and Jews can agree about the Jewishness of Jesus. That Jesus the Jew was born, lived, and died in the land of Israel in what we call the

---

[1]*The Documents of Vatican II*, ed. W. M. Abbott (New York, 1966) p. 665.

first-century C.E. cannot be doubted. The Jewishness of Jesus' teaching is well summarized by the distinguished German NT scholar Franz Mussner: Jesus of Nazareth stood for the great religious ideas of Israel as they are found in the Hebrew Bible and the Jewish tradition. His teachings on God, obedience to God's will, creation, expiation for sin, Covenant, the piety of the poor, the better righteousness, eschatology, and fidelity are consistent with his Jewish heritage. Through Jesus the great heritage of Israel has been mediated to all nations.[2]

The Jewishness of Jesus fascinates both Christians and Jews today. Christians recognize the Jewishness of Jesus as a bridge not only to Jews but also to other Christians. It is a starting-point for conversation, something about which mutual understanding and even agreement seem possible. It connects Christians with the humanity of Jesus and helps them avoid a longtime tendency to docetism. Many Jews, for their part, are putting aside a tradition of defensiveness regarding Jesus and engaging in a kind of reclamation or "bringing home" of Jesus as Jew.[3]

The Jewishness of Jesus is bringing Christians and Jews together. The paradox, however, is that what most obviously still divides Christians and Jews is their assessment of Jesus. There is, of course, a wide spectrum of views about Jesus both in Christian circles and in Jewish circles. Nevertheless, any sampling of opinion about what distinguishes Judaism from Christianity quickly yields the answer, "Jesus."

In the renewed relationship between Christians and Jews, biblical scholars have played a major role. One of the great achievements in religious studies during the past twenty years has been the willingness of scholars from varying religious backgrounds and commitments to work together. And the Jewishness of Jesus has been a major concern in this development.

Attention to the Jewishness of Jesus has also sharpened the problems involved in understanding Jesus. This sharpening of

---

[2]"Der Jude Jesus," *FrRu* 23 (1971) 3–7; *Traktat über die Juden* (Munich, 1979) p. 183; *Tractate on the Jews: The Significance of Judaism for Christian Faith* (Philadelphia, 1984) p. 113. See P. Lapide and U. Luz, *Jesus in Two Perspectives: A Jewish-Christian Dialogue* (Minneapolis, 1985).

[3]The idea of "reclaiming" or "bringing home" Jesus became prominent with S. Ben Chorin's *Bruder Jesus: Der Nazarener in jüdischer Sicht* (3rd ed.; Munich, 1970). For a full discussion from an evangelical perspective, see D. A. Hagner, *The Jewish Reclamation of Jesus: An Analysis and Critique of Modern Jewish Study of Jesus* (Grand Rapids, Mich., 1984). A harsh critique of Hagner's work is B. Young, "Jewish Scholarship and Jesus," *Immanuel* 19 (1984–85) 102–6.

issues is my concern in this paper. As a scholar trained in Second Temple Judaism and as a New Testament specialist, I would like to focus on three methodological difficulties that have emerged from recent study of the Jewishness of Jesus: Judaism in Jesus' time, our sources about Jesus the Jew, and theological assessments of Jesus. My hope is that investigation of these issues will clarify the new shape of the so-called quest for the historical Jesus. This new shape has emerged in part as a result of the labors undertaken in common by Christian and Jewish scholars.

The Jewishness of Jesus in Recent Scholarship

Before taking up these three methodological difficulties, it may be helpful to illustrate what I have described as the new shape of the so-called quest for the historical Jesus. That new shape comes from taking very seriously the Jewishness of Jesus and trying to understand him within the limits of first-century Judaism.

I will first describe in some detail the work of three scholars who explain Jesus' historical setting, intention, and death in the context of first-century Judaism. They are Geza Vermes (a distinguished Jewish specialist in the Dead Sea Scrolls, Jewish history, and rabbinic literature), E. P. Sanders (a Christian NT scholar well known for his contributions to Synoptic and Pauline studies and his work on the character of first-century Judaism), and Harvey Falk (an American rabbi from a very traditional Jewish background). What unites these three very different scholars is their resolute attempt to explain Jesus *within* the context of *Judaism*. In offering these summaries, I wish only to illustrate a trend in research on the historical Jesus and to prepare for a more general consideration of methodology. I will not provide detailed critiques of the individual authors.

In his *Jesus the Jew*, Geza Vermes seeks to set the scene of Jesus' activity and determine what kind of Jew he was.[4] Using texts from Josephus' writings and rabbinic literature about Galilee, Vermes places Jesus alongside such charismatic holy men as Ḥoni the Circle-Drawer and Ḥanina ben Dosa. Then he examines five christological titles (Prophet, Lord, Messiah, Son of man, and Son of God) with regard to their possible meanings during Jesus' ministry in Galilee and before their development by the early Church.

---

[4]G. Vermes, *Jesus the Jew: A Historian's Reading of the Gospels* (rev. ed.; Philadelphia, 1981). [Also, see Vermes' chapter in the present volume. J. H. C.].

In a booklet entitled *The Gospel of Jesus the Jew*, Vermes describes Jesus as a first-century Jewish holy man entirely dedicated to the call for repentance and the coming Kingdom of God, as someone uniquely aware of his filial relationship to God and eager to communicate it to others.[5] Although Jesus' charismatic teaching and life-style attracted some Jewish opponents, Jews did not bear the ultimate responsibility for Jesus' execution: "It was not on a Jewish religious indictment, but on a secular accusation that he was condemned by the emperor's delegate to die shamefully on a Roman cross."[6]

E. P. Sanders' *Jesus and Judaism* is important for its sharp criticism of scholars who refuse to take seriously the Jewishness of Jesus and for its effort to explain Jesus within the confines of first-century Judaism.[7] Describing himself as "a liberal, modern, secularized Protestant," Sanders understands Jesus as an eschatological prophet and focuses on what Jesus did in the Jerusalem Temple (see Mk 11:15–19 par.) and said about the Temple (see Mk 13:2; 14:58; par.). According to Sanders, Jesus' action in the Temple symbolized his expectation that God would soon give a new temple from heaven, in line with other Jewish forms of restoration eschatology. Jesus called sinners to accept his promise of the Kingdom, without demanding their repentance (which would involve restitution and/or sacrifice). The combination of Jesus' demonstration against the Jerusalem Temple and the questionable character of the following that he attracted led to his death at the hands of the Romans (with the urging of at least the Jewish high priests).

In *Jesus the Pharisee*, Harvey Falk situates Jesus in the Pharisaic struggle between the school of Shammai and the school of Hillel.[8] He claims that about 20 B.C.E. the school of Shammai gained control of the Jewish community in Palestine and the Hillelites joined the Essenes. Jesus' background was in the Essene branch of the Pharisaic movement gathered around Hillel. Jesus, according to Falk, remained an Orthodox Jew all his life and never

---

[5]Idem, *The Gospel of Jesus the Jew* (Newcastle upon Tyne, 1981). See also his *Jesus and the World of Judaism* (Philadelphia, 1984).

[6]*Jesus the Jew*, p. 37.

[7]E. P. Sanders, *Jesus and Judaism* (Philadelphia, 1985).

[8]H. Falk, *Jesus the Pharisee: A New Look at the Jewishness of Jesus* (New York/Mahwah, N.J., 1985). Though not of the same scholarly caliber as the works of Vermes and Sanders, Falk's book is noteworthy (see *Time* [July 22, 1985] 57) because of the author's Orthodox Judaism, his use of traditional Jewish sources, and the Catholic publisher.

wished his fellow Jews to change any aspect of their traditional faith. What got Jesus into trouble with the regnant Shammaites was his desire to establish a religion for gentiles on the basis of the seven Noahide commandments (prohibitions against idolatry, blasphemy, killing, stealing, sexual sins, and eating a limb from a living animal, as well as the obligation to establish courts of justice). Jesus' criticisms of the Scribes and Pharisees were really directed only at the school of Shammai and in fact upheld the views of Hillel. Although the Romans executed Jesus, it was the Sanhedrin dominated by the school of Shammai, the Zealots, and violent Temple priests who were the prime movers in getting Jesus killed. They did so because they feared that the Romans would embrace "Christianity" and destroy the Temple and the Jewish government (see Jn 11:47).

These three scholars situate Jesus in different contexts: Galilean charismatic Hasidism (Vermes), apocalyptic restoration movements (Sanders), and Pharisaism with its debate between the schools of Hillel and Shammai (Falk). They attribute different intentions to Jesus: calling for repentance in light of the coming Kingdom and communicating the experience of God as Father (Vermes), preparing for the restoration of Judaism (Sanders), and establishing a new religion for gentiles on the basis of the seven Noahide commandments (Falk). All three agree that the Roman officials bear ultimate responsibility for Jesus' death but give different reasons why Jesus' Jewish opponents may have collaborated with the Romans: his charismatic style (Vermes), the threat posed to the Jerusalem Temple and by the kinds of people that Jesus attracted (Sanders), and Shammaite fears about the new religion for gentiles that Jesus proposed (Falk).[9]

Judaism in Jesus' Time

There was a time not too long ago when it seemed easy to understand the Judaism of Jesus' days. The major sources were the gospels and the rabbinic corpus. Jews could be divided into two primary groups — Pharisees and Sadducees, with some other

---

[9]Some significant Christian attempts at dealing with the Jewishness of Jesus include A. E. Harvey, *Jesus and the Constraints of History* (Philadelphia, 1982); M. Hengel, *The Charismatic Leader and His Followers* (New York, 1981); C. Perrot, *Jésus et l'histoire* (Tournai, 1979); J. Riches, *Jesus and the Transformation of Judaism* (London, 1980).

shadowy entities such as the Essenes, the Zealots, and the "people of the land" at the margins.

That simple picture of Palestinian Judaism in Jesus' time no longer exists. Perhaps the best known factor in breaking down the old consensus was the discovery of the Dead Sea Scrolls in the late 1940s and early 1950s. All of a sudden, we had access to the library of a Jewish religious community organized along quasi-monastic lines and preparing itself for the coming of God's Kingdom (see Illus. 21). The community was quickly and correctly identified as the Essenes, thus leaving the sociological map of Palestinian Judaism relatively intact.

The Qumran discoveries (= Dead Sea Scrolls), however, soon led to a full-scale review of other evidence for Second Temple Judaism. We have learned some interesting and important things from this review, though the result can be stated in the following paradox: The more we know, the less we know.[10]

Among the documents found in the Qumran library,[11] in addition to the sect's own literature, were some of the OT Pseudepigrapha: 1 Enoch, Jubilees, and Testaments of the Patriarchs. Such documents were apparently not composed by the Essenes. Other Jewish groups lay behind them, some of which shared the Qumran sect's keen interest in eschatology. Once a neglected field, study of the OT Pseudepigrapha is now enriched by ample bibliographic resources, critical editions of texts, new translations in various languages, and reliable introductions.[12] This wealth of scholarly resources has furthered the impression of Second Temple Judaism's rich diversity.

Still another piece in the revision of our picture of Palestinian Judaism around the turn of the era has been the growing recognition that Jews had been part of the hellenistic world since the time of Alexander the Great. From the late fourth century B.C.E. onward, Jews were using Greek language, economic patterns, military formations, and cultural expressions to some extent. Even

[10]For a good popular presentation, see M. E. Stone, *Scriptures, Sects and Visions: A Profile of Judaism from Ezra to the Jewish Revolts* (Philadelphia, 1980). For bibliographic information, see my *The New Testament: A Bibliography* (Wilmington, Del., 1985) pp. 193–232.

[11]G. Vermes, *The Dead Sea Scrolls: Qumran in Perspective* (Cleveland, 1978). For more recent publications, see C. Koester, "A Qumran Bibliography: 1974–84," *BTB* 15 (1985) 110–20.

[12]J. H. Charlesworth (ed.), *The Old Testament Pseudepigrapha* (2 vols.; Garden City, N.Y., 1983, 1985); H. F. D. Sparks (ed.), *The Apocryphal Old Testament* (New York, 1984). For a general introduction to this literature and the Qumran writings, see M. E. Stone (ed.), *Jewish Writings of the Second Temple Period* (Philadelphia, 1984).

the Hasmonean family, which did so much to revitalize Jewish life in the second century B.C.E. against the inroads of hellenization, ended up adopting many hellenistic ways. The upshot of all this is that Palestinian Judaism can now only be seen as part of the wider Greco-Roman world, not as a hermetically sealed Jewish enclave.[13] Meanwhile, the archaeologists and historians have been busy in making our picture even more complicated. Perhaps their most interesting general finding here has been the recognition of regionalism in Palestine at the turn of the era, i.e., that life differed between Galilee and Jerusalem, and even between northern and southern Galilee.[14]

At the same time, there has been an ongoing reassessment of the rabbinic writings. On the one hand, we are now much more cautious in retrojecting into Jesus' day what is found in the Mishnah (put in final form around 200 C.E.) or the Palestinian and Babylonian Talmuds (from the fourth and fifth centuries), and still more cautious with regard to what is found in the midrashic collections. On the other hand, there is greater appreciation of the creativity and coherent vision of the rabbis as they worked out their vision of Jewish life in the second and third centuries, and more than a little doubt as to whether it is proper to look upon them as the lineal continuation of the Pharisaic movement.[15] Meanwhile, there has arisen a fairly large body of scholars who maintain that the targums are witnesses to the way in which the Hebrew Bible was read and interpreted in Jesus' time, though some serious methodological difficulties stand in the way of such claims.[16]

The more we know, the less we know. The "more" includes the discovery of the Dead Sea Scrolls, the restudy of the OT Pseu-

---

[13]M. Hengel, *Judaism and Hellenism: Studies in Their Encounter in Palestine During the Early Hellenistic Period* (2 vols.; Philadelphia, 1974); V. Tcherikover, *Hellenistic Civilization and the Jews* (Philadelphia, 1959).

[14]See E. M. Meyers and J. F. Strange, *Archaeology, the Rabbis, and Early Christianity: The Social and Historical Setting of Palestinian Judaism and Christianity* (Nashville, 1981); S. Freyne, *Galilee from Alexander the Great to Hadrian, 323 B.C.E. to 135 C.E.: A Study of Second Temple Judaism* (Wilmington, Del., 1980); R. A. Horsley, "Popular Messianic Movements around the Time of Jesus," *CBQ* 46 (1984) 471–95; idem, " 'Like One of the Prophets of Old': Two Types of Popular Prophets at the Time of Jesus," *CBQ* 47 (1985) 435–63.

[15]J. Neusner, *Judaism: The Evidence of the Mishnah* (Chicago/London, 1981). See also S. J. D. Cohen, "The Significance of Yavneh: Pharisees, Rabbis, and the End of Sectarianism," *HUCA* 55 (1984) 27–53.

[16]M. McNamara, *The New Testament and the Palestinian Targum to the Pentateuch* (Rome, 1966); *Targum and Testament* (Shannon/Grand Rapids, Mich., 1972); R. Le Déaut, *The Message of the New Testament and the Aramaic Bible* (Rome, 1982); A. D. York, "The Dating of Targumic Literature," *JSJ* 5 (1974) 49–62; S. A. Kaufman, "On Methodology in the Study of Targums and Chronology," *JSNT* 23 (1985) 117–24.

depigrapha, the recognition of Palestine as part of the hellenistic world and of distinct cultural regions in the land of Israel, and the revised picture of the rabbinic writings. A good deal more is known about Palestinian Judaism in Jesus' day than was known forty years ago. But in another sense we *know less*. Or at least we are less confident about simple and neat pictures. What emerges from all this research is a variety of Judaisms and some doubt about whether one can speak of any center or core. The most obvious candidates as the core, of course, are the Torah, the Jerusalem Temple, and the land itself. Yet even here there is debate about whether and to what extent these can be taken as unifying factors for the various Judaisms.[17]

In light of these developments during the past forty years in the study of Palestinian Judaism, the obvious question is this: What was the Jewish context of Jesus? It is not surprising that, in accord with the new developments, there have emerged new approaches to the context of Jesus. The following is a list of images of Jesus with (parenthetically) Jewish or other "background" material proposed in recent years as a basis for the image: eschatological prophet (apocalyptic writings),[18] political revolutionary (reports about rebels against Rome),[19] magician (Greek magical papyri),[20] Essene (Dead Sea Scrolls),[21] Galilean charismatic (rabbinic accounts),[22] Hillelite (Hillel-Shammai debates),[23] and Galilean rabbi (targums).[24]

The list could be extended. I have stopped at seven images and "backgrounds." Some of these I take more seriously (eschatological prophet, Galilean charismatic) than others. Nevertheless, there are at least shreds of evidence for each image and background. The point in making such a list is to illustrate how difficult it is to be exact about the precise Jewish context of Jesus. The root of the problem is that the new discoveries and the restudy of al-

---

[17]See the debate between N. J. McEleney, "Orthodoxy in Judaism of the First Christian Century," *JSJ* 4 (1973) 19–42, and D. E. Aune, "Orthodoxy in First Century Judaism? A Response to N. J. McEleney," *JSJ* 7 (1976) 1–10.

[18]Sanders, *Jesus and Judaism*.

[19]S. F. G. Brandon, *Jesus and the Zealots: A Study of the Political Factor in Primitive Christianity* (New York/Manchester, U.K., 1967); H. Maccoby, *Revolution in Judaea: Jesus and the Jewish Resistance* (London, 1973; New York, 1981).

[20]M. Smith, *Jesus the Magician* (New York, San Francisco, 1978).

[21]Falk, *Jesus the Pharisee*.

[22]Vermes, *Jesus the Jew*.

[23]Falk, *Jesus the Pharisee*.

[24]B. D. Chilton, *A Galilean Rabbi and His Bible: Jesus' Use of the Interpreted Scripture of His Time* (Wilmington, Del., 1984).

ready available material have revealed a much more complicated and diverse picture of Palestinian Judaism in Jesus' time than was imagined forty or fifty years ago. Since we know more now than we did then, we also know how little we do really know about Judaism in Jesus' time and how hard it is to put together what we already know in a coherent package.

So the first methodological problem pertaining to Jesus in his Jewish context is the nature of Palestinian Judaism in Jesus' time; it appears to have been quite diverse and multifaceted. Our increased understanding of its diversity has made it even more difficult to be sure precisely what kind of Jew Jesus was and against which historical background we should try to understand him.

Sources about Jesus the Jew

The second methodological problem involved in placing Jesus the Jew in his context concerns the nature of the ancient sources that speak about Jesus. On the Jewish side, there is not much. The few talmudic passages and the Toledot Jeshu tradition are fascinating examples of religious parody and polemic but tell us practically nothing of any value for understanding Jesus in the first century C.E.[25] The description of Jesus by Josephus in *Ant* 18.3.3. §63–64 may well be a later interpolation into the text. At least some of its statements ("he was the Messiah . . . on the third day he appeared to them restored to life") sound like the products of a Christian editor.[26]

The most extensive ancient sources about Jesus are the four gospels. These gospels are complicated documents for twentieth-century historians. The gospels describe Jesus of Nazareth, who exercised a public ministry of preaching and healing and was put to death as "King of the Jews" around 30 C.E. But these gospels were written some forty to sixty years after Jesus' death. They presupposed the Easter event. They spoke mainly to those who already believed in the decisive significance of Jesus. They were expressed in such a way as not only to describe Jesus in his orig-

---

[25] For a recent survey, see J. Maier, *Jesus von Nazareth in der talmudischen Überlieferung* (Darmstadt, 1978).

[26] For a survey of scholarship, see L. H. Feldman, *Josephus and Modern Scholarship (1937–1980)* (Berlin, New York, 1984) pp. 679–703; J. N. Birdsall, "The Continuing Enigma of Josephus' Testimony about Jesus," *BJRL* 67 (1985) 609–22. [See Charlesworth's detailed analysis of the pertinent texts on pp. 189–92 of the present volume.]

inal setting but also to address the problems facing the Christian communities of a later time. Between the time of Jesus and the final composition of the gospels, the traditions about Jesus were handed on in a complex and probably unsystematic process and were reshaped in light of the needs and concerns of various Christian groups. This complicated process of tradition — from Jesus through the early communities to the gospels — over a fairly long period of time has been widely accepted by Christians today.

Recognition of the complex nature of our chief sources about Jesus has been one of the factors that led historians and theologians over the past two hundred years on the so-called quest for the historical Jesus.[27] The idea behind this quest is to go beneath the surface of the gospels, to peel away the accretions made in the process of transmission, and so to arrive at Jesus of Nazareth — as he really was.

The quest for the historical Jesus seems to some a circular and speculative task. Some of us despair of its success and prefer to assume a continuity between Jesus, the early Church, and the gospels. Many NT specialists, however, are not satisfied with the assumption in favor of such organic continuity. In an effort to get back to the teaching of the historical Jesus, these scholars have devised several "authenticating" criteria: (1) A gospel saying must reflect the conditions of Palestine in Jesus' time and/or be capable of translation back into Aramaic or Hebrew. (2) It should be found in several independent early Christian strands of tradition. (3) It must be coherent or consistent with what is known about Jesus. (4) And most decisively, it must be so unique that it cannot be ascribed to Judaism or to the early Church.[28]

There are many problems with the logic of these criteria and their application. I wish to focus only on the fourth criterion, the so-called criterion of dissimilarity or discontinuity: A saying that is so unique that it cannot be ascribed to Judaism or to the early Church may be ascribed to Jesus. The problem with this criterion is that it makes Jesus dissimilar to or discontinuous with Judaism

[27]See A. Schweitzer, *The Quest of the Historical Jesus: A Critical Study of Its Progress from Reimarus to Wrede* (New York, 1910, 1961); G. Bornkamm, *Jesus of Nazareth* (New York, 1960); J. M. Robinson, *A New Quest of the Historical Jesus and other Essays* (Philadelphia, 1983 [a reprint of the 1959 work]).

[28]Good examples of the application of these criteria are found in N. Perrin, *Rediscovering the Teaching of Jesus* (New York, Evanston, Ill., 1967).

(and with the early Church). It wrenches Jesus out of his Jewish context and turns him into a kind of creative genius or eccentric (depending on one's perspective), transcending his culture. It fails to acknowledge the Jewishness of Jesus, or at least dismisses it as uninteresting and unimportant.

The quest for the historical Jesus has also attracted Jewish scholars. And here we usually encounter the opposite problem. Those Jews who do not dismiss Jesus as an apostate but approach him sympathetically as a brother often do so on the assumption that Jesus the Jew remained entirely within the boundaries of Judaism. They employ a criterion of similarity or continuity and assign whatever does not fit into their idea of Judaism in Jesus' time to the early Church or to the evangelists. They will argue that Jesus' teaching has been misunderstood or mistranslated, that it was only part of an inner-Jewish conflict, and that it has been distorted by the early Church's mission to the gentiles. The picture of Jesus that emerges from such arguments is that of a basically loyal and observant Jew, with perhaps a few odd ideas. Whatever differs from Judaism is dismissed as uninteresting or unimportant or simply mistaken.[29]

Thus, in placing Jesus the Jew in his context we have a problem of sources. What Jewish sources we have are either late or suspect. The Christian sources have passed through a complicated process of tradition. Those who attempt to get behind the gospels and thus discover the "real" Jesus involve themselves in a speculative and often circular enterprise. Modern Christian proponents of the quest for the historical Jesus take Jesus out of his Jewish context and focus mainly on his "un-Jewish" teachings. Modern Jewish proponents of the quest leave Jesus in the confines of Judaism as they understand them and thus echo the famous statement made by Claude G. Montefiore: "His teaching, where good, was not original, and where original was not Jewish or good."[30] Some go further than Montefiore and attribute the so-called original teachings to the early Church rather than to Jesus. Others assign these "original" teachings to Jesus' eccentricity with respect to his Jewish heritage.

---

[29]See T. Weiss-Rosmarin (ed.), *Jewish Expressions on Jesus: An Anthology* (New York, 1977); and P. Lapide, *Israelis, Jews and Jesus* (New York, 1979). For comprehensive bibliographic coverage and a critique from a Christian evangelical perspective, see Hagner, *The Jewish Reclamation of Jesus.*

[30]C. G. Montefiore, "Jewish Conceptions of Christianity," *HibJ* 28 (1929–30) 249.

Theological Assessments of Jesus

Our varying assessments about the theological significance of
Jesus constitute the third methodological problem. That Christians and Jews differ with respect to the significance of Jesus is
clear. For Jews, Jesus is another Jewish teacher and another victim
of oppression. For Christians, Jesus is that and more. He is the
authoritative interpreter of the Law, whose death brought about
the possibility of right relationship with God.

Jesus was a Jewish teacher. Much of his teaching according to
the gospels stands well within the boundaries of the Torah and the
wisdom tradition. Nevertheless, the gospels present Jesus as the
climactic revelation of God, surpassing and fulfilling the revelations accorded previously to the people of God. In this theological
perspective, Jesus emerges as the authoritative interpreter of the
Torah.[31] Not only can he say what it means (as Hillel and Shammai
did), but he can even abrogate it or bypass it.

The six antitheses in the Sermon on the Mount (Mt 5:21–48)
illustrate this point. In some cases, Jesus extends a biblical precept
in order to get at the root disposition. Thus Jesus forbids anger
and lust in order to avoid murder and adultery. But his antithesis
on divorce seems to repeal or reject the permission and procedure found in Deuteronomy 24:1. His statement regarding oaths
goes beyond the biblical prohibition against swearing falsely in
Leviticus 19:12; Numbers 30:2; Deuteronomy 23:21. His teaching on nonretaliation pushes the biblical law of retaliation (see Ex
21:23–24; Lev 24:19–20; Deut 19:21) to the point of abrogation.

Those who situate Jesus entirely within the confines of first-
century Judaism must attribute such an attitude toward the Torah
to the early Church or the evangelists. The evangelists themselves, however, present these and similar teachings as flowing
from Jesus' authority as the one sent from God and having authority over the Torah and its interpretation. The issue for them
was not how Jesus stood with respect to the Torah but how the
Torah stood with respect to Jesus. Here those who use the criterion
of dissimilarity appear to have the upper hand.

Jesus was a victim of oppression. The trial and death of Jesus
have been lively topics of discussion over the past thirty years.[32]

---

[31]R. Banks, *Jesus and the Law in the Synoptic Tradition* (London, New York, Melbourne,
1975).

[32]Some influential studies include J. Blinzler, *The Trial of Jesus* (Westminster, Md., 1959);

What has emerged from this discussion has been almost a consensus on the following matters: The final legal responsibility for Jesus' death lay with Pontius Pilate, the Roman prefect (see Illus. 11). Jesus was executed as a perceived political threat ("the King of the Jews") according to a Roman mode of punishment. The evangelists deliberately played down Roman responsibility and played up Jewish involvement. The precise degree of Jewish involvement in the events leading up to Jesus' death is still disputed. Were the chief priests and elders the initiators of the procedure, merely active collaborators, passive spectators, or unwilling agents? At any rate, it is now recognized that, when the Passion narratives begin, the Pharisees almost entirely drop out of sight.

Jesus was another Jewish victim of oppression. Like John the Baptist, Jesus the son of Ananias, Theudas, the Egyptian prophet, and other prophetic figures of his day, Jesus was perceived as a threat to the political stability of Judea.[33] In the light of Hitler's Holocaust, there has developed among Jews and Christians an attractive approach to Jesus of Nazareth as a symbol of Jewish victimization throughout the ages. Not only does such an approach bring Jesus back into his Jewish context, but it also brings into that same context the many Christians in our world today who suffer with Jesus and for his name. It is an arresting thought and deserves further reflections by Christians and Jews together.

Again, however, the gospels and other NT writings go beyond this common Christian-Jewish theology of martyrdom. They portray Jesus as savior of the world. They see his death as carried out according to God's will and a divine plan. They use such terms as redemption, reconciliation, justification, and atonement to express what has happened as a result of Jesus' death.

I do not raise these differences regarding the Torah and the significance of Jesus' death to argue for the superiority of the Christian view. I do so only to help us recognize the theological differences between Christians and Jews. Jesus was a Jewish

---

S. F. G. Brandon, *The Trial of Jesus of Nazareth* (New York, 1968); the various articles in R. Gordis (ed.), *The Trial of Jesus in the Light of History*, a special issue of *Judaism* 20 (1971) 6–74; E. Rivkin, *What Crucified Jesus?* (Nashville, 1984 [also see his chapter in this collection]); G. S. Sloyan, *Jesus on Trial* (Philadelphia, 1973); W. R. Wilson, *The Execution of Jesus* (New York, 1970); and P. Winter, *On the Trial of Jesus* (SJ 1; 2nd ed., rev. by T. A. Burkill and G. Vermes; Berlin, New York, 1974).

[33] A full treatment appears in J. S. Hanson and R. A. Horsley, *Bandits, Prophets, and Messiahs: Popular Movements at the Time of Jesus* (Minneapolis, 1985). See also F. Watson, "Why Was Jesus Crucified?," *Theology* 88 (1985) 105–12; Horsley, "Popular Messianic Movements."

teacher. Jesus was a victim. From these two facts, Christians and Jews have drawn different conclusions and can stay together regarding Jesus' identity only part of the way. At some point along that way we necessarily confront the theological issues raised so eloquently from the Jewish perspective by Samuel Sandmel: "We [Jews] have not believed that Jesus was the Messiah; we have not been willing to call him Lord; we have not believed that the *Logos* became incarnate as Jesus; we have not believed that Jesus was, or is, the very Godness of God.... we believe that man must make his own atonement, not have atonement wrought for him."[34]

Conclusion

Jews and Christians should welcome the recent attention given to the Jewishness of Jesus as a help to mutual understanding and religious cooperation. But it is important for us to come to grips with some problems involved in talking about the Jewishness of Jesus. (1) Our increased understanding of the diversity within Palestinian Judaism in Jesus' time makes it difficult to know precisely what kind of Jew Jesus was and against which background we should try to interpret him. (2) Jewish sources about Jesus are either late or suspect; Christian sources have passed through a complicated process of tradition. Those who try to get behind the sources either take Jesus out of Judaism or interpret him entirely within Judaism. (3) Both Jews and Christians view Jesus as a teacher and a victim of oppression. However, their ultimate theological assessments of Jesus differ. The recognition of our theological differences about Jesus demands that we continue to work together on the pertinent historical, methodological, and theological issues.

---

[34]*We Jews and Jesus* (New York, 1965), pp. 44, 46–47.

1. "YŠU'," "Jesus," in Semitic (Aramaic or Hebrew) script. The name was inscribed on an ostracon which dates from the time and place of Jesus of Nazareth. Appreciations expressed to the art staff, Doubleday & Company, Inc., Garden City, New York.

2. The terrain at Bethlehem, where some early Christian traditions place the birth of Jesus. Appreciations expressed to the Israel Government Tourist Office.

3. Sea of Kinneret or Sea of Galilee. Peter, Andrew, James, and John, Jesus' first disciples, were fishermen in this region of Galilee. Courtesy of Alan Oddie and PhotoEdit.

4. Shepherds even today are seen pasturing sheep in Galilee. Courtesy of Alan Oddie and PhotoEdit.

5. Spring in Galilee. This blossoming landscape is north of the Sea of Kinneret or Sea of Galilee and just southeast of Safed. Courtesy of Erich Lessing and PhotoEdit.

6. Mt. Tabor in Southern Galilee. Some early Christian traditions place Jesus' transfiguration on this mountain, which rises 568 meters impressively above the Plain of Israel. Courtesy of Erich Lessing and PhotoEdit.

7. View eastward from Samaria. Observe the olive groves in the foreground and the hills in the background. Courtesy of Erich Lessing and PhotoEdit.

8. The Judean desert. Robbers, lawless folk, rebels against Rome, and probably a few mystics dwelt or wandered in this barren land not far from the cosmopolitan Jerusalem. The parable of the Good Samaritan is set in such a locale. Courtesy of Erich Lessing and PhotoEdit.

9. Strato's Tower, or lighthouse, on the eastern shore of the Mediterranean Sea. Here, in the latter part of the first century B.C.E., Herod the Great built one of the most majestic cities in the Near East; he called it Caesarea after the Emperor. Courtesy of Erich Lessing and PhotoEdit.

10. Caesarea, Roman aqueduct. Courtesy of James H. Charlesworth.

11. This inscription, found at Caesarea, honors the Emperor Tiberius. The name Pontius Pilate, prefect of Judea, can be seen on the second line. The stone was inscribed in the first century C.E. Appreciations expressed to the Israel Museum, Jerusalem.

12. Jerusalem, the so-called Tomb of Absalom, which probably belonged to some wealthy Jews who lived during the time of Jesus. It is situated just below and to the east of the Temple Mount in the Kedron Valley. Courtesy of Zev Radovan and PhotoEdit.

13. Old Jerusalem, the Turkish wall, and the beautiful golden dome on the Temple Mount, as seen from the Mount of Olives (or Garden of Gethsemane). Courtesy of Alan Oddie and PhotoEdit.

14. Jerusalem and the Church of the Holy Sepulchre, which enshrines the traditional site for Jesus' crucifixion. Courtesy of Alan Oddie and PhotoEdit.

15. The interior of the Church of the Holy Sepulchre; view towards the apse.
Courtesy of Erich Lessing and PhotoEdit.

16. Jerusalem, the Wailing Wall. The massive stones in the foreground were placed there by King Herod's builders about two decades before the birth of Jesus. Courtesy of Alan Oddie and PhotoEdit.

17 Jesus washing the feet of Peter, according to an eight-century-C.E. Greek manuscript in the Palatine Library, Parma, Italy (Cod. No. 7). Courtesy of Erich Lessing and PhotoEdit.

18. Samuel anointing David king, according to a Byzantine silver dish found
on Cyprus (10 7/16 in. in diameter). The silverwork dates from the seventh
century C.E. Appreciations expressed to the Metropolitan Museum of Art,
gift of J. Pierpont Morgan, 1916. Some early Christian traditions claimed that
Jesus was a descendant of David; it is conceivable that he was considered
"Messiah" — "the Anointed one" — because of this relationship.

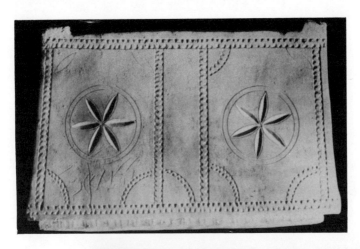

19. Photographs of a stone ossuary with an inscription (ŠLBY DWD) indicating that the individual whose bones were placed inside belonged to the lineage of David. See the discussion by Professor David Flusser in this volume (pp. 157–59). Appreciations expressed to the Israel Department of Antiquities and Museums.

20. Caesarea, Crusader walls. Courtesy of James H. Charlesworth.

21. Qumran, Cave IV. Courtesy of the Zuckermanns and the West Semitic
    Research Project.

22. Sepphoris in Lower Galilee; Roman amphitheater. Courtesy of James H. Charlesworth.

23. See of Galilee, western shore. Courtesy of James H. Charlesworth.

CHAPTER SIX

Jesus, His Ancestry, and the Commandment of Love

David Flusser

Introduction

It is possible to write the story of Jesus' life. We certainly have fuller records about the lives of contemporary emperors and some of the Roman poets; but among the Jews of post–Old Testament times, with the exception of the Jewish historian Flavius Josephus, and possibly St. Paul, Jesus is the one about whom we know most.

Every biography has its own peculiar problems. We can hardly expect to find information about Jesus in non-Christian documents. He shares this fate with Moses, Buddha, and Mohammed, who likewise received no mention in the so-called secular reports; and so, the only important Christian sources concerning Jesus are the four gospels: Matthew, Mark, Luke, and John. The rest of the New Testament tells us almost nothing about his life, and the Fourth Gospel is correctly regarded as biographically unreliable. The first three gospels are, in the main, based upon common historical material. Therefore, they can be — and have been — printed in a three-columned format. Such a book is called a "synopsis" — hence the name "synoptic gospels" given to the first three books of the New Testament. Is, then, the absence of non-Christian documents an insuperable obstacle in the way of knowledge of the life of Jesus?

When a religious genius appears within an environment that allows of precise documentation of his development, and of the circumstances of his life, there is always a temptation to try to uncover the psychological background leading up to this religious phenomenon. The reason why such psychological studies are often unsatisfactory is because the Spirit blows where he wills. This is especially true of personalities that are possessed by the Spirit. Who, for example, would dare to give a psychological analysis of the mystery of the personality of St. Francis? Our inability to provide a psychology of Jesus that does not sound a jarring note arises not from the type of sources at our disposal so much as from the nature of Jesus' personality.

That is the way it is: even if objective documentation is plentiful, the most genuine sources concerning a charismatic personality are his own utterances and actions, and the accounts of the faithful — read critically, of course. Thereafter the testimony of outsiders serves as an essential control. Let us take two modern examples. All that is significant about Joseph Smith (1805–1844), founder of the Mormons, can only be learned from him, and from Mormon documents. Then there is the case of Simon Kimbangu, the African who performed miracles of healing in the Belgian Congo from March 18 to September 14, 1921. He died in exile in 1950. Following the Christian model, his followers believed him to be the Son of God; but the documents do not make it clear what he thought of himself. Because of the brevity of his public activity, no unequivocal answer can be given to the question of his own self-assessment; and the testimony of the Belgian authorities in the Congo are as helpful in his case as the imagined archives of Pilate or records in the chancellery of the high priest would be in the case of Jesus.

The early Christian accounts about Jesus are *not* as *untrustworthy* as people today often think. The first three gospels not only present a reasonably faithful picture of Jesus as a Jew of his own time, but consistently maintain his style of speaking about himself in the third person. An impartial reading of the three gospels results in a picture, not so much of a redeemer of humankind as of a Jewish miracle-worker and preacher. There can be little doubt that even the latter picture does not do full justice to the historical Jesus. Obviously such a picture did not require the resurrection experience of the post-Easter Church before it could be portrayed. A series of miracle-legends and sermons certainly cannot be dismissed as "kerygmatic" preaching of faith in the risen and glorified Lord, as most present-day scholars and theologians do. The only gospel that emphasizes a post-Easter Christology is

John, and so it is of less historical value than the three synoptic gospels.

The Jesus portrayed in the synoptic gospels is, therefore, the historical Jesus, not the "kerygmatic Christ." How is this to be explained? It is generally accepted that the main substance of the synoptic gospels comes from two sources: an old account of the life of Jesus which is reproduced in Mark, and a collection of *Sayings*, known and used by Matthew and Luke along with the old account. Both of these chief sources were produced in the earliest congregation at Jerusalem and were translated into Greek. They contained the picture of Jesus as seen by the disciples who knew him. In addition, there was a certain amount of secondary material that came from the Jewish-Christian community. This had emerged out of dialogue — and later conflict — between Palestinian, and perhaps Syrian, congregations, and non-Christian Jewry. This material would seem to be reflected chiefly in Matthew.

For Jewish Christianity, even in later centuries when the Church in general regarded the view as heretical, Jesus the miracle-worker, teacher, prophet, and Messiah, was more important than the risen Lord of the kerygma. At a very early date, things had been different among the hellenistic Christian congregations founded by Greek Jews and composed predominantly of non-Jews. In these congregations, redemption through the crucified and risen Christ was the heart of preaching. It is no accident that the writings originating in these communities — for example, the letters of Paul — scarcely mention the life and preaching of Jesus. It is perhaps a stroke of luck, as far as our knowledge of Jesus is concerned, that the synoptic gospels were written fairly late — apparently after 70 C.E. — when the mighty creative power within the Pauline congregations had died down. For the most part, this later stratum of the synoptic tradition found its first echo in the redactions of the separate evangelists. If we examine this material with an unprejudiced mind, we learn from the content and the manner of expression that it is concerned not with kerygmatic statements, but with Christian platitudes.

The true facts are almost completely obscured, however, because in the present century people have tended more and more to identify the old account that lies behind Mark with our Gospel according to St. Mark. There are serious scholars today, it is true, who have isolated the secondary editing of Mark; but, as a rule, they refuse to draw the logical conclusions. If Mark's Gospel is a thorough revision of the original material, it can scarcely be identical with the old account upon which it is based. We may assume, therefore, that this old account, and not the revision, was known to both Luke and Matthew. Upon these presuppositions, R. Lindsey has freshly examined the synoptic problems and come to the following conclusions, which find support from other arguments too: Matthew and Luke, besides drawing upon the *Sayings*, also drew directly upon the old account; the editor of Mark used Luke for his version, and Matthew, besides using the old account, often drew upon Mark. It follows that when Matthew and Mark used almost the very same words it is Mark, and not the old account, that is reproduced in Matthew.

Even if we refuse to accept Lindsey's arguments and regard Mark as the model used by Matthew and Luke, it is not so difficult for modern scholars to distinguish the work of editing from the original traditional material in the gospels. This is an important fruit yielded by redaction criticism, which seems to be gaining more and more supporters. The adherents of this approach often seem to be quite unaware of the fact that they have opened up the way to sounder research into the life of Jesus. This study intends to make the conclusions of this approach, and Lindsey's solution, bear fruit by unlocking both of these ancient sources: the old account and the *Sayings*. Thus, we shall often leave the separate gospels and try to separate the original material from its editorial framework in all three gospels. In these cases, we will use the abbreviation "cf." The reader will be able to follow our method by using a synopsis. In order to understand Jesus, we have to know about the Judaism contemporaneous with him. The Jewish material is important, therefore, not just because it allows us to place Jesus in his own time, but because it allows us to interpret his sayings aright. If, then, we can be sure that there is a Hebrew phrase behind the Greek text of the gospels, we translate that Hebrew phrase and not the literal Greek.

Ancestry

Jesus is the common Greek form of the name Joshua. In Jesus' time the name was pronounced "Yeshua" (see Illus. 1); and Jesus of Nazareth was often called by that name in ancient Jewish literature. He was also called "Yeshu." Almost certainly, the latter was the Galilean pronunciation. After the arrest of Jesus, Peter betrayed himself by his peculiarly Galilean pronunciation (Mt 26:73). In those days, Jesus was one of the most common of Jewish names. The ancient Jewish historian, Flavius Josephus, for example, mentions twenty men with this name. The first is Joshua of the Bible, Moses' successor who conquered the Holy Land. Out of religious awe, the ancient Jews avoided certain important biblical names such as David, Solomon, Moses, and Aaron. In those days, it may be that the name Yeshua — Jesus — had gained popularity as a kind of substitute for Moses.

Jesus' father, and his brothers likewise, bore very popular names. His brothers[1] were called James, Joses, Judah, and Simon (Mk 6:3) — the names of the biblical patriarch Jacob and his three sons, as common in those days as "Jack" and "Bill" today. Joses is short for Joseph — the name of Jesus' father. Today it would be almost impossible for a Jewish child to be named after his own father, were he alive. In ancient times, by contrast, this was a fairly widespread custom. Jesus' mother was called Mary, which corresponds to the Hebrew Miriam, in those days also a common name. Although we know few women's names from ancient times — none of the names of Jesus' sisters has come down to us — Josephus mentions eight women called Miriam. The first is the sister of Moses, and the others are all named after her.

The marvelous story of Jesus' birth is to be found in the two literary, independent versions of Matthew and Luke. It is not found in Mark and John and is not presupposed in any other part of the New Testament. Apart from the New Testament writers, the first to mention the virgin birth is Ignatius of Antioch (d. 107).

As is well known, Jesus Christ means "Jesus the Messiah," and according to ancient Jewish belief, the Messiah was to be a descendant of David — the "Son of David." Both Matthew (1:2–16) and Luke (3:23–28) provide a genealogical tree leading back to David.[2] According to both of these genealogies, it is Joseph, not Mary, who is descended from King David. The decisive point is that both of Joseph's genealogies are found in those gospels that tell the story of the virgin birth: Matthew and Luke. It seems, therefore, that neither of these evangelists sensed any tension

---

[1] On the view that Jesus' brothers and sisters were, in fact, his cousins, or children of Joseph by a previous marriage, see the excellent book by the Catholic scholar, J. Blinzler, *Die Brüder und Schwestern Jesu* (Stuttgart, 1967).

[2] See J. Carmichael, *Death of Jesus* (New York, 1962) pp. 59–66.

between the descent of Jesus from David through Joseph, and the conception of Jesus without the agency of a human father. We must consider also that the two genealogies agree only from Abraham down to David.[3] The internal problems of both lists, and their considerable differences, leave us with the impression that both genealogies were constructed *ad hoc*, so to speak, in order to prove descent from David.

We know of no one at that time except Jesus[4] whose family was said to be Davidic. It was quite natural that any expected Messiah would retrospectively be legitimized by his followers as the Son of David (see Illus. 18). This happened to the Messianic pretender Bar Kokhba (d. 135), and it seems to have happened to Jesus also. Even were it possible that the family of Jesus possessed a tradition that they were of David's line, this could hardly have conditioned Jesus' self-consciousness. Jesus of Nazareth as a prince in disguise is highly improbable. However, if it can be shown that in the last century of the Second Temple period there were families that claimed to be of Davidic origin, then it will make us less suspicious about Jesus' Davidic lineage. If the Davidic families were numerous, then there is no place for the absurd image of Jesus as a prince in disguise.

An ancient rabbinic source (t.Ta'an 3.5) reports a venerable custom whereby the members of a family were entitled to bring wood to the Temple altar. The list itself is preserved in Mishnah Ta'anit 4.5. We have every reason to assume that this list preserves the names of eminent patrician families whose precedence was based on a centuries-old privilege: "The wood offering of the priests and the people was brought nine times (in the year). On the first of Nissan by the family of Arah of the tribe of Judah. On the twentieth of Tammuz by the family of David of the tribe of Judah...."

The final evidence of the existence of Davidids in Jesus' time was adduced at the end of 1971, when a burial cave was discovered in Jerusalem. The cave had been used in the first half of the first century B.C.E. An ossuary from this cave bears the following inscription: *šlby dwd* (see Illus. 19). Thus the inscription indicates that the bones contained in the ossuary belong to "those who are

---

[3]See W. Bauer, *Das Leben Jesu im Zeitalter der neutestamentlichen Apocryphen* (Darmstadt, 1967) pp. 21–29. On the sonship of David, see A. Suhl, *Die Funktion der alttestamentlichen Zitate und Anspielungen im Markusevangelium* (Gütersloh, 1965) pp. 89–94; F. Hahn, *Christologische Hoheitstitel* (Göttingen, 1964) pp. 242–79.

[4]See J. Liver, *The House of David...The Fall of the Second Commonwealth and After* (Jerusalem, 1959).

from the house of David." Now it becomes manifestly impossible to deny the existence of Davidic families in the last century of the Jerusalem Temple.[5]

Matthew and Luke provide the Davidic genealogy of Jesus; it is they who set the place of his birth in the city of David's birth, Bethlehem (see Illus. 2). Nevertheless, here the two accounts display important differences. According to Luke (2:4) Jesus' family traveled to Bethlehem only on account of the census. Before the birth of Jesus they lived in Nazareth, to which they returned. According to Matthew, however, the family resided in Bethlehem in Judea before the birth of Jesus, settling in Nazareth only on their return from Egypt (2:23).[6] It seems, then, that both the tradition that Jesus was born in Bethlehem, and the proof of his Davidic ancestry, arose because many believed that the Messiah would be of David's line and that, like David, the Messiah would be born in Bethlehem. This follows plainly from John 7:41–42. This passage tells of some who deny that Jesus is the Messiah, saying: "Is the Christ to come from Galilee? Has not the scripture said that the Christ is descended from David, and comes from Bethlehem, the village where David was?" The author of John, therefore, knew neither that Jesus had been born in Bethlehem nor that he was descended from David. At the same time, this incident shows how people demanded the fulfillment of these two conditions as legitimization of the messianic claim.

Jesus, then, was a Galilean Jew, probably born in Nazareth (see Illus. 3–5). Certainly that was where he lived for about thirty years until the time of his baptism by John (Lk 3:23). He was baptized either in 27/28 C.E. or 28/29 C.E.[7] It is more difficult to determine the duration of his public ministry, the period between his baptism and crucifixion. On the evidence of the first three gospels, it appears that this period extended to no more than one year. Following John, on the other hand, we would have to assume that it ran to two or even three years. It has become fairly clear today that John the theologian had little intention of being a historian, and so it would be unwise to accept his chronology or his geo-

---

[5]D. Flusser, " 'The House of David' on an Ossuary," *IMJ* 5 (Spring 1986) 37–40.

[6]See Bauer, *Das Leben Jesu*, p. 59.

[7]On the chronology of Jesus, see M. Dibelius, *From Tradition to Gospel* (New York, 1965); K. L. Schmidt, *Der Rahmen der Geschichte Jesu*, (Darmstadt, 1964) pp. 1–17; Bauer, *Das Leben Jesu*, pp. 279–310.

graphical framework without examination.[8] In any case we have
to ask also whether the first three gospels do intend to provide
a historical and geographical scheme and to what extent such a
scheme is conditioned by the theological presuppositions of the
individual evangelists.[9] There is material evidence to suggest that
on these points the synoptists are to be trusted. Jesus may have
worked in Judea and in Jerusalem before his final journey to death,
but his real sphere of operation was in Galilee on the northwest
shore of Lake Kinneret (see Illus. 3). It will also become evident
that the events are best understood on the presumption that the
baptism and the crucifixion were separated by only a short space
of time. Some scholars conclude that Jesus died in the year 30 or
33. Most probably, then, Jesus was baptized in 28/29 and died
in the year 30.

As we have seen, Jesus had four brothers, and some sisters.
The family at Nazareth, therefore, included at least seven children. If one accepts the virgin birth as historical and also concedes
that Jesus' brothers and sisters were his real blood brothers and
sisters, the conclusion must be accepted that Jesus was Mary's
first-born child. Even those who regard the nativity narratives of
Matthew and Luke as unhistorical must consider that Jesus may
well have been the eldest of the family. Luke (2:22–24) reports
that the parents of Jesus took him to Jerusalem shortly after his
birth to present him to the Lord, as the Law prescribed: "Every
male that opens the womb shall be called holy to the Lord." It is
true that one could redeem one's first-born through an offering
to a priest anywhere,[10] but there were devout people who took
this opportunity of making a pilgrimage with their young son to
the Temple of God, Jerusalem. Did Luke or his source invent this
story to proclaim the virgin birth, or was Jesus, in fact, Mary's
eldest child?

It is almost certain that Jesus' father died before Jesus was baptized. He may have died when Jesus was still quite a child. When
Jesus' public ministry begins, we meet his mother and his brothers
and sisters, but there is no mention of his father. According to Luke
(2:41–51), Joseph was still alive when Jesus was twelve years old:

---

[8]On the historical value of John's Gospel, see C. H. Dodd, *Historical Tradition in the
Fourth Gospel* (New York, 1963).
[9]On Mark, see W. Marxsen, *Der Evangelist Markus* (2nd ed.; Göttingen, 1959). On Luke,
see H. Conzelmann, *The Theology of St. Luke* (New York, 1961).
[10]See Num 18:15.

Now his parents went to Jerusalem every year at the feast of the Passover. And when he was twelve years old, they went up according to the custom; and when the feast was ended, as they were returning, the boy Jesus stayed behind in Jerusalem. His parents did not know it, but supposing him to be in the company they went a day's journey, and they sought him among their kinsfolk and acquaintances; and when they did not find him, they returned to Jerusalem, seeking him. After three days they found him in the Temple, sitting among the teachers, listening to them and asking them questions; and all who heard him were amazed at his understanding and his answers.

This anecdote from the life of the boy Jesus has special significance: it is a story of the precocious scholar; one might almost say, of a young talmudist. Today a Jewish boy is regarded as an adult when he turns thirteen; but in those days a boy of twelve could be regarded as grown up. Luke's story may well be true. I myself have heard the widow of a great rabbinic scholar, A. Aptowitzer, tell how her husband was lost when his parents were visiting an annual fair. In the early hours of the morning, they found him in a school keenly disputing scholarly problems with the rabbis. This woman had certainly never read Luke. If I am not mistaken, the Indian philosopher Gupta tells a similar story in his autobiography.

The anecdote Luke tells of the boy Jesus does not contradict the rest of what we know about Jesus' Jewish education. It will be affirmed with some justification that Jesus' disciples were "uneducated, common men" (Acts 4:13). This led to the assertion — made, indeed, by the historically less reliable John (7:15) — that Jesus himself was uneducated, that he had "never studied." Viewing Jesus' sayings against the background of contemporary Jewish learning, however, it is easy to observe that Jesus was far from uneducated. He was perfectly at home both in Holy Scripture and in oral tradition and knew how to apply this scholarly heritage. Jesus' Jewish education was incomparably superior to that of Paul.

External corroboration of Jesus' Jewish scholarship is provided by the fact that, although he was not an approved scribe,[11] people were accustomed to address him as "Rabbi" (my teacher).[12] "The form of address 'Rabbi' was in common use in those days,

---

[11]Mt 21:23–27 and Lk 20:1–8. See D. Daube, *The New Testament and Rabbinic Judaism* (London, 1956).

[12]Hahn, *Christologische Hoheitstitel*, pp. 74–81.

and was specially in favor to describe scholars and teachers of the Torah. It had not yet become restricted to expert and ordained teachers."[13] The generation following Jesus was the first to know the title as an academic degree. Jesus did not approve of the pleasure so many Pharisees took in being addressed as rabbi. "And," he said, "call no man your father on earth, for you have one Father, who is in heaven" (Mt 23:6–12). In those days "Abba" was another common form of address. In the generation before Jesus, a scribe had said much the same thing: "Love manual work and hate rabbinism."[14] Many shared this view. Arrogance may often have been found among the scribes, but they were not effete academicians. They demanded that everyone teach his son a trade, and many of them were themselves artisans. Carpenters were regarded as particularly learned. If a difficult problem was under discussion, they would ask: "Is there a carpenter among us, or the son of a carpenter, who can solve the problem for us?"[15] Jesus was either a carpenter or the son of a carpenter; most likely he was both. This in itself is no proof that either he or his father was learned, but it counts against the common, sweetly idyllic notion of Jesus as a naïve and amiable, simple manual workman.

Neitzsche was right when we wrote: "All the attempts I know of to construct the history of a 'soul' from the Gospels seem to me to imply a deplorable levity in psychological matters."[16] There is, however, a psychological element in the life of Jesus that we may not ignore: his rejection of the family into which he was born. This element is to be found even in the historically less reliable John. At the marriage feast in Cana, Jesus' mother asked him to produce wine, and he replied: "O woman, what have you to do with me?" (2:4).[17] In a freshly discovered apocryphal narrative, this theme of tension between Jesus and his family is heightened almost intolerably. This source[18] tells that, as Jesus was being crucified, his mother Mary and her sons James, Simon, and Judah, came and stood before him. Hanging upon the cross, he said to her: "Take your sons and go away!" The synoptists, too, tell us

---

[13] Hahn, *Christologische Hoheitstitel*, pp. 75–76.

[14] *Sayings of the Fathers* 1.10.

[15] J. Levy, *Wörterbuch über die Talmudin und Midraschim* (Berlin, 1924), vol. 3, p. 338.

[16] F. W. Neitzsche, *Antichrist*, para. 29, in *Complete Works*, 18 vols. (New York, 1964).

[17] The expression, which appears frequently in the gospels, comes from 1 Kgs 17:18. See also R. E. Brown, *The Gospel according to John I–XII* (AB; New York, 1966) p. 99.

[18] S. Pinès, "The Jewish Christians of the Early Centuries of Christianity according to a New Source," *The Israel Academy of Sciences and Humanities Proceedings* (Jerusalem, 1966), vol. 2, p. 61.

something about this tension. On one occasion, his mother and his brothers came and asked to speak to him. He turned to the disciples and said: "Here are my mother and my brothers! For whoever does the will of my Father in heaven is my brother, and sister, and mother" (Mt 12:46–50; cf. Lk 11:27–28). Jesus applied this experience to others as well; "Truly, I say to you, there is no man who has left house or wife or brothers or parents or children, for the sake of the Kingdom of God, who will not receive man-ifold more in this time, and in the age to come eternal life" (Lk 18:28–30). There is another saying on the same subject that does not sound so inhuman in Hebrew as in translation: "If any one comes to me and does not hate his own father and mother and wife and children and brothers and sisters . . . he cannot be my disciple" (Lk 14:26). Jesus knew that uncompromising religious commitment was bound to break family ties, all the more as he was certain that the end was very near.

> To another he said, "Follow me." But he said, "Lord, let me first go and bury my father." But he said to him, "Leave the dead to bury their own dead. . . . " Another said, "I will follow you Lord; but let me first say farewell to those at my home." Jesus said to him, "No one who puts his hand to the plough and looks back is fit for the Kingdom of God." (Lk 9:59–62)

As we have seen, an emotion-laden tension seems to have arisen between Jesus and his family, and it would appear to have been this psychological fact — the background to which we do not know — that powerfully contributed to his personal decision that was so decisive for humankind. Mark reduces this psychological background to a very simple formula: when Jesus left his work-shop and set off to preach the Kingdom of God, his family thought he had gone mad. Mark reports that his family "went out to seize him, for they said, 'he is beside himself ' " (Mk 3:21). This passage is unreliable, however, for it is a rather abstruse contribution of the evangelist.[19] The real core of all this is probably the fact that his family regarded the mission that led the eldest son to death as a dangerous illusion (Jn 7:5). Jesus correctly anticipated that his own kith and kin would not believe in him. For this reason, he did not return home after his baptism, but went to Capernaum. When he left that town to visit his native town, he only proved that no

---

[19]V. Taylor, *The Gospel according to St. Mark* (New York, 1966) pp. 235–36; see also Schmidt, *Der Rahmen der Geschichte Jesu*, pp. 122–23.

one is a prophet in his own country; for when he taught in the synagogue at Nazareth, the people asked where the son of Joseph had obtained all of his wisdom; and he was unable to perform any miracles there on account of their unbelief. If psychology is right, this is all quite intelligible.

What happened to Jesus' family after his death? A doubtful report (Acts 1:14)[20] tells us that Mary, the mother of Jesus, and his brothers joined the apostles in Jerusalem. Jesus' brother, James, came to believe as a result of a resurrection appearance.[21] In 62 C.E. James died for faith in his brother. He was murdered by a Sadducean high priest.[22] The other brothers were later converted to the faith, and they, with their wives, accepted the hospitality of the congregations (1 Cor 9:5). Having recognized their dead brother as the Messiah, the "brothers of the Lord" then realized that they too were of David's line. An old account[23] tells us that the Emperor Domitian regarded the grandsons of Jesus' brother, Judah, with suspicion because they belonged to the Jewish royal house. The Emperor is supposed to have interrogated them in Rome, but set them free when he discovered that they were only poor peasants. They were leaders of Christian churches, apparently in Galilee, and they lived until the reign of Trajan. James, the "brother of the Lord," was succeeded as head of the Church in Jerusalem by Simeon, a cousin of Jesus. After Jesus' death, his family had, therefore, overcome their disbelief and took an honorable place in the young Jewish-Christian community. We can understand their action: it might be dangerous, indeed, to live as their Master's relative within an ordered society; but it was simpler to do so than to see a brother or a son as different from themselves. Despite all her inability to understand her son, Jesus' mother behaved very properly. The dreaded catastrophe came, and her own heart was pierced by a sword.[24] Did she find complete consolation later through faith in her risen son, and in the hope that she would see him again?

[20]See E. Haenchen, *Die Apostelgeschichte* (2nd ed.; Göttingen, 1959); E. Meyer, *Ursprung und Anfänge des Christentums* (Stuttgart, Berlin, 1921–24) pp. 44–45.

[21]1 Cor 15:7; Gal 2:9; on the history of Jesus' family see E. Hennecke and W. Schneemelcher, *New Testament Apocrypha*, vol. 1, *Gospels and Related Writings* (Philadelphia, 1963).

[22]*Ant* 20.9.1.

[23]*HE* 3.11.19–20, 32.

[24]Lk 2:35.

Love

The revolutionary germ in Jesus' preaching — if we may speak thus — does not emerge from Jesus' criticism of the Law, but from other premises altogether. Jesus was not the first to provide these; his attack developed from attitudes already established before his time. Revolution broke out precisely with the radical commandment of love.

In about the year 175 B.C.E., a Jewish scribe bearing the Greek name Antigonos of Socho used to say: "Be not like slaves who serve their master for the sake of reward, but like slaves who serve their master with no eye on any reward; and may the fear of heaven be among you."[25] This saying is characteristic of the change in intellectual and moral atmosphere that had taken place in Judaism since the time of the Old Testament.[26] At the same time, it is the expression of a new and deeper sensitivity within Judaism, which was an important precondition for the preaching of Jesus.

The religion of Israel stressed the existence of *one* righteous God; his iconoclastic exclusiveness was linked with his inflexible moral will. The righteousness of the Old Testament seeks concrete expression in a new and just social order. God's righteousness is also his compassion; he espouses especially the cause of the poor and oppressed. He does not desire other people's physical power and strength, but their fear of him. The Jewish religion is a religion of morality in which the principle of justice is indispensable. That is why the division of human beings into just and sinners is so important. For the Jew, the concept that God rewards the just and punishes the wicked is the confirmation of God's steadfast truth. How, otherwise, could the righteousness of God prevail in the world?

Human destiny, however, seldom corresponds to human moral endeavor; often guilt obviously goes unpunished and virtue unrewarded. It is thus easy to see that something is amiss; but no ethics and no religion has yet succeeded in solving the problem of evil. In the Old Testament, the Book of Job is devoted to the topic of the bitter lot of the righteous; and Eastern heathen wisdom literature too knows the cry: "They walk on a lucky path those who

---

[25] *Sayings of the Fathers* 1.3. See K. Schlesinger, *Die Gesetzeslehrer* (Berlin, 1934) p. 25. On what follows, see D. Flusser, "A New Sensitivity in Judaism and the Christian Message," *HTR* 61 (1968) 107–27.

[26] See also the legends in *Aboth de R. Nathan*, 5.1, in Schlesinger, *Die Gesetzeslehrer*, p. 25.

do not seek a god. Those who devoutly pray to a goddess become poor and weak."[27]

It was not this problem that caused the revolution that led to the moral imperative of Jesus. As we have said, the moral religious maxim according to which the righteous flourish and the evil come to a bad end is constantly refuted by life. For the Jew of ancient times, however, the statement was doubtful from another point of view also. Even if the maxim had been confirmed by experience, the question would still have to be asked: Is the simple division of people into righteous and sinners itself appropriate? We know, it is true, that no one is perfectly just or utterly evil, for good and evil struggle within the heart of everyone. Also, there arises the question of the limits of the mercy of God and of his love for human beings. Even if there were no problems about the reward of the just and the punishment of the sinner, would they be performing a truly moral act if they performed it because they knew that they would be rewarded? As we have said, Antigonos of Socho believed this should be the morality of the humble slave: You ought to act morally, and at the same time give no thought to the reward that will surely come to you.

The strict morality of the old Covenant was clearly inadequate for the new sensitivity of the Jews of Jesus' time. Having now recognized that human beings are not sharply divisible into righteous and sinners, it was practically impossible for one to love the good and hate the wicked. Because it had become difficult to know how far God's love and mercy extended, many concluded that one ought to show love and mercy toward one's neighbor, thus imitating God himself. Luke (6:36) puts this saying into the mouth of Jesus: "Be merciful, even as your Father is merciful." This is an old rabbinical saying.[28]

In circles in which, at that time, the new Jewish sensitivity was especially well developed, love of one's neighbor was regarded as a precondition of reconciliation with God. "Transgressions between a man and his neighbor are not expiated by the Day of Atonement unless the man first makes peace with his neighbor." Thus spoke a rabbi a few years after Jesus.[29] And Jesus

---

[27]J. B. Pritchard (ed.), *Ancient Near Eastern Texts Relating to the Old Testament* (Princeton, 1955) p. 439.

[28]H. L. Strack and J. Billerbeck, *Kommentar zum Neuen Testament aus Talmud und Midrasch* (Munich, 1922–61), vol. 2, p. 159.

[29]Yoma 8.9; see R. Mayer, *Der Babylonische Talmud* (Munich, 1963).

said: "For if you forgive others their trespasses, your heavenly Father also will forgive you; but if you do not forgive others their trespasses, neither will your Father forgive your trespasses" (Mt 6:14–15).

The best summary of the new Jewish ethics is found in its oldest manifesto, Ecclesiasticus, or The Wisdom of Jesus the Son of Sirach (27:30–28:7), which was written about the year 185 B.C.E.

> Anger and wrath, these also are abominations, and the godless man will possess them.
> He that takes vengeance will suffer vengeance from the Lord, and he will firmly establish his sins.
> Forgive your neighbor the wrong he has done, and then your sins will be pardoned when you pray.
> Does a man harbor anger against another, and yet seek for healing from the Lord?
> Does he have no mercy towards a man like himself, and yet pray for his own sins?
> If he himself, being flesh, maintains wrath, who will forgive him his sins?
> Remember the end of your life, and cease from enmity, remember destruction and death, and be true to the commandments.
> Remember the commandments, and do not be angry with your neighbor; remember the covenant of the Most High, and overlook trespass.

The notion we have already encountered, that a man must be reconciled with his brother before praying for himself, is linked in Sirach with a modification of the old idea of reward that is typical of the period. The old compensatory justice whereby the righteous were rewarded according to the measure of their righteousness, and the sinners punished according to the measure of their sins, filled many in those days with uneasiness; and so they began to think: If you love your neighbor, God will reward you with good; if you hate your neighbor, God will visit you with evil. Jesus too said something like this: "Judge not, and you will not be judged; condemn not and you will not be condemned; forgive, and you will be forgiven; give, and it will be given to you, good measure, pressed down, shaken together, running over, will be put into your lap. For the measure you give will be the measure you get back" (Lk 6:37–38).

The beginning of this saying reminds us of the saying of the celebrated Hillel, who had already said: "Judge not your neighbor, lest you find yourself in his place!"[30] The saying, "The measure you give will be the measure you get back" was a proverb among the Jews in those days.[31] The saying of Jesus reported by Luke finds an important parallel in Jesus' words as reproduced by Clement of Rome about 96 C.E.: "Be merciful, and you will find mercy; forgive, and you will be forgiven; as you do, so it will be done to you; as you give, so it will be given to you; as you judge, so you will be judged; as you do good, so will good be done to you; with the same measure in which you give, it will be given to you" (1 Clem 13:2). This saying came from the early Church or perhaps from Jesus himself.[32]

The themes in which the new sensitivity in Judaism expressed itself in those days were closely interwoven. These themes interrelate many of the sayings of Jesus, and also relate his sayings with many Jewish proverbs. Thus Clement of Rome reports him as saying: "As you do, so it will be done to you," that is to say, as you treat your neighbor, so God will treat you. This is a most interesting variation on the so-called Golden Rule accepted as a moral imperative by many nations, and among the Jews;[33] even before the time of Jesus (Mt 7:12), it was regarded as the sum of all the Law. Hillel had said: "What is distasteful to yourself, do not do to your neighbor; that is the whole Law, the rest is but commentary." The Jews of that time probably put his interpretation upon the maxim also: God metes out to you in the same measure in which you mete out to your neighbor. The conclusion follows: "As a man pleads before God for his own soul, so should he plead for every living soul."[34]

Both Jesus and Hillel before him saw the Golden Rule as a summary of the Law of Moses. This becomes intelligible when we consider that the biblical saying, "You shall love your neighbor as yourself" (Lev 19:18), was esteemed by Jesus and by the Jews in general as a great chief commandment of the Law.[35] An old

---

[30] *Sayings of the Fathers*, 2.3; see Mayer, *Der Babylonische Talmud*, p. 328.

[31] Billerbeck, *Kommentar*, vol. 1, pp. 444–46.

[32] It certainly was not first compiled from the Greek synoptic gospels; its Semitisms, among other things, prove this. *Polycarp* 2.3 is dependent upon Clement, as the introduction to Jesus' saying shows (1 Clem 13.1b).

[33] Billerbeck, *Kommentar*, vol. 1, pp. 459–60. On Hillel's dictum in Shabbat 31a see W. Bacher, *Die Agada der Tannaiten* (Strasburg, 1890), vol. 1, p. 4.

[34] 2 Enoch 61:1. See Billerbeck, *Kommentar*, vol. 1, p. 460.

[35] See Billerbeck, *Kommentar*, vol. 1, p. 358. Earlier (p. 354) he argues against the assertion of modern Jewish scholars "that the old synagogue, even in New Testament times, had understood the command to love one's neighbor to be contained in the universal obligation

Aramaic translation of this biblical precept runs like this: "Love your neighbor, for whatever displeases you, do not to him!" This paraphrastic translation turns the phrase "as yourself" into the negative style of the Golden Rule. The saying "Love your neighbor" was understood as a positive commandment, and the words "as yourself" as a negative commandment included in it: you are not to treat your neighbor with hatred, because you would not like him to treat you in that way. Therefore, by means of Jewish parallels we have been able to see how the Golden Rule (Mt 7:12) and the commandment to love our neighbor (Mt 22:39) are related within Jesus' teaching.

There was yet another explanation of the phrase "as yourself" in the biblical commandment to love one's neighbor, so important in those days. In Hebrew the phrase can also mean "as though he were yourself." The commandment then reads: "Love your neighbor for he is like yourself." Ben Sirach knew of this interpretation when he demanded that one forgive one's neighbor his trespasses, for it is a sin to withhold mercy from "a man like himself" (Sir 28:3–5). Rabbi Ḥanina, who lived approximately one generation after Jesus, explicitly taught that this commandment to love one's neighbor is: "A saying upon which the whole world hangs, a mighty oath from Mount Sinai. If you hate your neighbor whose deeds are wicked like your own, I, the Lord, will punish you as your judge; and if you love your neighbor whose deeds are good like your own, I, the Lord, will be faithful to you and have mercy on you."[36] Our relationship to our neighbor ought, therefore, to be determined by the fact that we are one with him both in good and in evil characteristics. This is not far from Jesus' commandment to love; but Jesus went further and broke the last fetters still restricting the ancient Jewish commandment to love one's neighbor. Rabbi Ḥanina believed that one ought to love the righteous and not to hate the sinner, but Jesus said: "I say to you, Love your enemies and pray for those who persecute you" (Mt 5:44).

We shall see, it is true, that in those days the semi-Essene circles had reached similar conclusions from different presuppositions and that Jesus' moral teaching was influenced by these circles also; but influences do not explain everything. He who avoided

---

to love others." Let us assume that he is right; but with what certainty may we conclude that Jesus specifically extended the command to love one's neighbor to embrace gentiles?

[36] *Aboth de R. Nathan* (2nd version) p. 53.

his parental home in Nazareth and became the "friend of publicans and sinners" felt himself sent only to "the lost sheep of the house of Israel." It was not simply his total picture of life that urged Jesus on to loving devotion to sinners: this inclination was deeply linked with the purpose of his message. Moreover, from his infancy until his death on the cross the preaching of Jesus was, in turn, linked with his total picture of life. The commandment to love one's enemies is so much his definitive characteristic that his are the only lips from which we hear the commandment in the whole of the New Testament. Elsewhere we hear only of mutual love and blessing one's persecutors. In those days it was obviously very difficult for people to rise up to the heights of Jesus' commandment.

Jesus mentioned the biblical commandment when he was explaining the sum and substance of the Law of Moses:

> "Teacher, which is the great commandment in the Law?" And he said to him, "You shall love the Lord your God with all your heart, and with all your soul, and with all your mind (Deut 6:5). This is the great and first commandment. And the second is like it, You shall love your neighbor as yourself (Lev 9:18). On these two commandments depend all the Law and the prophets" (Mt 22:35–40).[37]

It is almost certain that here Jesus was teaching a proverb probably popular in oral tradition, because he saw it as important for his own message. This happened on other occasions too: he simply took over a saying of some scribe. "And he said to them, 'Therefore every scribe[38] who has been trained for the kingdom of heaven is like a householder who brings out of his treasure what is new and what is old' " (Mt 13:52). Jesus' saying about the double commandment of love clearly was coined before the time of Jesus. We have already seen that the biblical saying about love of one's neighbor was also described elsewhere as "the great commandment in the Law,"[39] and this commandment is truly like the other — the commandment to love God — for both verses from the Bible (Deut 6:5 and Lev 19:18) begin with the same phrase.

---

[37]The phrase "and the prophets" was added later. We have tried to reconstruct the beginning of Jesus' saying according to the manner of speech of that time. The saying could be possible in its present form only if the enquirer had been wanting to discover whether Jesus knew the answer. Luke (10:25–28) spotted this difficulty and wanted to overcome it.

[38]The saying does not come from Jesus; it has undergone Christian elaboration.

[39]See note 35.

It was typical of rabbinical scholarship to see similarly phrased passages from the Bible as connected in content also. The first great commandment of Jesus — love of God — was thus in harmony with the spirit of contemporary Pharisaism.[40] In the list of the seven kinds of Pharisee,[41] two positive types are named: the Pharisee of fear like Job and the Pharisee of love like Abraham. The many rabbinical documents that compare fear of God and love of God set love much higher than fear, for it was in harmony with the new Jewish sensitivity to serve God out of unconditional love rather than out of fear of punishment.[42]

All that has been said explains how the double commandment of love existed in Early Judaism before and contemporaneously with Jesus.[43] The fact that it does not appear in the rabbinical documents that have come down to us is probably a sheer accident; for Mark (12:28–34) and Luke (10:25–28) show that on the question of "the great commandment" Jesus and the scribes were in agreement.

The saying before us is but one example of many in which the uninitiated reader thinks he finds a specially characteristic teaching of Jesus and in so doing fails to observe the significance of the really revolutionary sayings. All the same, such sayings as the great commandment fulfill a significant function within the total preaching of Jesus. From early Jewish writings we could easily construct a whole gospel without using a single word that originated with Jesus. This could only be done, however, because we do in fact possess the gospels.

The same is true of the section of the Sermon on the Mount in which Jesus allegedly defines his own personal attitude toward the Law of Moses (Mt 5:17–48). There, so to speak, he brings things old and new out of his treasure.

The sensitivity of Early Judaism evolved, in contrast to the simple view of the Old Testament, a whole dialectic of sin; for when a human being ceases to be regarded as an unproblematical being, sins themselves become a problem. If we are not careful, one sin can lead to another; and even an action that does not appear sinful can cause us to become entangled in a real sin. There was

---

[40]*Sayings of the Fathers*, 1.3.

[41]Sota 22b; Ber 14b.

[42]Sifre on Deut 6:5. The correct text according to Midrash Tannaim on this passage.

[43]See Jub 36; the Jewish "'Two Ways," in the Didache; TDan 5:3; TIss 5:2; 7:6; TZeb 5:1. See also F. M. Braun, "Les Testaments des XII Patriarches," *RB* 67 (1960) 531–32.

a saying: "Flee from what is evil and from what resembles evil."
If we apply this concept to the commandments, we discover that
the lesser commandments are as serious as the greater.

Jesus' exegesis on the Law in Mt 5:17–48 should be understood in this sense also. The interpretation proper is preceded
by a preamble (Mt 5:17–20) in which Jesus justifies his method. It
seems that exaggerated importance has been attached to the first
sentence (Mt 5:17) of this introduction. Jesus only seemed to say:
"Think not that I have come to abolish the Law;[44] I have come
not to abolish, but to fulfill," and thus, following the customary
language[45] of his time, he avoided the reproach that the exegesis of the Law which followed abrogated the original meaning
of the words of the Bible. He could not have wanted to do this
because the Law, as written, is mysteriously bound up with the
existence of this world; so, even the minor commandments are
to be obeyed. This implies a tightening up of the Law, not in respect of ritual, but in respect of the relationships among people.
This attitude was present in Early Judaism too, as the following
saying exemplifies: "Everyone who publicly shames his neighbor
(and who thereby makes him turn pale) sheds his blood."[46] The
first two biblical exegeses of Jesus in the Sermon on the Mount
are constructed on this conceptual and formal scheme: it is not
just the murderer, but he who is angry with his brother, who is
condemned (Mt 5:21–22), and "every one who looks at a woman
lustfully has already committed adultery with her in his heart"
(Mt 5:28). According to a later traditional Jewish saying,[47] three
classes of sinners are consigned to hell for all eternity: the adul-
terer, those who publicly put their neighbor to shame, and those
who curse their neighbor. Jesus, too, had something to say on
this last type: "Whoever insults his brother shall be liable to the
council, and whoever says, 'You fool!' shall be liable to hell" (Mt
5:22). The continuation (Mt 5:29–30) has an interesting parallel
in rabbinical literature. Jesus said (cf. Mk 9:43–48):[48] "If your eye
causes you to sin, pluck it out, for it is better to lose it than for
your whole body to go into hell." The same is said about the hand
and the foot. Earlier (Mt 5:28) Jesus said that every one who had

---

[44]The phrase "or the prophets" does not seem to be original.
[45]On the idiom see Rom 3:31.
[46]Baba Metzia, 58b.
[47]Baba Metzia, 58b.
[48]Matthew abridges the saying, and Mark has elaborated it.

looked at a woman lustfully had already committed adultery with her in his heart. There was a Jewish opinion[49] that the word "to commit adultery" in Hebrew had four letters in order to warn us that adultery could be committed by hand, foot, eye, and heart.

Jesus began his exegesis of the Scriptures by stressing the importance of the lesser commandments. In this spirit he is then able to equate anger with murder and lust with adultery. In the Jewish "Two Ways" theme, preserved in the early Christian document[50] the *Didache*, we read: "My child, flee all evil, and from all that is like unto it. Be not soon angry, for anger leadeth to murder. . . . My child, be not lustful, for lust leadeth to fornication . . . for from all these are generated adulteries."[51] Here we encounter the two applications of the rule corresponding to the sixth and the seventh of the ten commandments, which Jesus expounds in exactly the same way in the Sermon on the Mount. In this the second table of the Decalogue can be seen in the background of Jesus' scriptural exegesis, and it is seen even more clearly in the "Two Ways." These biblical commandments speak of our relation to our neighbor, and so the real conclusion of Jesus' exegesis is his commentary (Mt 5:43–48) on the great commandment, "Love your neighbor as yourself."

Those who listened to Jesus' preaching of love might well have been moved by it. Many in those days would have agreed with him. Nonetheless, in the clear purity of his love they must have detected something very special. Jesus did not accept all that was thought and taught in the Judaism of his time. Although not really a Pharisee himself, he was closest to the Pharisees of the school of Hillel, who preached love, but he pointed the way further to unconditional love — even of one's enemies and of sinners. This was no sentimental doctrine.

Conclusion

The present age seems especially well disposed to understand Jesus and his interests. A new sensitivity has been awakened in us by profound anxiety over the future, and over the present. Today we are receptive to Jesus' reappraisal of all our usual values, and

---

[49] Midrash Haggadol on Ex 20:14.

[50] See J. P. Audet, "Affinités litteraires et doctrinales du 'Manuel de Discipline,'" *RB* 59 (1952) 219–38.

[51] Did 3:1–3.

many of us have become aware of the questioning of the moral norm, which is his starting point too. Like Jesus, we feel drawn to social pariahs, to the sinners. When he says that we must not resist evil because, even by our denial, we only encourage the intrinsically indifferent play of forces within society and the world at large, we Jews and Christians of today at least can understand. If we free ourselves from the chains of dead prejudice, we are able to appreciate his demand for undivided love, not as philanthropic weakness, but as a true psychological consequence.

The enormity of his life, too, speaks to us today: the call of his baptism; the severing of ties with his estranged family and his discovery of a new, sublime sonship; the pandemonium of the sick and possessed; and his death on the cross. Therefore, the words which Matthew (28:20) puts into the mouth of his risen Lord take on for us a new, non-ecclesiastical meaning: "Lo, I am with you always, to the close of the age."

Selected Bibliography of David Flusser's Publications*

A. Books

Jesus in Selbstzeugnissen und Bilddokumenten. Hamburg, 1968. E.T. New York, 1969.
The Josippon (Josephus Gorionides), ed. with an intro. and notes, vol. 1. Jerusalem, 1978; vol. 2. Jerusalem, 1980 [Hebrew].
Jewish Sources in Early Christianity. Tel Aviv, 1979 [Hebrew]. E.T. New York, 1987 (Collected Papers).
Die Rabbinischen Gleichnisse und der Gleichniserzähler Jesus. Bern, 1981.
Die Letzten Tage Jesu in Jerusalem. Stuttgart, 1982.
Bemerkungen eines Juden zu christlichen Theologie. Freiburg, 1984 (Collected Papers).
Tussen Oorsprong en Schisma. Hilversum, 1984 (Collected Papers).
The Spiritual History of the Dead Sea Sect. Ministry of Defense, Israel, 1985 [Hebrew].
Entdeckungen im Neuen Testament; vol. 1: *Jesusworte und ihre Überlieferung.* Neukirchen, 1987 (Collected Papers).
Collected Papers, vols. 1–2. Jerusalem, 1988.

---

*Provided by the editors to encourage further study.

B. Articles

"The Sect of the Judean Desert and Its Opinions," *Zion* 19 (1954) 89–103 [Hebrew].

"'Do not Commit Adultery,' 'Do not Murder,'" *Textus* 4 (1964) 220–24.

"The Pharisees and the Stoics according to Josephus," *Iyun* 14 (1964) 318–29 [Hebrew].

"The Son of Man, Jesus in the Context of History," *The Crucible of Christianity*, ed. A. Toynbee. London, 1969; pp. 215–34.

"Das jüdische Martyrium im Zeitalter des Zweiten Tempels und die Christologie," *FrRu* 25 (1971) 187–94.

"Die jüdische und griechische Bildung des Paulus," *Paulus*. Freiburg, 1971; pp. 19–37.

"The Liberation of Jerusalem: A Prophecy in the New Testament," *EI* 10 (1971) 226–36 [Hebrew].

"Jesus ein Revolutionär," *KG* 28 (1972) 25–30.

"New Christian Understanding of Judaism," *Orot* (1973) 2–16 [Hebrew].

"Biblical Literature, Intertestamental Literature," *Encyclopaedia Britannica, Macropaedia*. Chicago, 1974; vol. 1, pp. 931–38.

"Der lateinische Josephus und der hebräische Josippon," *Josephus-Studien*, eds. O. Betz, K. Haacker, and M. Hengel. Göttingen, 1974; pp. 122–32.

"Jerusalem in the Literature from the Second Temple Period," *R. Mass Jubilee Volume*. Jerusalem, 1974; pp. 263–93 [Hebrew].

"The Great Goddess of Samaria," *IEJ* 25 (1975) 13–20.

"Paganism in Palestine," *The Jewish People in the First Century*, eds. Sh. Safrai and M. Stern. CRINT; Assen, 1976; section 1, vol. 2, pp. 1065–1100.

"Who Sanctified the Well-Beloved in the Womb?" *Studies in Bible and the Ancient Near East*, eds. Y. Avishur and J. Blau. Jerusalem, 1978; pp. 329–36 [Hebrew with Sh. Safrai].

"Apocalyptic Elements in the War Scroll," *Jerusalem in the Second Temple Period: Abraham Schalit Memorial Volume*, eds. A. Openhaimer, U. Rapaport, and M. Stern. Jerusalem, 1980; pp. 434–51 [Hebrew].

"Das Erlebnis, ein Jude zu sein," *Richte unsere Füsse auf den Weg des Friedens: Helmut Gollwitzer zum 70. Geburtstag*, eds. A. Baudis et al. Munich, 1980; pp. 15–25.

"Reflections of a Jew on a Christian Theology of Judaism," *A Christian Theology of Judaism*, ed. Cl. Thoma. New York, 1980; pp. 1–19.

"Pharisaer, Sadduzaer und Essener in Pescher Nahum," *Qumran*. Darmstadt, 1981; pp. 121–66.

"The Apocryphal Songs of David," *The Memorial Volume for Y. M. Grintz*, ed. B. Ufenhaimer. Tel Aviv, 1982; pp. 83–103 [Hebrew with Sh. Safrai].

"The Jewish Origins of Christianity," *JQ* 24 (1982) 78–98.

"Jewish Messianic Figures in the New Testament," *Messianism and Eschatology*, ed. T. Baras. Jerusalem, 1983; pp. 103–34 [Hebrew].

"Notes on the Jewish Marriage Liturgy," *I. A. Seeligman Volume*. Jerusalem, 1983; pp. 543–61 [Hebrew with Sh. Safrai].

"The Roman Empire as Seen by the Hasmonaeans and the Essenes," *Zion* 48 (1983) 151–76 [Hebrew].

"Nadab and Abihu in the Midrash and in Philo's Writings," *To Millet*. Tel Aviv, 1984; pp. 79–84 [Hebrew with Sh. Safrai].

"Psalms, Hymns and Prayers," *Jewish Writings of the Second Temple Period*, ed. M. E. Stone. CRINT; Assen, 1984; section 2, vol. 2, pp. 551–77.

"Maria und Israel," *Maria*. Freiburg, 1985; pp. 12–16.

"The Ten Commandments and the New Testament," *The Ten Commandments*. Jerusalem, 1985; pp. 118–87 [Hebrew].

"Das Aposteldekret und die Noachitischen Gebote," *Wer Tora mehrt, mehrt Leben: Festgabe für Heinz Kremers zum 60. Geburtstag*, eds. E. Brocke and H.-J. Barkenings. Neukirchen, 1986; pp. 173–92 [with Sh. Safrai].

"The 'House of David' on an Ossuary," *IMJ* 5 (1986) 37–40.

"The Ossuary of Yehohanah Granddaughter of the Highpriest Theophilus," *IEJ* 36 (1986) 39–44 [with Dan Barag].

" 'Durch das Gesetz dem Gesetz gestorben' (Gal 2, 19)," *Judaica* 43 (1987) 30–46.

"Paul's Jewish-Christian Opponents in the Didache," *Gilgul: Dedicated to R. J. Zwi Werblowsky*, eds. S. Shaked, D. Shulman, and G. G. Stroumsa. Leiden, 1987; pp. 71–90.

"Qumran and the Famine During the Reign of Herod," *IMJ* 6 (1987) 7–10.

"Christianity," *Contemporary Jewish Religious Thought*, eds. A. A. Cohen and P. Mendes-Flohr. New York, 1987; pp. 61–66.

"Die Sünde gegen den heiligen Geist," *Wie gut sind deiene Zelte, Jaakow ...*, *Festschrift zum 60. Geburtstag von Reinhold Mayer*, eds. E. L. Ehrlich and B. Kappert. Gerlingen, 1986; pp. 139–44.

CHAPTER SEVEN

Jesus, Early Jewish Literature, and Archaeology

James H. Charlesworth

Introduction

Informed Jews and Christians no longer approach the gospels as if they are biographies. But in the face of what is perceived to be insensitive or excessively liberal criticism of the gospels, some students do tend to read the New Testament as if Jesus' actions and words are recorded without alteration. This approach has been exposed as improper by New Testament scholars for well over one hundred years. Unfortunately, many today are confused by what they perceive to be a choice between Jesus' "authentic" actions and the Church's "inauthentic" redactions. I shall attempt to show why these are false alternatives.

Some scholars will assuredly wish to ask the following question: Is it not obvious that one conclusion of New Testament research is that nothing can be known assuredly about the Jesus of history? The answer seems to be "no": not even Bultmann and Tillich espoused that utter pessimism. Their ideas are not to be confused with those of Bruno Bauer, Paul Couchoud, G. Gurev, R. Augstein, and G. A. Wells, all of whom denied the existence of Jesus. Bultmann and Tillich, as radical as they were, affirmed the existence of Jesus and the undeniable fact of his crucifixion in Jerusalem before 70 C.E. Moreover, failure to grasp the historical particularity of Jesus, and all the scandals this entails, reduces a religion to a philosophy of existence, precisely as intended by Fritz Buri in his critique of Bultmann.

The major impediments in our search for the historical Jesus have lightened. First, the theological one has crumbled. It had been constructed out of a twofold claim: some critics argued that faith alone is sufficient for the Christian, others added that Jesus the Christ is known solely existentially. Now, the best minds perceive that faith without some historical knowledge is faithless to Jesus. Only responses to him that, like the early creeds and hymns, are impregnated by historical data, are paradigmatically different from superstition, no matter how sophisticated they appear.

Second, it is now obvious to the leading New Testament scholars that pre-Easter data are preserved in the gospels. If we are impeded in our search by the confessional dimension of the gospels, that is because the early Christians were not crippled by the crucifixion but empowered by the resurrection. Embarrassing data, moreover, are preserved in the narratives — notably, Judas' betrayal, Peter's denial, and Jesus' crucifixion. Such data shaped the Church; they were not created to serve the needs of the Church. The only persuasive explanation for Simon of Cyrene's identification as the father of Alexander and Rufus (Mk 15:21) is because of their importance to — perhaps presence in — Mark's community.

We must grasp that history is accessible only via tradition, and it is comprehensible only via interpretation. Redaction criticism is possible only because traditions were extant to be edited.

Third, formerly we were lost in a wasteland of history, which was caused by the paucity of sources from pre-70 Judaism. Now — since the 1940s — we possess hundreds of documents that are pre-70 and Jewish.

Somehow, in the decades of confused apologetics and well-meaning attempts to refine an infallible methodology, we forgot two essential dimensions of the search for Joseph's son. Historical research is scientific by method but not by conclusion; the historian at best can provide us not with certainty but with probability. Hence any discourse on searching for *ipsissima verba Jesu* (Jesus' own *exact* words) and absolute certainty about recovering them is imprecise, imperceptive, and impossible.

The new research on Jesus will be different from and more informed than previous attempts primarily because of the increased documentary evidence and the phenomenal archaeological discoveries; hence, it is pertinent to organize an assessment of where we are according to these categories. Our discussion will focus on the Old Testament Pseudepigrapha, the Dead Sea Scrolls, the Nag Hammadi Codices, Josephus, and Archaeology. Since the field to be covered is broad and complex, the approach must be focused and selective; and this course obviously demands many personal judgments which cannot be explained here. Suffice it to state that only two questions will be addressed to each of these divisions in research: Are the data significant in our search for the Jesus of history? If so, why and in what important ways?

The Old Testament Pseudepigrapha

In 1913 Clarendon published the first English edition of the Old Testament Pseudepigrapha.[1] It was selective and directed to scholars. In 1983 and 1985 Doubleday published the two volumes of *The Old Testament Pseudepigrapha*.[2] The first English edition contained seventeen pseudepigrapha; the new one has fifty-two documents plus thirteen writings preserved only in ancient quotations and added as a supplement to volume 2. The astronomical leap from seventeen to sixty-five documents will upset scholars who have grown content with a normative view of Early Judaism; younger scholars excited by new challenges will thrive on the vast new territory for exploration. They will find that it is now even more difficult to separate Jewish from Christians writings; and they will grow to perceive what it means to state that "Christianity" for at least forty years, from 30 to 70 C.E., was a group within Judaism. In seeking to understand the Pseudepigrapha they will ultimately be forced to confront the issues related to Jesus and his place in first-century Judaism.

As always with sensationally new and exciting developments, there have been misrepresentative statements. It is clear that Jesus' warning to let an answer be merely "yes, yes" or "no, no," according to Matthew, and his reference to many mansions in heaven, according to John, is paralleled impressively in one pseudepigraphon from the first century. It is called 2 Enoch. One author (C. F. Potter, in *Did Jesus Write This Book?*) became so excited about these parallels that he claimed "it may well be that" Jesus "wrote" 2 Enoch, or part of it."[3] Fortunately, no scholar has been guilty of such false claims.

---

[1] R. H. Charles (ed.), *The Apocrypha and Pseudepigrapha of the Old Testament in English*, 2 vols. (Oxford, 1913; reprinted frequently since 1963).

[2] J. H. Charlesworth (ed.), *The Old Testament Pseudepigrapha*, 2 vols. (Garden City, N.Y., 1983–85).

[3] C. F. Potter, *Did Jesus Write This Book?* (New York, 1965) p. 27.

In assessing the significance of the Pseudepigrapha for Jesus research, one aspect is noncontroversial and indeed obvious. Many of the Pseudepigrapha are roughly contemporaneous with Jesus and are Palestinian. Along with the Dead Sea Scrolls, they are major new sources for describing the religious phenomena in pre-70 Judaism. Unlike the Dead Sea Scrolls, however, the Pseudepigrapha are not primarily or merely the literary products of one small Jewish group which had withdrawn and isolated itself in the desert. The early Jewish Pseudepigrapha clarify the intellectual landscape of first-century, pre-70 Jews, like Jesus. And that is exceedingly important because creative geniuses like Jesus enjoy horizons that extend beyond one country. They live in an intellectual world.

What is the significance of the early Jewish Pseudepigrapha for Jesus research? It is amply demonstrated by considering the ways these writings help us understand Jewish apocalypticism and eschatology.

E. Käsemann, as is well known, concluded that the mother of all Christian theology is "apocalyptic" thought.[4] The brilliant German New Testament scholar reminisced that the study of apocalyptic thought was simply not a suitable topic during his years as a student and almost all of his long career as a professor. Today, however, this vast field is a focal point for New Testament research. For example, Professor J. Christiaan Beker has astutely seen that the heart of Paul's theology is shaped by Jewish apocalyptic thought.[5]

In essence, the unearthly vision of the apocalyptists is that the righteous can go home again. They can return home, not into the womb à la Freud, and not back to an esoteric world via *gnosis*. They can return back to paradise that is to be — or is already — reopened for them (see esp. 4 Ezra 8, 2 En 8–9). Then and there they shall have full and peaceful fellowship with all, especially once again with God.

The Pseudepigrapha, and the apocalyptic literature collected within it, is decisive for understanding Jesus of Nazareth; but he obviously was *not* one of the apocalyptists. They were repeatedly exhorted to write down what they had seen and heard. Jesus wrote

---

[4]E. Käsemann, "On the Subject of Primitive Christian Apocalyptic," in *New Testament Questions of Today*, trans. W. J. Montague (Philadelphia, London, 1969) pp. 108–37.

[5]J. Chris. Beker, *Paul the Apostle: The Triumph of God in Life and Thought* (Philadelphia, 1980; reprinted 1984).

nothing. The apocalyptists were often scribes, who worked in a *beth midrash*, were influenced by Wisdom literature, and were preoccupied with encyclopedic and scientific knowledge. Jesus was an itinerant teacher, who proclaimed the nearness and importance of God's Kingdom. The apocalyptists were vengeful, often calling upon God to destroy the Jews' enemies. Jesus was more concerned with inward dispositions and an attitude of compassion and outgoing love (but see 2 En 52) — he even exhorted his followers to "love your enemies" (Mt 5:43). The apocalyptists tended to denigrate the earth. Jesus celebrated God's creation, and used the lilies of the field as examples of God's concern for his people (Mt 6:25–33). The apocalyptists talked about the future age drawing closer. Jesus — sometimes in conflicting ways, according to the evangelists — affirmed that only God really knew the time of the end (Mk 13:32), but that it appeared already to be dawning in his ministry (Mk 9:1), especially in the miracles and proclamations (Mk 1:14–15). Most importantly, the apocalyptists tended to situate God far from the living world of humanity. Jesus stressed the nearness, indeed the presence, of a compassionate Father, who should be called *Abba* (the Semitic noun for "father").

Yet the apocalypses and apocalyptic literature are important for understanding Jesus. Both the apocalyptists and Jesus shared a feeling for the oppressed (cf. 1 En 102–04 and 2 En 63); and both uttered woes against the complacent and oppressive rich (1 En 94:8–9, 96:4–8, 97:8–10; Mk 10:23–25). Both presupposed a profound dualism, especially of two categorically different ages. Both were ultimately optimistic; God's promises and the greatest of all human dreams — peace and harmony throughout the universe — would be realized by God's own actions, perhaps through an intermediary. Both transferred allegiance to another world and redefined priorities. For example, Jesus claimed the first shall be last (Mk 10:3). Both sided with the poor (Mk 10:21) against the wealthy, exhorted righteous conduct (e.g., 1 En 104:6; 2 En 61), uttered beatitudes (viz. 2 En 42, 52; Mt 5), and demanded purity of hearts (cf. 2 En 45; Mk 7:14–23).

The most surprising — and, to many, astounding — development in research on the Pseudepigrapha is a paradigm shift on the evaluation of the date and character of the Parables of Enoch (1 En 37–71). This book is exceedingly important for New Testament scholars because it describes the heavenly Son of man, the

Messiah, the Elect One, and the Righteous One. I am convinced these are four terms for the same intermediary of God.

J. T. Milik, who was responsible for publishing the Aramaic Enoch fragments found among the Dead Sea Scrolls, emphasized that the Parables of Enoch, so clearly aligned with Jesus' reputed words, was unattested among the Aramaic fragments. He judged that it was a Christian composition from around the beginning of the third century C.E. Practically all New Testament scholars were persuaded by his judgment and refused to use 1 Enoch 37–71 to assess Jesus' life and the theology of the earliest Christians.

Today, no specialist on the Parables of Enoch accepts Milik's judgment without major qualifications. During international seminars in Tübingen and Paris, more than a dozen experts on this book agreed that it is certainly a Jewish document.[6] All members of these seminars except one were convinced the Jewish work — the Parables of Enoch — must predate the destruction of Jerusalem in 70 C.E. Hence the term, and perhaps title, "Son of man" was already developed by Palestinian Jews long before 70.

Since the Son of man is almost always found in the New Testament in collections of Jesus' words, is it not possible that this phrase derives authentically from Jesus himself? Are there not some of these Son of man sayings that may help us understand Jesus and his perception of his mission? Is it not difficult to categorize all the Son of man sayings either as circumlocutions for the first-person-singular pronoun, or as another means of referring generically to humanity? What indeed was denoted and connoted by the title "Son of man" during the early decades of the first century C.E.? And what did Jesus mean by these words?

One additional comment should be made in passing. As is well known, Jude 14–15 contains a quotation from what was considered long ago to be — perhaps — a lost Jewish document. Now we know the author of Jude quoted from "1 Enoch," chapter 1. And unexpectedly, the very quotation is now discovered in Aramaic on a strip of leather found among the Dead Sea Scrolls.[7]

Biblical theologians, and others, will now be forced to reassess our understanding of canon, since a book in the Christian canon

---

[6]See the proceedings in J. H. Charlesworth, *The Old Testament Pseudepigrapha and the New Testament: Prolegomena for the Study of Christian Origins* (SNTS MS 54; Cambridge, 1985; reprinted 1987, 1988).

[7]For a photograph and further discussion see Charlesworth, *Jesus within Judaism* (Anchor Bible Reference Library 1; Garden City, N.Y., 1988) pp. 44–45.

quotes as prophecy a passage in a book rejected from the Protestant and Catholic canon, although it is in the Falasha canon. Obviously, in the first century there was considerable fluidity regarding the limits of canon, Scripture, and inspired words.

The Dead Sea Scrolls

The so-called Dead Sea Scrolls were first discovered in the late 1940s in caves just to the west of the Dead Sea (see Illus. 21). The first photographs and translations appeared shortly thereafter, but the largest Scroll was obtained by Y. Yadin in the mid-1960s and was not translated into English until 1983. A voluminous body of fragments has not yet been published; as of the present I count more than 170 important "sectarian" Scrolls and portions of documents; less than a dozen of these are well known.[8]

No collection of ancient literature has excited the imagination of our contemporaries so fully as the Dead Sea Scrolls. This excitement has led to sensational claims and ideological counterclaims. The scholarly jargon for the exchange is the "Qumran fever."

The claims about the importance of the Scrolls for Jesus research have been excessive; some critics recently revived the old justly discarded opinion that Jesus or John the Baptist was really the founder of the Qumran community, the *Môrēh haṣ-Ṣedek*, or Righteous Teacher. Those who hold these views are writers masquerading as scholars.

The Scrolls do not support the opinion that Jesus was an Essene or even significantly influenced by them. Yet, it is difficult to agree with William S. LaSor's judgment, in *The Dead Sea Scrolls and the New Testament*, that the Essenes and Jesus, along with the early Christians, simply represent Jewish "sectarian" movements "moving in different orbits."[9]

One must distinguish between what is in the New Testament from what is behind it. What is *in* the New Testament are the theologically edited reflections of the early Christians; what is *behind* the New Testament are the earliest historical individuals and communities that were created out of historical events, namely the experience and memory of Jesus' life and horrifying death,

---

[8]See the comprehensive edition of previously published Dead Sea Scrolls, being edited by Charlesworth and to be published by Princeton University Press.

[9]W. S. LaSor, *The Dead Sea Scrolls and the New Testament* (Grand Rapids, Mich., 1972) p. 254.

and the claim to having been confronted by a resurrected Jesus. The "in" is not a categorical antithesis to the "behind" but they are distinguishable categories. The failure to perceive this distinction has invalidated much New Testament research over the last two hundred years.

Jesus' death in 30 C.E. predates the first gospel by about forty years. The crucial issue is not the comparison of documents, namely the Scrolls which predate 70, and the gospels which postdate it. The critical questions concern Jesus and the Essenes and the more than forty years when the Essenes and Jesus and his followers shared the same territory, nationality, chronological period, and adversaries — namely, the Romans and Sadducees, and intermittently the Pharisees and the Zealots. Can there have been no relationships between the Essenes and the Palestinian Jesus Movement when both emphasized the sinfulness of all humanity and the need for God's grace, the eschatological time, the establishment of the New Covenant according to Jeremiah 39, the presence and power of Satan and the demons, and the clarion call of Isaiah 40:3? Is it not clear that both groups emphasized essentially the same hermeneutical principle: all Scripture and prophecy pointed to the present — the endtime — and directly and especially to their own special group? Did not both groups, *mutatis mutandis*, exhort a sharing of possessions? Has it not become palpable lately that both groups were products, and to a certain extent examples, of Jewish apocalypticism. Do not both groups, and only they, stress the living presence of "the Holy Spirit" in their community? Can all these similarities be dismissed legitimately as mere coincidences? These reflections thrust before us one major question: What *were* the relationships between Jesus and the Essenes?[10]

According to both Philo and Josephus, four thousand Essenes lived in Palestine. Since no more than approximately three hundred Essenes could have lived at Qumran and nearby, the vast majority, or around thirty-seven hundred, dwelt elsewhere. Philo and Josephus also stressed that the Essenes lived in villages and cities, preferring to congregate on the fringes. The reference to the Essene gate in the walls of Jerusalem by Josephus is now apparently confirmed by recent archaeological discoveries and a

---

[10]The question is now being explored by a team of international experts; their work will be published by Charlesworth in *Jesus and the Dead Sea Scrolls* (Anchor Bible Reference Library; Garden City, N.Y., in preparation).

passage in the Temple Scroll.[11] We must confront the growing evidence that Essenes lived in the southwestern sector of Jerusalem.

These perspectives are significant. Jesus probably would have met Essenes during his itineraries, maybe he talked with many of them. Perhaps they discussed common values and the need for full dedication to God and his Covenant.

Four similarities between Jesus and the Essenes may be briefly sketched. First, Jesus shared with the Essenes a theology that was thoroughgoingly monotheistic and paradigmatically eschatological. The present was the end of time. He, of course, preached a somewhat more imminent eschatology, but one should talk about the difference between the Essenes and Jesus in such a way that Jesus' eschatology was more "realizing" in terms of degree, not kind.

Second, Jesus shared the Essenes' utter dedication to God and Torah. Perhaps he was referring to the Essenes, the only celibate group known in Early Judaism, when he praised the men who became eunuchs for God's Kingdom (cf. Mt 19:10–12).

Third, according to Mark, Jesus proclaimed that divorce is forbidden. This apodictic statement is difficult to comprehend and so Matthew relaxed it and made it casuistic (Mt 5:31–32, 19:9). Jesus' view on divorce, according to Mark, was until recently unparalleled in the history of Jewish thought.

Now, a prohibition of divorce is found in the Temple Scroll. According to this document, the king must remain married to only one woman: "and he [the king] must not select in addition to her another woman because she, herself alone, will remain with him all the days of her life" (11 QTemple 57:17–18). What is demanded of the king is even more stringently required of others.

Only two Jews denied the possibility of divorce: Jesus, according to Mark, and the author of the Temple Scroll. Since the Temple Scroll antedates Jesus and appears to be the quintessential Torah for some Essenes, the relationships that may have existed between Jesus and the Essenes should be raised again for fresh discussion.[12]

Any comparisons between Jesus and the Essenes must ultimately be grounded in a recognition of vast differences. The Essenes were extreme legalists and, for the sake of purity, they quarantined themselves from all others; Jesus rejected the legal-

---

[11]See the article by R. Riesner in *Jesus and the Dead Sea Scrolls*.
[12]See the article by O. Betz in *Jesus and the Dead Sea Scrolls*.

istic rules that choked the Sabbath, and involved himself with all ranks of humanity.

Most importantly, he emphasized the need to love others, an attitude illustrated in Luke by the Parable of the Good Samaritan, and developed into a new commandment in the Johannine writings. It is conceivable that Jesus may have been thinking about and rejecting the exhortation to hate the sons of darkness, when he stated, "You have heard that it was said, 'You shall love your neighbor and hate the enemy'" (Mt 5:43). The best, and possibly only real Jewish parallel to the rule to hate others is found in the Dead Sea Scrolls. In fact, according to the Rule of the Community at the time of the yearly renewal, Essenes chanted curses on all the sons of darkness, specifically those who were not Essenes, including Jews who masqueraded as Essenes.

Without a doubt the most significant and uncontroversial importance of the Dead Sea Scrolls for Jesus research is the light they shine on a previously dark period. To enter into the world of the Dead Sea Scrolls is to become immersed in Jesus' theological environment. The Scrolls do more than simply either provide the ideological landscape of Jesus' life or disclose the *Zeitgeist* he knew. Along with the data unearthed by the archaeological excavations of Qumran, they give us some indication of the social settings of pre-70 Palestinian Jews.

In addition to these brief comments, the Dead Sea Scrolls — along with the Pseudepigrapha — enable us to begin to appreciate the distinctive features of Jesus' theology. These early Jewish texts supply the framework from which the theologian can evaluate the uniqueness of Jesus of Nazareth. The contours of the historical Jesus begin to appear, and it is startling to discern how true it is that the genesis and genius of earliest Christianity, and the one reason it became distinguishable from Judaism, is found primarily in one particular life.

In summation, we can report that Ernest Renan's oft-quoted dictum, that Christianity is an Essenism that succeeded, is simplistic and distortionistic. Christianity did not evolve out of one "sect" on the fringes of a normative Judaism. Christianity developed out of many Jewish currents. There was no one source or trajectory. Jesus, of course, was not an Essene; but he may have shared more with the Essenes than the same nation, time, and place.

The Nag Hammadi Codices

In the late 1940s, shortly before the discovery of the Dead Sea Scrolls in Jordan, an Arab peasant found in Egypt, not far from Nag Hammadi, thirteen Coptic codices that preserved ancient writings. Considerable excitement surrounded this discovery, because many of the documents were previously unknown, and because sayings of Jesus were preserved in some codices.

Unfortunately, many scholars made rash and sensational claims about the importance of the Nag Hammadi Codices. Some even judged that Bultmann's historical speculations were now receiving proof. In *The Promise of Bultmann*, Norman Perrin argued that:

> Bultmann's particular view of a pre-Christian Gnostic redeemer myth (the myth of a heavenly figure coming down to earth to secure salvation for men and opening a way for them into the heavenly realm) as an influence upon John has been strenuously resisted on the grounds that we have no evidence that such a myth is pre-Christian. But now recent discoveries in Egypt would seem to prove that Bultmann has been right all through the years on this matter.[13]

In my estimation, most scholars today would agree with Perrin's statement "that we have no evidence that such a myth is pre-Christian.[14]

Critics may feel that it is unfair to cite Perrin, because his opinion may once have been valid but is obviously impossible today. Yet a revered scholar, James Robinson, has just expressed a similar evaluation. In a foreword to the recently published English translation of E. Haenchen's *A Commentary on the Gospel of John*, Robinson disparages W. F. Albright's claim that the Dead Sea Scrolls and not the Nag Hammadi Codices are significant for understanding the Gospel of John. Robinson announces that "Haenchen's commentary serves in a way to mark the transition from the Qumranian orientation characteristic of much Johannine study in the first decades after World War II to the Nag Hammadi orientation that has become increasingly prominent in recent years."[15] The image of a mass exodus of Johannine scholars from Qumran to Nag Hammadi, evoked by this statement, is a mirage. The best Johannine scholars know we are faced not with an "either/or,"

---

[13]N. Perrin, *The Promise of Bultmann* (Philadelphia, 1969; reprinted 1979) p. 110.
[14]See especially G. Quispel, "Gnosis," *VoxT* 39 (1969) 27–35.
[15]J. M. Robinson, "Foreword," in E. Haenchen, *A Commentary on the Gospel of John*, trans. R. W. Funk, 2 vols. (Hermeneia; Philadelphia, 1984), vol. 1, p. x.

but with a "both/and": *both* collections must be studied. Moreover, the Dead Sea Scrolls, unlike the Nag Hammadi Codices, are clearly Jewish and anterior to the group of Jews converted to Christianity that produced the Gospel of John.

What is the significance of the Nag Hammadi Codices for Jesus research? What document can be singled out as essential in our search for the historical Jesus? The answer is clear and readily available. It is the Gospel of Thomas.

The interest in this gospel among scholars is phenomenal. I have counted 397 publications on it alone.[16] Its significance for gospel research is placarded by the inclusion of translations of it in K. Aland's *Synopsis*.

The Gospel of Thomas is significant in the search for the historical Jesus because of the following factors: (1) It is a document of Jesus' sayings reminiscent of the lost source (Q) used independently by both Matthew and Luke. (2) It contains sayings of Jesus that, at least in some passages, are independent of the so-called canonical gospels. (3) It is now becoming well recognized that it is improper to discard the Gospel of Thomas as late, derivative, and gnostic.

Since the early 1960s one saying in the Gospel of Thomas has caught my eye, and I have found it difficult to shake the possibility that it may have been more accurately preserved in the Gospel of Thomas than in the corresponding pericope in Luke. The passage is in Logion 101 (cf. 55):

> [Jesus said], "Whoever does not hate his fath[er] and his mother in my way will not be able to be a d[isciple] to me. And whoever does [not] love h[is father] and his mother in my way will not be able to be a d[isciple t]o me...."

A significantly different but better known version of this saying is found in a section unique to Luke:

> If anyone comes to me and does not hate his father and mother and wife and children and brothers and sisters, and even his own soul, he is not able to be my disciple. (Lk 14:26)

Matthew has an even different version: "he who loves father or mother more than me is not worthy of me; and he who loves a son or daughter more than me is not worthy of me. And he who does

---

[16]See Charlesworth, *The New Testament Apocrypha and Pseudepigrapha: A Guide to Publications and Excursuses on Apocalypses* (Metuchen, N.J., London, 1985).

not take up his cross and follow after me, is not worthy of me" (Mt 10:37–38; Matthew is closer to a doublet in Thomas, Logion 55).

The major issue concerns the appearance of "in my way" twice in Thomas and not once in Luke. It is difficult to dismiss this phrase as merely an explanatory gloss in Thomas.

The logion in Thomas seems either to be an early Palestinian reflection on Jesus' way, or a statement from Jesus, perhaps somewhat altered, that is in line with his wisdom sayings. In any case, it is obvious how significant the Gospel of Thomas may be in our search for the sayings of the historical Jesus.

Here we have paused briefly to look at one saying of Jesus and its transmission and redaction in the first one hundred years after his death. Before continuing it is necessary at least to stress that many other sections of Thomas deserve much more careful study than customarily given to them by New Testament scholars. For example, the study of Jesus' parables is frustrated by a myopic focus on only Matthew and Luke. The Parable of the Great Supper is so thoroughly altered by Matthew and his school that we are left wondering about reverence for tradition and reliable transmission (see Mt 22:1–14; Lk 14:15–24). The parable reappears in Thomas (Logion 64) and is not nearly so edited there as in Matthew. Most importantly, it is now relatively certain that Luke's and Thomas' parable about a supper or dinner is changed by Matthew and his school into an allegory about a king's wedding feast for his son.

Josephus

Josephus' writings are well known and have been important for New Testament studies for over one thousand years. Some early Christian scholars before Chalcedon (451) revered him excessively. Jerome (c. 342–420) saluted him as "the Greek Livy" (*Ep. 22 ad Eustochium* 35.8).

Josephus and Jesus were Palestinian Jews who were intimately linked with Galilee. Although Josephus lived later in the first century than Jesus, his early career was characterized by the struggle against, and eventually the war with, Rome. It is difficult to discern what transpired during the fifteen hours prior to the crucifixion, but it is clear that Jesus was crucified by the Romans, probably because he seemed to them a political insurrectionist. He and his followers were certainly seen as a threat to the precarious peace that existed around 30 C.E. in Palestine.

The significance of Josephus for Jesus research does *not* reside in the man Josephus, however; it lies in his literature. He is the historian of Early Judaism. He describes the turbulent times in which Jesus lived.

Most significantly, he referred to Jesus. His reference to Jesus, the *Testimonium Flavianum*, may be translated from the Greek as follows (clearly Christian words are in italics):

> About this time there was Jesus, a wise man, *if indeed one ought to call him a man*. For he was one who performed surprising[17] works (and) a teacher of people who with pleasure received the unusual.[18] He stirred up[19] both many Jews and also many of the Greeks. He *was the Christ*.[20] And[21] when Pilate condemned him to the cross, since he was accused by the first-rate men among us, those who had been loving (him from) the first did not cease (to cause trouble),[22] *for he appeared to them on the third day, having life again, as the prophets of God had foretold these and countless other marvelous[23] things about him*. And until now the tribe of Christians, so named from him, is not (yet?) extinct.
>
> (*Ant* 18.63–64)

The above translation attempts to bring out the meaning most likely intended by the first-century Jew. We can be assured that either a Christian scribe added this passage *in toto*, or that one or more Christian scribes edited and expanded it.

---

[17] Gk. *paradoxos*, "strange, surprising, wonderful." Josephus would have meant "surprising"; a Christian would have assumed he meant "wonderful." The Slavonic version mentions "astonishing and powerful miracles."

[18] Following H. St. J. Thackeray's emendation suggested in *Josephus, the Man and the Historian* (New York, 1929) pp. 144–45. Christian scribes would have changed *taēthē*, "unusual, strange," to *talēthē*, "truth."

[19] The Greek verb, *epagō*, has a pejorative innuendo; however, as a strong aorist middle, it could have been interpreted "win over" (to himself).

[20] As some scholars have speculated, something like "according to their opinion" preceded, and was deleted from, the confession, which obviously in its extant form in Greek cannot be attributed to Josephus. Another suggestion is that the Greek *legomenous*, "so-called," may have been before *christos*, but was omitted intentionally. See G. C. Richards and R. J. H. Shutt, "Critical Notes on Josephus' Antiquities," *Classical Quarterly* 31 (1937) 176.

[21] An adversative *kai* is possible: "but."

[22] Not "did not forsake him." One must add something to explain what Jesus' followers did not cease to do. See F. F. Bruce, "The Evidence of Josephus," in *Jesus and Christian Origins Outside the New Testament* (Grand Rapids, Mich., 1974) pp. 39–40. Immediately prior to this passage Josephus discusses a riot (*he stasis*), immediately after it he discusses "another affliction" (*heteron ti deinon*). One must see the framework for the *Testimonium Flavianum*.

[23] Gk. *thaumasios*, "wonderful, admirable": hence probably not an assessment of Jesus by Josephus.

A study of the *Testimonium Flavianum* leads to speculations, on either option, that ultimately fall short of convincing proof. It appears probably that Josephus referred to Jesus, but certainly not in the form preserved in the Greek manuscripts. Hence, many critics refuse to take a stand on the issue of reliable Josephus words in this section of the *Antiquities*. The passage is virtually ignored in research on the Jesus of history.

For years I yearned for the discovery of a text of Josephus' *Antiquities* that would contain variants in the *Testimonium Flavianum*. Then perhaps we could support scholarly speculations with textual evidence.

In fact, this very dream was recently realized when a tenth-century Arabic version of the *Testimonium Flavianum* was discovered in Agapius' *Kitāb al-'Unwān*. The translation of this passage by S. Pinès,[24] who drew attention to it, is as follows:

> Similarly Josephus (*Yūsīfūs*), the Hebrew. For he says in the treatises that he has written on the governance (?) of the Jews: "At this time there was a wise man who was called Jesus. His conduct was good, and (he) was known to be virtuous. And many people from among the Jews and the other nations became his disciples. Pilate condemned him to be crucified and to die. But those who had become his disciples did not abandon his discipleship. They reported that he had appeared to them three days after his crucifixion, and that he was alive; accordingly he was perhaps the Messiah, concerning whom the prophets have recounted wonders."[25]

What is immediately obvious — when one compares the Arabic recension with the Greek one — is that the clearly Christian passages are conspicuously absent in the Arabic version.

The two recensions of the *Testimonium Flavianum* should be studied by theological students, clergy, the laity, and seminary professors. The Greek recension, minus the Christian interpolations, reveals how a first-century Jew probably categorized Jesus: He was a rebellious person and disturber of the elusive peace; but he was also a wise person who performed "surprising," perhaps even wonderful works. And he was followed by many Jews and gentiles. The Arabic version provides textual justification for excis-

---

[24]S. Pinès, *An Arabic Version of the Testimonium Flavianum and Its Implications* (Jerusalem, 1971).

[25]The last sentence could also be translated, "He was thought to be the Messiah, concerning whom the prophets have recorded wonders." See Pinès, *An Arabic Version*, p. 71. I favor this rendering; it is supported by the Syriac recensions of the *Testimonium Flavianum*.

ing the Christian interpolations and demonstrating that Josephus probably discussed Jesus in *Antiquities* 18; but, in its "complete" form, it is certainly too favorable to Jesus. The focus of both recensions then helps shift the spotlight back on the Jesus of history, and that fact is of phenomenal importance. Our gaze is pulled away from preoccupations with ideas to confrontations with a first-century Galilean. We are momentarily protected from the perennial threat of docetic dogmas and freed to reflect on the scandalous particularity of one person, Jesus. Neat paradigms are scrambled by an unnerving confrontation with *realia*. Historic dreams become anchored in historical drama.

Archaeology

The search for the historical Jesus has been predominantly a German-centered European concern: from Reimarus to Strauss, from Strauss to Schweitzer, from Schweitzer to Bultmann, and from Bultmann to Käsemann, Bornkamm, and Hengel. This entire area of research has focused upon the New Testament writings, a study of the meaning of myth, the literary sources inherited by the evangelists, and the pre-gospel origin of the Jesus tradition. Except in the publications by J. Jeremias and M. Hengel, singularly absent has been an awareness of the importance of archaeology for a perception of Jesus' time and the early Palestinian Jesus Movement.

In the last three decades, however, spectacular discoveries are proving to be significant in our search for the historical Jesus. I shall draw attention to only two that I am personally convinced are unusually important for Jesus research. At the outset, however, I must caution that it is very difficult to move from the first-century Palestinian milieu, now being partly revealed by archaeologists, to Jesus' own thoughts and actions.

A most significant archaeological discovery for Jesus research is the recovery of the bones of a man, named Jehohanan, who had been crucified.[26] His heels (*tuber calcanei*) remain attached to the wood portions of the *simplex*, because the spike driven through them bent when it hit a knot in the olive wood cross. His forearms, or his wrists, were tied to the *patibulum*. The man was crucified in his thirties, in Jerusalem, and near the time of Jesus'

---

[26]See Charlesworth, "Jesus and Jehohanan: An Archaeological Note on Crucifixion," *ExpT* 84 (1973) 147–50.

own crucifixion. Previous to this archaeological find, we possessed no remains of one who had been crucified.

The significance of this discovery for Jesus research is obvious. We have a grim reminder of the horrors of crucifixion. Jehohanan's legs had been bent, and his torso twisted on the cross. The resulting muscular spasms would have caused excruciating pains. Death could have come far more rapidly than we had imagined. We can now better understand a report found *only* in Mark; this verse was not copied from Mark by either Matthew or Luke because they did not understand it or — more probably — were disturbed by the polemical use of it. Mark reported that Pilate could not believe that Jesus was "already dead" (*ēdē tethnēken*, Mk 15:44).

Also, the old hypothesis that Jesus' corpse must have been dumped into a pit set aside for the corpses of criminals and insurrectionists and not buried is disproved. Jehohanan's bones had received a proper Jewish burial.

As I stated fifteen years ago:

> It is not a confession of faith to affirm that Jesus died on Golgotha that Friday afternoon; it is a probability obtained by the highest canons of scientific historical research.[27]

Before the crucifixion Jesus had been nearly beaten to death by Roman soldiers during approximately ten hours of all-night scourging. Reflections on this dark episode in history are difficult and disturbing for the Christian; but they expose the weakness in the claim — revived in 1982 by G. Cornfeld — that Jesus only appeared to die: "Jesus never died."[28] Such a position cannot derive from sane and critical reflection; it emanates from polemics and was promulgated in the second century by Celsus, the Roman polemicist against Christianity (see Origen, *Contra Celsus* 2.56).

The most significant archaeological discovery for Jesus research is the growing proof for the site of the crucifixion. Jesus was crucified around 30 C.E. just outside Jerusalem's walls, as the author of Hebrews stated (Heb 13:12).

Today pilgrims are shown "The Garden Tomb" near Gordon's Calvary; both are just north of the present Turkish walls of the Old City. Most lay Christians choose this serene spot, clearly outside

---

[27]Charlesworth, *ExpT* 84 (1973) 150.
[28]G. Cornfeld (ed.), *The Historical Jesus: A Scholarly View of the Man and His World* (New York, London, 1982) p. 187.

the present walls, as the location of Jesus' own burial. Calvary is assumed to be nearby.

The traditional site for Calvary is not attractive. It is a noisy menagerie of competing ecclesiastical authorities within the Church of the Holy Sepulchre, and within the present walls of the Old City (see Illus. 14, 15).

When I was living in Jerusalem, K. Kenyon discovered proof that the wall now encompassing the traditional site lies, in places, on a foundation that was constructed probably in 41 by Herod Agrippa. Hence, in 30 the traditional site would have been outside the city. Also, in the late 1960s Père C. Coüasnon showed me in the Church of the Holy Sepulchre columns *in situ* from the fourth-century Church of Constantine;[29] hence, the traditional place can be traced architecturally to the early centuries of Christianity. And, moreover, prior to the nineteenth century there were no competing sites for Golgotha.

In the late 1970s excavators exposed part of the foundations of Hadrian's Roman Forum in which the Temple of Aphrodite was constructed around 135 C.E. This temple had buried Golgotha, and perhaps Jesus' tomb. Now, major discoveries confirm, in my opinion, that the Church of the Holy Sepulchre houses the rock on which Jesus was crucified (see Illus. 14, 15).

It is now clear, thanks to excavations in the late 1970s, that a rock inside the Church of the Holy Sepulchre, and traditionally called Calvary, still rises approximately thirteen meters above bedrock. The exposed rock, moreover, bears the marks of ancient quarrying: It is a rejected portion of an ancient pre-exilic Israelite white stone (*malaki*) quarry.[30] By the first century B.C.E. this area had evolved from a seventh- or eighth-century rock quarry, to a refuse dump, and finally to a burial site, since Jewish tombs clearly predating 70 are visible. It is possible that the final phase in the first century before 70 was a garden as described by the author of John (see Jn 19:41).

I am convinced that it is on this exposed fist of rejected rock that Jesus had been crucified. It was outside the walls and near a public road in 30; hence it fits all the Jewish (see Lev 24:14, and Mishnah Sanh 6.1) and Roman requirements of a spot for executions.

Perhaps the early Christians living in Jerusalem knew what ar-

---

[29] C. Coüasnon, *The Church of the Holy Sepulchre in Jerusalem*, trans. J.-P. B. and C. Ross (London, 1974) p. 29 and Plates XVI, XVIII, XIX.
[30] See the photographs in Cornfeld (ed.), *The Historical Jesus*, pp. 202, 212.

chaeologists only recently have discovered. It is possible that they celebrated Jesus' crucifixion by reciting Psalm 118:22,

> The stone which the builders rejected;
> this has become the head of the corner.

In fact this tradition, recorded in 1 Peter (2:7), is also attributed by Luke to Peter, when he spoke to the high priest in Jerusalem: "this is the stone which was rejected by you builders, but which has become the head of the corner" (Acts 4:11). The pronoun "this" could be a *double entendre* for both Calvary and Jesus.

Although we must not succumb to the naive fascination and lure of "the holy places," as have unenlightened pilgrims, we must not miss the significance for New Testament research of recent archaeological discoveries. These have been simply phenomenal.

The foregoing discussion reveals that a purely theological and literary approach to the New Testament or Christian origins is improper and misleading, and results in unscholarly conclusions and bankrupt theology. An examination of documents roughly contemporaneous with Jesus and archaeology, of course, must never be portrayed improperly as if they can prove or support any faith or theology. Authentic faith certainly needs no such shoring up. Philologists, historians, and archaeologists cannot give Christians a risen Lord, but they can help Christians better understand Jesus' life, thought, and death.

Summary

The search for the historical Jesus over the last two hundred years has been a rocky road with many dead ends and detours. Many Jewish and Christians scholars have served us well; and it is now obvious the journey is both possible and necessary. From D. F. Strauss we learned about the multidimensional nature of myth and the importance of honest methodology. From M. Kähler we apprehended that the gospels are post-Easter confessionals; but from P. Benoit, N. Dahl, and E. Käsemann we perceived that pre-Easter tradition did come to the post-Easter community and shaped its redaction.

From A. Schweitzer we recognized that any attempt to understand Jesus must allow him to belong to the first century; we must not throw around him the garb of modern respectability. Moving away from Schweitzer's exaggerated emphasis on eschatology and confused perception of apocalyptic thought, we are on the right track in stressing, with E. Käsemann, G. Bornkamm, H. Anderson, G. Vermes, and D. Flusser, that we can know more of the historical Jesus than the form critics, especially R. Bultmann, had allowed.

The search for *ipsissima verba Jesu* evolved from a misperception of the circumscribed arena of probabilities in which the historian works. Jesus' teaching was characterized by parables and the proclamation of God's rule (or the Kingdom of God). These two phenomena, and the Lord's Prayer itself, however, are deeply Jewish and paralleled abundantly in literature roughly contemporaneous with Jesus.

In this chapter I have focused on the Dead Sea Scrolls and the Pseudepigrapha. This limitation should not be taken to undermine my firm, and published, conviction that rabbinic literature also preserves many edited essentials for grasping the religious life and the liturgy of first-century Jews, like Jesus.

Certainly N. Perrin, and the large group of scholars who followed him, had the proper intent but the wrong perception of Early Judaism, and — most importantly — a misleading methodology. Jesus' authentic words were sought within a net that released all Jesus' sayings that were paralleled either in Judaism or in the Church. A strict application of this method produces a Jesus who was not a Jew and who had no followers. Yet, if two facts are unassailable today, they are Jesus' deep Jewishness — he was a Jew — and his paradigmatic effect on Jews and gentiles.

Jesus did exist. He was a real person who lived in Palestine, grew up in Galilee (see Illus. 3–6), had some relationship with John the Baptist (who certainly baptized him), centered his public ministry in Capernaum, healed the sick, and finally moved southward to Jerusalem, where his life ended ignominiously on a cross outside the western wall of Jerusalem in 30.

Past research and present data contain tacitly a demand for a renewed dedication to Jesus research; a request for an unbiased exploration of Jesus and his time by Jews and Christians; an appeal to be informed methodologically, textually, and archaeologically; a call to enjoy the inclusiveness and preponderance of the interrogatives within the elusive probabilities of the historian's sphere; and a plea to realize that the historian and the theologian are not necessarily antagonists.

Conclusion

In the latter part of the twentieth century a new appreciation of Jesus and of his Jewish roots has been acknowledged by more than the specialists. In fact, this perspective is coming to be assumed by most of those who are interested in the creative forces that defined the first century C.E. and in turn shaped Western culture. It may be too early to report that Jesus is no longer a major impediment on the road to better relations among Jews and Christians (see Küng's chapter in this volume). It can be stated, however, that no longer is it considered intelligent and informed to claim that he was an Aryan, or to question the fact that he was a Jew. It is also no longer popular to disparage Jesus' teachings, as if they are often silly and impractical. These two gross distortions of historical truth are no longer typical of what is deemed the product of careful research and reflections.[31]

Today every New Testament scholar I know realizes that Jesus was a first-century Jew. Most of these scholars are Christians, and many are ordained Protestant ministers or Roman Catholic priests. Jewish scholars today, using scientific methodologies, stress the brilliance of much of Jesus' teachings. Some see him as one who emphasized in his life and thought the extreme demands of the Law (Torah). Each group of scholars is working non-confessionally with historical and scientific methods. Neither began moving in this direction in order to improve the relations among Jews and Christians. The conclusion is not dictated by such contemporary concerns. The perspective, which is now a presupposition underlying much research on first-century times, does, however, become the foundation for bridge building among contemporary Jews and Christians.[32]

The task now is to instill in the mind of the public these refreshing new insights. Surely our world and culture will be more peaceful, enjoyable, and protected from past gross injustices and fears if it becomes common knowledge that Jesus was a first-century Jew, that his proclamation of God's Rule (or the Kingdom of God) and his prayer are clearly Jewish. His disciples were all Jews, and many other Jews were attracted to his life and thought. Like the Pharisees, Sadducees, and Essenes,

---

[31] See now the following important works: R. K. Ericksen, *Theologians under Hitler: Gerhard Kittel, Paul Althaus, and Emmanuel Hirsch* (New Haven, London, 1985) and T. Weiss-Rosmarin (ed.), *Jewish Expressions on Jesus: An Anthology* (New York, 1977).

[32] See the excellent chapter in this volume by D. J. Harrington, S.J. (pp. 123–36).

the Palestinian Jesus Movement was a distinct Jewish group which helped shape the vibrant world of pre-70 Jewish culture. Jesus — and the origins of Christianity — are inextricably linked with Judaism.

CHAPTER EIGHT

Jesus, the Jewish Revolutionary

Alan F. Segal

Although Christianity's destiny brought it to Rome and world prominence, its beginnings were in "sectarian" Judaism. Like the other "sects," Christianity was based on an interpretation of the Torah constitution, as is evident in the term "New Testament," from the Latin term meaning "new covenant" which in turn came from the Greek, itself an interpretation of Jeremiah 31. Jeremiah's consoling prophecy that God would renew the destroyed country of Israel with a new covenant was reunderstood as a prophecy of Jesus' incarnation. This reinterpretation was advanced by the Church, not by Jesus himself. Jesus' own message is often more difficult to isolate. But it is certain that Jesus headed an apocalyptic movement, not just a movement of educational social reform.[1]

In his own day many of Jesus' hearers understood his meaning to be apocalyptic. This does not mean that all of Jesus' teaching was apocalyptic. He was also a preeminent teacher of wisdom. But the part of his teaching that can be identified as uniquely his own and that most affected his contemporaries was apocalyptic. Since the later Church would not eliminate authentic Jesus traditions yet at the same time did not favor apocalypticism, the presence of apocalyptic in early Christianity must be attributed to Jesus himself.

Tracing the apocalyptic traditions in Christianity reveals an irony in New Testament methodology: the historicity of teachings ascribed to Jesus can confidently be asserted only when they conflict with the teachings of the Church that followed him. In Norman Perrin's phrase, every statement about Jesus must pass a "criterion of dissimilarity" before it can be accepted

---

[1] A. Schweitzer, *The Quest for the Historical Jesus* (1910; 3rd ed., London, 1954).

as historical.[2] Clearly, this test of evidence can call into question many authentic traditions about Jesus. It is nevertheless necessary, because Christian tradition was transmitted by well-meaning followers who found it inconceivable that Jesus had not spoken directly about every one of the Church's fundamental beliefs. If any non-Christian or anti-Christian reports of the mission of Jesus had survived, the criterion of dissimilarity might have been unnecessary. But the only extant historical reports about Jesus come from his followers, all of whom had accepted similar ideas about the meaning of his mission before they wrote.

Apocalypticism

Until recently, apocalypticism was defined solely by the literary apocalypses, especially the Book of Daniel in the Hebrew Bible and the Revelation of Saint John in the New Testament. Apocalypticism, coming from the Greek verb meaning to "disclose," "uncover," or "bring to light," has always implied the revelation of the secret of the coming endtime. Apocalyptic books have in common the violent end of the world and the establishment of God's Kingdom. They are replete with arcane symbolism and puzzling visions, the meaning of which is hardly clear from a first reading. And they are often pseudepigraphical, fictitiously ascribed to an earlier hero or patriarch.

Discovery and renewed study of many noncanonical apocryphal and pseudepigraphical books of the Old and New Testaments has changed the definition of apocalypticism by providing insight into the conditions that produced the literary genre.[3] The Dead Sea Scrolls give a totally unexpected glimpse of Jewish sectarian life, for they are concerned with the nature of the actual community as well as its expectations about the endtime. Since the Dead Sea Scrolls reflect an Essene group, they make it possible for the first time to view the workings of an actual ancient apocalyptic community, comparing their social organization with their apocalyptic writings.

Although the sociological picture of ancient apocalypticism is incomplete, apocalyptic movements in the modern period, partic-

---

[2]See N. Perrin, *Rediscovering the Teaching of Jesus* (New York, 1967).
[3]See J. Charlesworth, *The Pseudepigrapha in Modern Research* (Missoula, Mont., 1976); M. Stone, *Scriptures, Sects, and Visions: A Profile of Judaism from Ezra to the Jewish Revolts* (Philadelphia, 1980).

ularly those in Melanesian and North American Indian religions, evidence clear sociological commonalities. The modern data also have limitations, but because they are complete by comparison to data in the ancient period, they serve as a practical guide. The Melanesian and native American Indian societies during the last century, though far removed from the world of first-century Judaism in history, geography, and material culture, exhibited some of the same social forces. They, too, had to deal with problems of acculturation and disorganization brought on by European domination, in ways similar to those used by ancient Jewish society in dealing with the problem of Greek culture and Roman domination.

The most important similarity between ancient and modern apocalypticism is that both movements characterize time as a linear process which leads to the future destruction of the evil world order. For both modern and ancient apocalypticists there will be an "end of days," a decisive consummation of history. As opposed to holding an optimistic view of progress, which moves toward the final goal by slow approximations, apocalypticists are totally impatient with the corrupt present, seeing it as a series of unprecedented calamities. Usually, the "end of days" is viewed as a sudden, revolutionary leap into an idealized future state, when the believers will finally be rewarded for their years of suffering, while their oppressors and the other evil infidels will be justly punished.

There are important analogies between apocalyptic movements and political revolutions. Though the apocalyptic view of the ideal future is not always revolutionary in a political sense, it necessarily entails the destruction of the present evil political order. The new order is always an idealization, often of a recaptured past state of perfection, as the term "paradise" implies in the West.[4]

Though ancient apocalypticism and modern millennial cults have perceptible similarities, the relevance of the modern data becomes clear only when seeking the causes and motivations of apocalypticism from the refractory and incomplete ancient record.

---

[4]See Y. Talmon, "Pursuit of the Millennium: The Relationship between Religions and Social Change," in W. Lessa and E. Vogt (eds.), *Reader in Comparative Religion: An Anthropological Approach* (2nd ed.; New York, 1965) pp. 522–37; B. Barber, "Acculturation and Messianic Movements," in Lessa and Vogt (eds.), *Reader in Comparative Religion: An Anthropological Approach* (3rd ed., New York, 1972) pp. 512–16; R. Linton, A. F. C. Wallace, W. W. Hill, J. S. Slotkin, C. S. Belshaw, D. Aberle, and C. Geertz, "Dynamics in Religion," in Lessa and Vogt (eds.), *Reader* (3rd ed.) pp. 496–543.

Among the underlying commonalities in apocalyptic and millennial cults is the role of the leader. His individual skills and talents, as well as his ideals, necessarily have a strong effect on the movement. The leader must be revered by the community, not necessarily as a strong political leader but as a person whose example dramatizes the movement for the believer.[5] The leader should be the best moral example of the values that the movement endorses. Normally, the leader fulfills the function of modeling the ideals of the group.

Common motivations also underlie any millennial movement. People who join apocalyptic groups feel deprived of something meaningful or valuable to the society but unavailable to all people equally. Marxism stresses the appeal of apocalypticism to colonized peoples who have no access to the rewards of their labor, since it has been disassociated from the rewards of production. There are more varieties of deprivation than the economic. Epidemics, famine, war, or other disasters may stimulate millenarian movements, for the disaster can be seen as the penultimate stage before the victory of the good. Relative deprivation can also lead to the formation of apocalyptic movements.[6] The group does not have to be deprived in absolute terms — by famine, war, or poverty — for apocalypticism is occasionally popular among affluent classes. There only has to be a lack of social or religious attainment commensurate with the economic level, or rising expectations without any real possibility for improvement in status.

Other motivations are involved as well. Deprivation, whether absolute or relative, is not enough to ensure the rise of an apocalyptic movement. Some of these movements arise out of ambiguities in the way a religion is interpreted by different classes. Though all people require norms for orienting their lives, reli-

---

[5]P. Worsley, *The Trumpet Shall Sound: A Study of "Cargo" Cults in Melanesia* (New York, 1968, 1979); K. Burridge, *New Heaven, New Earth: A Study of Millenarian Activities* (New York, 1969); J. Gager, *Kingdom and Community: The Social World of Early Christianity* (Englewood Cliffs, 1975); S. R. Isenberg, "Millenarism in Greco-Roman Palestine," *Religion* 4 (1974) 26–46; I. C. Jarvie, *The Revolution in Anthropology* (Chicago, 1967) p. 52; *Max Weber: Essays in Sociology*, trans. and ed. H. H. Gerth and C. Wright Mills (New York, 1946); Weber, *Ancient Judaism*, trans. H. H. Gerth and D. Martindale (New York, 1952); Weber, *Gesammelte Aufsaetze zur Religionssoziologie* (3 vols.; Tübingen, 1920–30); R. C. Tescher, "A Theory of Charismatic Leadership," *Daedalus: Journal of the American Academy of Arts and Sciences* (Summer 1968) 73–74.

[6]Worsley, *The Trumpet Shall Sound*; Vittorio Lantenari, *The Religions of the Oppressed: A Study of Modern Messianic Cults*, English ed. (New York, 1963); D. Aberle, "A Note on Relative Deprivation Theory as Applied to Millenarian and Other Cult Movements," in S. Thrupp (ed.), *Millennial Dreams in Action: Studies in Revolutionary Religious Movements* (New York, 1970); Gager, *Kingdom and Community*.

gious systems at times provide better norms for some parts of a society than for others. When groups see themselves as cut off from the goals of the society, in terms of power, ethics, or status, and from the feelings of self-worth that arise from achieving these goals, they may coalesce into antisocial movements of *communitas*, or communitarian idealism. Such movements, which stress an alternative social structure to that of the dominant majority, can appeal widely to one whose status is ambiguously defined by a society. Status ambiguities were common in Roman society because class was defined by law, not by occupation and buying power. Therefore, people who succeeded in a trade often achieved a status above their legal station in life. Reform of the basic social categories appeals to such people. While deprivation of both material needs or spiritual status is necessary for the development of apocalypticism, it, too, is not sufficient to produce an apocalyptic movement. To develop an apocalyptic cult, in contrast to a purely political movement, people must have a propensity to impose religious meanings upon events and must be searching for a more satisfactory system of religious values. The factors of need, deprivation, anxiety, leadership, and the propensity to interpret events in a religious framework all came together in first-century Judea. The result over the next two centuries was the rise of a variety of apocalyptic cults.[7]

Apocalyptic groups have the propensity to mix political and religious motives to such an extent that the actors in the drama have difficulty distinguishing between them. As a general rule, members of apocalyptic movements hold a variety of positions about political change. At times an apocalyptic movement has a retarding effect on simple political revolution because the ex-

---

[7]See V. Turner, *The Ritual Process: Structure and Anti-Structure* (Ithaca, 1977); Barber, "Acculturation and Messianic Movements," in Lessa and Vogt, ed., *Reader*, pp. 512–16; G. Theissen, *The First Followers of Jesus: A Sociological Analysis of the Earliest Christianity*, trans. J. Bowden (London, 1978), originally published in German and published again as *Sociology of Early Palestinian Christianity*; M. I. Finley, *The Ancient Economy* (Berkeley, 1973); W. Meeks, *The First Urban Christians* (New Haven, 1983) pp. 53–54. The movement of Sabbatianism in Judaism is an example of this phenomenon. Pogroms alone do not account for the rise of the messianic movement around Sabbatai Zevi in the years around 1666 in the Turkish Empire, for that was not the place where pogroms actually took place. Instead, the threat of pogroms, together with the rise of Lurianic Kabbalah, a mystical movement given to messianic speculation, accounts for the rise of the mystical messiah. See G. Scholem, *Sabbatai Zevi* (Princeton, 1976). The same is true of conversion to marginal religious sects in contemporary American life. See J. Lofland and R. Stark, "Becoming a World Saver: A Theory of Conversion to a Deviant Perspective," *American Sociological Review* 30 (1965) 862–75; B. Barber, "Function, Variability, and Change in Ideological Systems," in B. Barber and A. Inkeles (eds.), *Stability and Social Change* (Boston, 1971).

plicitly religious symbolism of its leaders tends to make the group more interested in theological goals than in political ones. At other times, even in the same movement, earnest political revolutionaries may be present among the apocalyptic cult members. These cults engage in a wide spectrum of political action, ranging from passive to active, and depending on the faction in the group that dominates at any one moment, their participation may change in character. But regardless of the disposition of a group toward political action, either active or passive, the distinction is lost on the ruling powers. The opposition of rulers to the group is constant, no matter what the group itself may think of armed intervention. The various actors within a society may interpret the movement differently, but the rulers almost always interpret the threat as a political one and deal with it accordingly. Moreover, since the political or nonpolitical aims of the movement start out fairly confused, often some historical development in the conflict between the apocalyptic group and the power structure confirms, disconfirms, or reaffirms the political intentions of the group.[8] Many of the apocalyptic groups of hellenistic Judea, including Christianity, underwent such a moment of political decision.

The Book of Daniel

The Book of Daniel purports to be the writings of a prophet who lived during the reigns of Nebuchadnezzar, Cyrus, and Xerxes, but the visions at the end of the book, in chapters 7–12, are from a much later time, during the Maccabean revolt. This dating is established by the prophecies in Daniel 7:8 and 8:9, where "the little horn speaking great things" is Antiochus Epiphanes.[9] In a perplexing vision a divine figure called "the Ancient of Days" (7:9) presides over the heavenly council at the last judgment and sentences the fourth kingdom, the one ruled by Antiochus, to destruction. Then there appears in the clouds of heaven "one like a Son of man" (7:13), an expression that in Aramaic means only "a

---

[8]See V. Lantenari, *Religions of the Oppressed: A Study of Modern Messianic Cults* (New York, 1963). Sabbatianism provided a clear example of the moment of political decision in Judaism. See Scholem, *Sabbatai Zevi*. The radically mystical and apolitical nature of Sabbatianism became clear only after Sabbatai Zevi was apprehended by the Sultan in Constantinople as a political threat and offered the choice of conversion to Islam or death. Zevi's choice of conversion began a reinterpretation of the mystical tradition to account for a Muslim messiah, and it also clarified a future nonpolitical role for Sabbatianism.

[9]See also SibOr 3.381–400.

human figure." His human appearance contrasts with the monstrous animal figures that have preceded him in the vision and is clearly designed to signify the good forces. An angel interprets the figure as symbolizing "the holy community, the saints of the most high" (7:27). Probably, the "Son of man" or manlike figure is simply an angel, since angels are human figures in heaven. It is even possible that the figure is one of the archangels, perhaps Michael or Gabriel, who are mentioned in other visions. In any case, the angelic status of the "Son of man" seems sure. Instead of a transient kingdom, he establishes an everlasting and universal dominion, which will begin after "a time, two times and a half a time of the little horn," which is a cryptic reference to the three and one-half years when Antiochus persecuted the Jews, 168–165 B.C.E. The mention of the abomination of desolation is probably a reference to the stationing of Syrian troops in the Temple and the desecration of the Temple purity (11:31, 12:11).

The fact that the author of the Book of Daniel was not making a prediction about the Babylonian Exile but rather was looking back at the Maccabean revolt as if that event of his recent experience had been predicted by Daniel, a legendary hero of the Babylonian captivity, has religious connotations. The writer is saying that the days of Antiochus are numbered, because he has insulted God by desecrating the altar. The clock is beginning to strike midnight, when God will intervene and set everything to rights. In fact, the author's skill in describing the events of the Maccabean revolt reveals when the book was written. The only prediction that did not come true, besides the final consummation, is the prophecy concerning the death of Antiochus on his return to Jerusalem after his war with Egypt (11:40–45). Antiochus in fact died in Persia in 163 B.C.E. Daniel is concerned not only with the fate of the world empires but with the aftermath of the judgment and the setting up of an ideal community on earth. In this earthly kingdom, the righteous and the illustrious dead will partake in everlasting harmony (12:2).[10]

According to modern observations of millenarianism, books like Daniel are normally written by an apocalyptic "sect." The identity of this particular "sect" cannot be fixed with accuracy, but some hints of its existence can be coaxed from the ancient documents. Although in Daniel the angelic princes of the evil na-

---

[10]D. S. Russell, *The Method and Message of Jewish Apocalyptic* (Philadelphia, 1964) pp. 286–87.

tions fight against Michael, "Prince of Israel," the protagonists are not the entire community of the Jews. Both the text of Daniel and the events of the Maccabean war suggest that a smaller group than the whole Jewish nation was intended.[11] When the book was being written, the Jewish state was in the midst of a civil war, with Antiochus intervening on the side of the most hellenizing party. The party of faithful Jews are identified in Daniel as *maskilim*, the "wise" or "enlighteners" (11:2, 34). The visionary identifies with this group of Jews. They are the ones who will be rewarded by shining as the stars in heaven (11:2). Their job is to impart to the many the apocalyptic teachings about the end of time and so save people from the coming annihilation. The "people of the saints of the most high" are likely to be the same group, who will share in the final victory, live in the reestablished state of Judah, and become what they are not when the book was written, the sole inhabitants of the land of Judah. The entire plan is predestined and has nothing to do with the ability of the group to fight in battle.

Although this apocalyptic group is opposed to Antiochus, it does not share the position of the Maccabees, for the religious goals of Daniel contrast with the political position taken by the Maccabees in their official history of the Maccabean revolt. In the First Book of Maccabees, an active militarist and political view is taken of the events that founded the Hasmonean house. There are few references to God's miraculous intervention in history. But there is indirect evidence for a second, more passive group of revolutionary allies to the Maccabees. Judas was joined by "a company of Hasideans" (Hasidim in Hebrew, though not related to the modern Hasidim), "mighty warriors of Israel, everyone who offered himself willingly for the Law" (1Mac 2). Shortly thereafter part of the force of Judas was caught in a cave and martyred, because they refused to fight. On account of the close juxtaposition of the two events, the martyrs of the cave are thought to have belonged to the Hasidim. As opposed to Judas, the Hasidim seem to have been more passive in their resistance and interested in restoring acceptable religious conditions, purifying the altar, and reinstating the legitimate priesthood. Although the Hasidim fought alongside the Maccabees, they also disputed with them. They gave up resisting once the Temple was restored, whereas the Maccabees continued much longer to fight for land and position.

---

[11] J. J. Collins, *The Apocalyptic Vision of the Book of Daniel* (Missoula, Mont., 1977) esp. pp. 167–70, 191–218.

The Hasidim broke decisively with the Maccabees in 142 B.C.E. when Simon Maccabee was proclaimed "high priest forever, until a faithful prophet should arise" (1Mac 14:41). The issue that set the Maccabees and Hasidim unalterably against each other was the founding of a new Maccabean high priesthood for their own political ends. According to Frank Cross, this incident led to the founding of the Dead Sea Scroll Essene community.[12] The Essene community at Qumran was thus an apocalyptic community historically related to the sentiments expressed in Daniel, founded after it became clear that the Maccabees would not bring about the religious reforms for which the authors of Daniel hoped. Indeed, the Maccabees were as cynical in the election of the high priesthood as Antiochus had been before them. But the Hasidim and subsequently the Essenes harbored eschatological expectations for the divine restoration of correct worship in Jerusalem.

Just as in the modern period, so too in the ancient world there were differences between active and passive revolutionaries. The Book of Daniel gives evidence of a more religious wing of the opposition to Antiochus, while 1 Maccabees suggest an overtly political group of militants. The subsequent efforts of the Maccabees to take over the high priesthood as well as the kingship led to the final break between the apocalypticists who wrote Daniel and the ruling Maccabean party. Historical events helped to differentiate the political and nonpolitical aims, but even before the events, the distinction was already moot.

The Book of Daniel is the first book in the Bible to stress the concept of resurrection, together with the idea that the *maskilim* will ascend to heaven for astral immortality. Through these ideas the apocalypticists both explained the years of persecution and kept true to their faith that God would intervene to reestablish justice. The form of immortality that was envisioned may well have been angelic. The angels had been identified with the stars as early as the First Temple period. Several strands of late hellenistic spirituality apparently involved the way in which astral immortality was gained. For instance, the Books of Enoch are obsessed with the notion of astral journey, as are the Hekhaloth texts of Jewish mysticism, which were traditionally thought to date from Islamic times but are now thought to have been written in the hellenistic period. Aramaic fragments of 1 Enoch have now

---

[12] F. Cross, *The Essene Library at Qumran and Modern Biblical Studies* (Garden City, N.Y., 1958) pp. 80–120.

been found at Qumran, giving witness to the earliest, Aramaic
version and showing that the Enoch literature was known to the
Dead Sea Scroll sectarians.[13] The so-called Mithras liturgy, found
in the third-century C.E. Paris Magical Papyrus, describes one such
heavenly journey in an Egyptian magical context, culminating in
a personal encounter with a heavenly god, Helios Mithras, and resulting in the "immortalization" (*apanathanatismos*) of the adept.
Astral mysticism permeated Judaism as well.

Talmudic texts hint that the earliest rabbis occasionally practiced mystical ascension techniques, but there is even clearer
evidence of apocalyptic Judaism's use of ascension techniques
and traditions.[14] For instance, Josephus reports that the Essenes
"immortalize" (*athanatizousin*) souls, almost the same term that
appears in the Mithras liturgy (*Ant* 18.18). In another phrase that
suggests the theme of the rivalry between angels and men over
the approach of a mystic making a heavenly ascent, Josephus says
that they "think the approach of the righteous to be much fought
over." The Dead Sea Scrolls also report that the members of the
Qumran group are "together with the angels of the Most High and
there is no need for an interpreter."[15] The location for this meeting
must be either heaven or the recreated ideal earth. The Qumran
community probably believed its forebears to have ascended to
heaven as angels after their deaths, as Daniel 12 implies.

The Qumran community held that the angels were their close
companions. The scroll entitled "The War of the Children of Light
against the Children of Darkness" describes a military plan in
which the angels of God descend to lead the numerically insignificant Qumran community to victory. Its priestly preoccupation
with ritual cleanliness is functional for a group that desired angelic company. Angels would not consent to enter an Essene camp
unless the Qumranites were in a sufficient state of ritual purity, the
same state recognized by the rabbis as a necessary precondition
for ascent to the heavenly Temple.

The Qumranites also cherished traditions about the angelic cap-
tain of the forces of light, who is named Melchizedek. Although
the identification of this angelic intermediary with Melchizedek

---

[13]See J. T. Milik, *The Books of Enoch* (Oxford, 1976); G. Scholem, *Major Trends in Jewish Mysticism* (New York, 1967); Scholem, *Jewish Gnosticism, Merkabah Mysticism, and
Talmudic Tradition* (New York, 1965).
[14]See Hag 14b; Sanh 38b.
[15]Hymns 6:13; 3:20; 11:10; 2:10; 1QS 2.5–10.

is an unusual aspect of the Dead Sea Scroll tradition, many other apocalyptic writings emphasize helping human or angelic figures in heaven. For instance, in Daniel 7:13 the figure of the "Son of man" appears to take over the role of punishing the evil. These mystical traditions in apocalyptic Judaism are of fundamental importance for the rise of Christianity.

Even the Greek Bible connected Adam's prelapsarian divine image — the image of God in which Adam was made and which, according to some legends, he lost after he sinned — with the image of God's glory seen in Ezekiel's chariot vision. Probably this manlike manifestation of divinity was associated with the angelic "Son of man" figure of Daniel as well. The association of the discussion of the heavenly man in Ezekiel with the description of God in Moses' vision on Sinai in Exodus 19–34 and even with the description of Adam before the fall in Genesis is an antique one. The First Book of Enoch, now known to be mostly pre-Christian, and the vision of Moses in the remaining fragments of the work of Ezekiel the Tragedian, a pre-Christian writer, evince well-developed enthronement traditions.[16] The Qumranites probably felt that they could ascend to the heavenly Temple before death and that they would one day be translated into angels who would help destroy the children of darkness on earth.

Christianity as Apocalyptic Judaism

Jesus also spoke of himself as a "Son of man." The early Church associated these statements with Daniel 7:13, prophesying the coming of an angelic Son of man. Yet what Jesus meant about himself is not at all clear. The most apocalyptic statements about "the Son of man" satisfy the criterion of dissimilarity, for the later Church knew that Jesus' return was not imminent. The only reason to preserve the apocalyptic "Son of man" statements in Church tradition was that they were already believed to be authentic, even when they appeared not to have come true as predicted. Some statements of the apocalyptic "Son of man" apparently came from the earliest, apocalyptic Church tradition:

> For whoever is ashamed of me and of my words in this adulterous and sinful generation, of him will the Son of man also be ashamed

---

[16]See G. Quispel, "Gnosis," in M. J. Vermaseren (ed.), *Die orientalischen Religionen im Roemmerreich* (Leiden, 1981).

when he comes in the glory of his father with the holy angels. (Mk 8:38)

And I tell you, every one who acknowledges me before men, the Son of man will acknowledge before the angels of God; but he who denies me before men will be denied before the angels of God. (Lk 12:8–9)

For truly I tell you, you will not have gone through the cities of Israel before the Son of man comes. (Mt 10:23)

Truly, I tell you that there are some of those standing here who will not taste death until they see the Son of man coming in his Kingdom. (Mt 16:28)

Truly, I tell you that in the generation when the Son of man shall sit on the throne of his glory, you also who have followed me shall sit on twelve thrones judging the twelve tribes of Israel. (Mt 19:28)[17]

These short statements have two salient characteristics: they cannot have been invented as a pious wish by the later Church, for they talk about an apocalyptic end which never happened, and they rely on the imagery of the apocalyptic past. The expression "Son of man" comes explicitly from Daniel. Jewish mystical concepts of the "glory" of God — connecting Genesis 1:28, Ezekiel 1 and 10, and Exodus 24:10 as human figures that somehow represent divine power — are crucial for the meaning of this passage.[18] But what Jesus meant by the term is impossible to decipher.

The "Son of man" problem represents one of the most mysterious and vexing of all New Testament quandaries. Jesus was presumably referring not to himself but to the apocalyptic passage in Daniel when he spoke these words. On the basis of the resurrection, his followers identified him with the passage he had discussed. But there is no unambiguous evidence of a preexistent title "Son of man." It may merely have been an allusion to a well-known vision of the endtime.[19]

In any event, there is little doubt that much of Jesus' message was apocalyptic. This probably explains why names reminiscent of the Zealot movement, which in 66 C.E. fomented the Jewish

---

[17]See A. J. B. Higgins, *Jesus and the Son of Man* (Philadelphia, 1964).

[18]See A. F. Segal, *Two Powers in Heaven* (Leiden, 1977).

[19]The "Son of man" was once mistakenly thought to be the Jewish name for a widespread Persian and Indian mythical figure who represented a less nationalistic and more universal messianic hope. Another theory has it that "Son of man" means merely "I," as does "that man" in Aramaic, and that Jesus only meant to be referring to himself. See G. Vermes, *Jesus the Jew* (London, 1973).

revolution against Rome, show up in reference to the Christian movement. Judas Iscariot and Simeon the Zealot have names suggesting the Sicarii and Zealots, two groups of radical revolutionaries in 66 C.E. Exactly what these people expected of Jesus or how closely they can be connected with a revolutionary movement that flourished thirty years after Jesus' death is a moot point. But for political revolutionaries to have been attracted by Jesus' message would not have been surprising. For one thing, like the Dead Sea Scroll community and the Hasidim before him, Jesus seems to have been aware of and extremely critical of the Temple: "I will destroy this Temple that is made with hands, and in three days, I will build another, not made with hands" (Mk 14:58).[20]

Opposition to the Temple is not unprecedented in Judaism. Nor is it innocent of political ramifications, considering that the Temple was the center of native government for Judea. On the contrary, this kind of action demonstrates the apocalyptic character of the message that Jesus taught. Because the earthly Temple is impure, Jesus and the apocalypticists maintained, only the Reign of God would put events right again. However, this view does not necessarily imply that Jesus intended a political revolution.

Jesus and Political Revolution

Early Christianity was a religious revolution, but its political aims were still inchoate. The active and nonviolent motives of a movement are not easily unscrambled, as the modern data has made clear. But from the point of view of the central authority, most threats have active political consequences. Some of Jesus' followers seem to have had revolutionary expectations, though passivity was the stronger tradition in Jewish apocalypticism. Both the Qumran community and the Hasidim had a negative view of actual military combat with the oppressive, demonic forces. Rather, God himself with his angelic host was the direct agent of vengeance against wrong-doers, who more often than not were viewed as satanic envoys. Although this attitude is not pacifistic, it is very passively hostile.[21]

Then there is the evidence of the New Testament itself. When Jesus was arrested, he did not resist. The Church followed his

---

[20]The Mt 26:61 version reads: "I am able to destroy the Temple of God, and to build it in three days." Jn 2:19 reads: "Destroy this Temple, and in three days, I will raise it up."

[21]M. Hengel, *Was Jesus a Revolutionist?* (Philadelphia, 1971).

example. The direction that the Christian movement took was governed by its desire not to antagonize further the Roman authorities. This course may not have been intended from the outset, but it was consistent with the evidence of Jesus' own actions.

Although Jesus recommended passive resistance, he was still an apocalypticist and had strong feelings of scorn for the putative rulers of his country. The pietistic figure of a "gentle Jesus meek and mild" was a creation of Victorian Bible scholarship and is belied by the gospels themselves at every turn. Jesus was a passionate advocate of political and individual justice who predicted a terrible and imminent end for the evil regime ruling Judea.

The mystery about the social message of early Christianity is not so complete as that about the Book of Daniel. As difficult as the gospels are to evaluate, they still give a remarkable amount of evidence about the life of Jesus and his effect on his contemporaries. Early Christianity was a movement primarily of the disadvantaged and, even more so, of people who had little hope of improving their position. This is not to say that no one else could have joined. Paul's writing shows that more privileged people were also attracted. Like the Sadducees' close association with the traditional priestly aristocracy and the Pharisees' association with urban tradespersons, the association of Christianity with the deprived or those of ambiguous status is only a generalization. But the gospels themselves testify that the early Christians had less access to the means of salvation than other people. For one reason or another they felt alienated from the roles that society had defined for them.

Jesus' original support came from the country folk of Galilee, whose ways and interests were different from those of the Jerusalemites. He appealed to a number of people in the society whose rank was inferior but whose economic situation was not hopeless, including prostitutes, tax collectors, and others considered disreputable or impure by Sadducees or Pharisees, as well as many ordinary Jews, Samaritans, and Galileans with no specific party affiliation. These people often had some economic standing in the community. But their status was relatively low as compared with their economic attainments.

In some cases, the low status was based on a moral judgment about the ways in which the money was made. However, the presence of prostitutes and tax collectors among Jesus' supporters is probably symbolic as well as actual, vividly expressing the apocalyptic ethic of overturning the established order. Quite a number of ordinary people, who had other disadvantages, must have been among Jesus' most enthusiastic audiences. The ethic of making the last to be first appears to be addressed not only to social outcasts, in hopes of converting them, but also to people more generally with ordinary feelings of low self-esteem (Mk 10:31; Mt 19:30; Lk 13:30).

The message of Jesus that, with repentance, all are equal before God is typical of all sectarian apocalypticism of the time. Christian practices of public repentance, baptism, and chaste communal living are likewise typical of the other contemporary apocalyptic groups. Yet the similarity only emphasizes the striking difference between Christianity and Essenism, for example. Essenism was priestly and largely interested in the cultic purity rules allowing priests to approach God's holy places. Christianity, in spite of its many similarities with other apocalyptic groups, was almost hostile to purity rules. Its corresponding emphasis on converting the distressed or sinful began in the teaching of John the Baptist, became characteristically Christian, and probably reflected the strong charismatic influence of Jesus. Through John the Baptist, baptism became the Christian rite uniquely demonstrating repentance, though there is no good evidence that Jesus performed it.

Jesus' unique lack of interest in purity rules was accompanied by another unique message: he did not stress a return to the old strict interpretations of Torah, as did the other apocalyptic groups. Although Jesus accepted the Jewish Law, he occasionally indulged in symbolic actions designed to provoke questions about the purpose of the Torah, such as healing the chronically ill or picking grain on the Sabbath. But these actions could have been directed at the Pharisees or other sectarian interpreters of the Torah without implying that the Torah itself was invalid.

Like many of the other apocalyptic groups around them, Christians often lived together and shared possessions. But Christian communalism stressed only chastity, not monasticism. Although asceticism and perhaps monasticism were associated with the movement of John the Baptist, the majority of Jesus' early followers lived within the fabric of society. As the Christian movement developed, some Christians showed signs of a primitive communism, implicit in their pooling of resources.[22] Early Christianity

---

[22]See M. Hengel, *Property and Riches in the Early Church: Aspects of a Social History of Early Christianity*, trans. J. Bowden (Philadelphia, 1974).

did not adhere to the social code of the Essenes, yet it did contain the seeds of a radical criticism of private property and believed strongly in sharing all economic resources. "No man can serve two masters.... You cannot serve God and mammon [money]" (Lk 16:13). Like the Pharisees and the Essenes, the Christians were equally religious and political in orientation.

Jesus was suspicious of people of means: "It is easier for a camel to go through the eye of a needle than for a rich man to enter the Kingdom of God" (Mk 10:24). This statement does not prevent a rich man from becoming part of the movement; but it establishes a higher price for the rich than the poor. Early Christianity thus exhibited a deep suspicion of property. Given the command to share all things with the poor, few confident and successful people would have entered the movement at first. Those whose wealth had not brought with it feelings of achievement or worth would have been better targets for evangelism. Entering the Christian community at the beginning was a total commitment: "Give to every one who begs from you; and of him who takes away your goods, do not ask them again" (Lk 6:30).

Jesus himself did not come from the lowest economic classes but rather came from the class that provided most members of the rabbinic movement.[23] He came from an environment that valued property and skilled professions. His teaching was designed to appeal to the poor and otherwise underprivileged people, like the Samaritans, Galileans, and ordinary Jews unskilled in the Torah, yet unlike John the Baptist, he was not an ascetic. There is no evidence of his favoring the sanctification of sexuality by means of marriage, as did the Pharisees, but he accepted the institution of marriage as a given and participated in fellowship meals with food and wine.

Each of Jesus' followers apprehended and interpreted the message according to his or her own powers and experience. Conflicting interpretations of Jesus' teachings were present from the very beginning. These different social responses competed with each other for dominance within the community. Some of Jesus' closest disciples and many of the apostles chose to live in a communal way, but others in his movement chose, or merely continued, to

---

[23]Like his father, Jesus was an artisan, a *tektōn*, a Greek word that means mason, carpenter, cartwright, and joiner all rolled into one (Mk 6:3). According to Justin Martyr, he had "made yokes and ploughs" (*DialTrypho* 88:8); Hengel, *Property and Riches*, p. 27.

live in less radical styles. There was not a single "orthodox" interpretation of Jesus' mission.

Christianity as a Messianic Movement

The Messiah was traditionally the reigning king of Israel, but after the Romans began to govern directly, claiming to be the Messiah was tantamount to fomenting revolution against Roman order. Furthermore, because of the apocalyptic expectation that God would repay the Romans for their cruelty, the Jewish community believed that a Messiah would, with supernatural assistance, bring about a victory against Roman government. "Messiah" was not a title that a Jew would have applied to himself lightly.

"Messiah" is also the most problematic of all titles to be applied to Jesus, because Jesus suffered and died before the coming of the Kingdom of God, which he prophesied, although the Messiah was supposed to bring about God's Kingdom, usually by succeeding to the throne of David and effecting great victories. Nowhere in pre-Christian Jewish tradition is there the slightest evidence of an expectation of a messiah whose suffering will be redemptive for the people. The Christian idea had to come from somewhere else.

The simplest explanation would be that Jesus really was of royal lineage; therefore his messianic role was a normal expectation. Yet the stories of Jesus' Davidic lineage are suspect. They could have been provided by the Church later, as part of a cycle of infancy stories. The shortest gospel, Mark, contains no record of the youth of Jesus. It may be that Matthew and Luke provided a messianic infancy to match Jesus' known messianic purpose. In short, the stories of Jesus' Davidic lineage do not satisfy the criterion of dissimilarity, because they may have been remembered by a Church which automatically supposed Jesus to be a scion of David.

The best explanation for the enigma of Jesus' messiahship is that the Christian community did exactly what the other Jewish groups of the first century had done: they read Scripture in the light of events. Philo read Scripture in the light of allegory, finding in it a philosophical tract. The Essenes read Scripture in the light of *pesher*, finding in it a prophecy for the coming judgment. The Pharisees read Scripture in the light of *midrash*, finding in it a platform for their interpretation of the purity laws and resurrection. Christianity became messianic instead of merely apocalyptic — the Messiah not being a necessary character for the coming of the apocalyptic millennium in Judaism — because the title was provided by a historic event experienced by the earliest Christian community. This event became the basis for a reinterpretation of Scripture.

N. A. Dahl has pointed out that the title "King of the Jews" on the cross has a high probability of historicity, because it was not one that the Church wished to have remembered about Jesus.[24] The Church preferred other titles of less nationalistic and more universal scope. Ironically, Jesus is called a messiah by the Church because he was executed by the Romans on the charge of being a candidate for the throne of Judea. This was not a charge that even traitorous Jews cooperating with Roman authorities would have invented. Whatever else his followers expected or desired from Jesus, they began after Easter Sunday, on account of the resurrection that they believed had then occurred, to preach of Jesus as the dying and rising Messiah.

Jesus was sometimes recognized as a possible Messiah even before his crucifixion, although there is little evidence that he sought the title for himself. In the Gospel of Mark, Jesus denies the title whenever it is applied to him except at his trial. However, some people besides the Romans must have understood Jesus as a messianic candidate, for neither the Romans nor their administrative advisers among the aristocrats in Judea would have fabricated a messianic role for Jesus, were he not already perceived to be a messianic threat. They would hardly have invented a title that so completely justified Jesus' opposition to them.

Jesus' movement presented a problem for the Romans and for members of the upper levels of Jewish administration, some of whom were cooperating with the Romans. Inasmuch as many of the other revolutionary movements destroyed by the Romans were not messianic, a revolutionary political movement did not have to be messianic in nature. Yet no matter how supernatural his actions, the Messiah was also a political figure. Thus, the Bar Kokhba Revolt of 132 C.E., barely a century after Jesus, contained strong messianic overtones. When the revolt was quelled, the death of its messianic leader, as in Christianity, brought about the rise of a tradition that the Messiah must suffer and die for the end to come.[25] But these examples only point up the anomaly of

---

[24]N. A. Dahl, *The Crucified Messiah* (Minneapolis, Minn., 1974).

[25]Messiah ben Joseph: "What is the cause of this wailing? Rabbi Dosa and the rabbis disagree. One says: It is on account of the killing of the Messiah son of Joseph. Another

a messianic movement when the strong, charismatic figure at its founding has pacifist goals in mind.

The paradoxical use of this title in Christianity is borne out in the situations when the term "Messiah" is used of Jesus. Jesus is usually called Messiah at his trial and death. But in prophecies of his return, Jesus is usually called the "Son of man," which identifies him with the angelic figure mentioned in Daniel. So Jesus is not called Messiah on the basis of his return; rather, he is called Messiah on the basis of his trial and death, which is in keeping with the hypothesis that he was arrested on this charge but is certainly not in keeping with the Jewish expectation of a Messiah. The best explanation for the title of Messiah, then, is that the historical events surrounding the trial accounted for the association, although it did not fit prior expectations. It was the charge leveled against Jesus by his detractors, with some justification from their point of view, once they were sure that he was in their power. But it was not a title that Jesus himself stressed in his ministry. Afterward, when Jesus was experienced as still alive by some of his disciples, the term "Messiah" was reunderstood by the community to make sense of Jesus' suffering and death.

It appears, then, that *Jesus was a Jew of powerful charisma whose teachings were innovative and popular;* that *he desired a quick apocalyptic end to this evil world,* and that some people, including some of his followers, took this to be a messianic claim and a political statement. The movement must have been strong enough to come to the attention of Roman and Jewish authorities in Jerusalem. Moreover, the explicit purposes of a millennial movement are never clear to the social actors until historical events remove the ambiguity. Some movements turn into apolitical, symbolic rebellions; others are largely political in orientation. Presumably the borderline between violent revolution and passive resistance was never reached before Jesus' arrest. Jesus' lessons probably emphasized patience with contemporary political events. But the Romans did not understand the teaching, as shown by Jesus' arrest and the Roman policy toward Christians for centuries after his death.

---

says: This is on account of the killing of the evil inclination. But the former interpretation is to be adopted, for it is written, 'And they shall look on him whom they have transpierced, and they shall wail over him as over an only child.' Why should he who says that it is on account of the killing of the evil inclination be sorrowful? He should rejoice rather than weep" (b.Sukk 52a). See also Vermes, *Jesus the Jew*, p. 139.

Resurrection was one of the controversies of sectarian life in the time of Jesus. But expectations of both resurrection from the dead and ascension to heaven were strongest wherever the context was religious persecution or martyrdom. One event that passes the criterion of dissimilarity is Jesus' death as a martyr, for he was unjustly accused and illegitimately executed. And he died trying to protect and fulfill his preaching of the meaning of the Law rather than to subvert it.

It is understandable that several of Jesus' followers came to feel that Jesus was resurrected and had ascended to a new order of being. Since ascension and enthronement were common motifs of resurrection stories at the time, especially of stories dealing with martyrdom, it was entirely appropriate to identify Jesus with the enthroned figure about whom he had preached. This idea caused some readjustment in later New Testament writings. For instance, the Letter to the Hebrews, which strongly affirms Jesus' divinity, must argue that he was raised higher than the angels and was, in fact, God. It is characteristic of the later Church that the Letter to the Hebrews does not mention the phrase "Son of man." Since the later Church was not particularly interested in this title for Jesus and it never acquired the same theological importance as "Messiah," "Son of man" is probably to be attributed to the earliest Christian tradition. Since Jesus distinguishes himself from the Son of man in the New Testament, he is not likely to have preached that he was the figure of the prophecy.

The evolution from Jesus' preaching of the coming end of the world to the Church's preaching of Jesus' return as the Son of man, the sign that the coming apocalypse has already begun in a spiritual way, is one of the most striking factors in the success of the early Christian movement. It allowed the movement to succeed in an area where almost every other apocalyptic movement is doomed to fail, namely in institutionalizing the original impulse for reform into a stable religious system. Although it is practically impossible to discover how the evolution of thought took place, one can see how the Church reunderstood the Hebrew Bible to make sense of the events of Jesus' life, and this is one major clue.

Christian Exegesis of the Hebrew Bible

The expectation of Jesus' ascension to heaven was given vivid actuality in the way that Christians brought the Scripture of the

Old Testament to bear on their experiences after the resurrection. The most commonly used Hebrew Scripture in the New Testament was not a traditional messianic prophecy. Indeed, no traditional prophecy would have solved the problem that history had given the Christians, to find a prophecy of messianic suffering. Psalm 110, however, contained the perplexing line:

> The LORD says to my lord: "Sit at my right hand, till I make your enemies your footstool."

This psalm was clearly intended to express something of the relationship between the Davidic, reigning king and God. Christians often interpreted this verse to imply that Jesus had been raised to the Father's right hand, giving it a new prophetic meaning which explained what God had intended for Jesus. When combined with the prophecy of Daniel that a manlike angelic figure, the Son of man, will be enthroned in heaven and take part in the final judgment, this passage became the basis for Christian eschatology.

Although the Christian interpretation was new, this kind of reinterpretation of Scripture was a standard procedure during the period and was absolutely justifiable from the perspective of any contemporary. Even though the verse might have meant something quite different in its original historical context, there was nothing impious or unusual in interpreting Scripture as a prophecy fulfilled by the immediate historical occurrences. On the contrary, all the groups in Early Judaism would have automatically searched for a scriptural grounding for any important event in the life of their community, similar to the way in which American society searches for legal precedents when a new or puzzling situation arises. Since biblical traditions were so widely known throughout the society, a large part of the earliest Christian community would have been able to search the Scriptures. In short, the reinterpretation of Scripture was normal for any group of the first century.

The most important idea implied in the reinterpretation of Psalm 110 is the divinity of the two figures, "God" and "my lord." "Lord" is a term by which the Jews designated God. In Hebrew the word "Lord" for God is different from but extremely close to the ordinary word "Lord." When translated into Greek or Aramaic, the two terms become one. In Christianity, the Greek word *Kyrios*, meaning "Lord," became a term describing not God himself, as in Judaism, but Christ. Thus, the earliest Christian exegesis already asserted the divinity of the figure of Jesus on the basis of his heavenly ascent and exaltation in Psalm 110. Hellenistic and mystical Judaism held similar views on the human form of God's glory (*kavod*), *logos*, the resemblance of Adam to God before sin, and the divine participation of some principal angels in God's divinity. The Qumran community asserted the "divinity" of Melchizedek, the angelic mediator, through a similar interpretation of the Hebrew word *El*, meaning "God" or "angel." Philo even describes Moses as divine when he ascends to Mount Sinai and, allegorically, to heaven itself.[26] Against this background, Christian innovations are both natural and fitted to the events of the crucifixion. The events unique to Jesus' biography account for a postresurrection identification of the mediator or angelic figure with him and hence create a messianic candidate who succeeded at his messianic mission in a totally new and unexpected way. Since the interpretation is so novel, not all followers of Jesus may have approved of it. Nevertheless, if the New Testament is an indication of the variety of Christian writing in the first century, there was little diversity in the community on this point.

Psalm 118:15–25 is also used by the Christian community to express its surprise about the way in which Jesus fulfilled the prophecies of the Hebrew Bible:

> Hark, glad songs of victory in the tents of the righteous;
> "The right hand of the Lord does valiantly, the right hand of the
>   Lord is exalted, the right hand of the Lord does valiantly!"
> I shall not die, but I shall live, and recount the deeds of the Lord.
> The Lord has chastened me sorely but he has not given me over to
>   death.
>
> Open to me the gates of righteousness, that I may enter through
>   them and give thanks to the Lord.
>
> This is the gate of the Lord, the righteous shall enter through it.
>
> I thank thee that thou hast answered me and hast become my
>   salvation.
> The stone which the builders rejected has become the head of the
>   corner.
> This is the Lord's doing; it is marvelous in our eyes.
> This is the day which the Lord has made; let us rejoice and be glad
>   in it.

---

[26]See the Dead Sea Scrolls, 11QMelch; Philo, *Life of Moses*; Philo, *Questions and Answers on Ex* 24:10–12.

Save us, we beseech thee, O LORD! O LORD, we beseech thee, give
us success!

This is not a messianic psalm but a psalm of thanksgiving after a
military victory. After it is applied to Jesus, however, it receives a
variety of new meanings. In 1 Corinthians 3:10–17, for instance,
Paul interprets Jesus straightforwardly as the foundation stone
of the Church. Acts 4:11 stresses another aspect of the verse, that
Jesus was the cornerstone whom the Jews have rejected. By then it
was necessary for the Church to maintain that the Jewish rejection
of their own Messiah was also grounded in scriptural prophecies.

Christians eventually saw that Isaiah 53, the Psalm of the Suffering Servant, was a prophecy applying to Jesus:

Who has believed what we have heard?
And to whom has the arm of the LORD been revealed?
For he grew up before him like a young plant, and like a root out
of dry ground;
he had no form or comeliness that we should look at him, and no
beauty that we should desire him.
He was despised and rejected by men; a man of sorrows, and ac-
quainted with grief;
And as one from whom men hide their faces he was despised, and
we esteemed him not.

Surely he has borne our griefs and carried our sorrows;
yet we esteemed him stricken, smitten by God, and afflicted.
But he was wounded for our transgressions, he was bruised for our
iniquities;
upon him was the chastisement that made us whole, and with his
stripes we are healed.
All we like sheep have gone astray; we have turned every one to
his own way;
and the LORD has laid upon him the iniquity of us all.

He was oppressed, and he was afflicted, yet he opened not his
mouth;
like a lamb that is led to the slaughter, and like a sheep that before
its shearers is dumb, so he opened not his mouth.

By oppression and judgment he was taken away; and as for his
generation, who considered
that he was cut off out of the land of the living, stricken for the
transgression of my people?
And they made his grave with the wicked and with the rich man
in his death,

although he had done no violence, and there was no deceit in his
mouth.

Yet it was the will of the LORD to bruise him, he has put him to grief;
when he makes himself an offering for sin, he shall see his off-
spring, he shall prolong his days;
the will of the LORD shall prosper in his hand; he shall see the fruit
of the travail of his soul and be satisfied;
by his knowledge shall the righteous one, my servant, make many
to be accounted righteous; and he shall bear their iniquities.
Therefore I will divide him a portion with the great, and he shall
divide the spoil with the strong;
because he poured out his soul to death, and was numbered with
the transgressors;
yet he bore the sin of many, and made intercession for the transgressors.

The easy applicability of this passage to Jesus' life obscures the
curious fact that it was not often used explicitly by the earliest
Church, and the New Testament never uses it to prove the vicarious atonement of the Messiah. Yet the theory that the passage
silently informs all of the New Testament is difficult to substan-
tiate. Paul, the earliest New Testament author, who is extremely
interested in the concept of vicarious atonement, does not quote
Isaiah 53 at all. Only relatively late writers of the New Testament
explicitly quote the passage. Luke, for instance, quotes Isaiah 53 in
Acts 8:26–40 when he relates the story of the Ethiopian eunuch:

But an angel of the LORD said to Philip, "Rise and go toward the south
to the road that goes down from Jerusalem to Gaza. This is a desert
road." And he rose and went. And behold, an Ethiopian, a eunuch,
a minister of Candace the queen of the Ethiopians, in charge of all
her treasure had come to Jerusalem to worship and was returning;
seated in his chariot, he was reading the prophet Isaiah. And the
Spirit said to Philip, "Go up and join this chariot." So Philip ran to
him, and heard him reading Isaiah the prophet, and asked, "Do you
understand what you are reading?" And he said, "How can I, unless
someone guides me?" And he invited Philip to come up and sit with
him. Now the passage of the Scripture which he was reading was
this:

As a sheep led to the slaughter or a lamb before its shearer is
dumb, so he opens not his mouth.
In his humiliation justice was denied him.

Who can describe his generation?
For his life is taken up from the earth.

And the eunuch said to Philip, "About whom, pray, does the prophet say this, about himself or about someone else?" Then Philip opened his mouth, and beginning with this scripture he told him the good news of Jesus. And as they went along the road they came to some water, and the eunuch said, "See, here is water! What is to prevent my being baptized?" And he commanded the chariot to stop, and they both went down into the water, Philip and the eunuch, and he baptized him. And when they came up out of the water, the Spirit of the LORD caught Philip; and the eunuch saw him no more, and went on his way rejoicing. But Philip was found at Azotus, and passing on he preached the gospel to all the towns till he came to Caesarea.

This passage reveals that before Christianity the meaning of Isaiah 53 was not clearly messianic. The eunuch asks whether the passage refers to the prophet himself or to someone else, never assuming it to apply to the Messiah.[27] Only then does Philip tell the eunuch that it refers to Jesus. Furthermore, Philip uses the passage to prove that Jesus, the Messiah, must die, not to prove that the suffering of Jesus was redemptive. It was the suffering of the Messiah, not the concept of vicarious atonement (redemptive suffering), which needed demonstration. Vicarious atonement was hardly in need of proof in first-century Judaism, for the Temple, with its system of vicarious animal sacrifice, was still operating. Paul, who stresses vicarious atonement in regard to Jesus, never feels the need to prove it by means of Scripture.

The novelty of the Christian exegesis of Isaiah 53 was to apply it exclusively to the Messiah. Judaism identifies many different people as servants of Yahweh. Rabbinic tradition tried to understand the identity of the figure by applying Isaiah 53 to anyone who was called a servant of Yahweh in the Hebrew Bible — Moses, Abraham, Phineas, Elijah, and the Messiah. But the Messiah is only called "servant" in an oblique way. Psalm 89 identifies David as servant. Zechariah 3:8 calls the "branch," which was a messianic term, a "servant." But the future Messiah is not explicitly called

[27] The servant in Isaiah 53 may have originally referred to a specific character, as opposed to other servant psalms, which are metaphorical descriptions of Israel. However, the death of this servant is not necessarily implied by the reference to his grave being dug, which may merely mean that he was expected to die.

a servant. The identification of the servant in Isaiah 53 with the Messiah is first attested by the Christians.[28]

In 1 Peter, Isaiah 53 is used to explain the death of the martyrs as an emulation of the Christ, but even here vicarious atonement is not proven by the scriptural passage. The Christian meaning of the Scripture arose in the same way as did the exegesis of the other Jewish groups, through the interplay between historical experience and the words of the Bible. This explains why Christianity had so much trouble persuading Jews that the Messiah had come. Nothing that the Christians maintained seemed self-evident to the majority of the Jewish community, and the Jews were the only ones who expected a Messiah. This situation illuminates the statement of Paul: "We preach Christ crucified, a stumbling block to Jews and folly to gentiles" (1Cor 1:23). He means that for a Christian to persuade a Jew to convert, the Christian has to overcome the Jewish expectation that no Messiah (Christ) can be crucified, and the Christian similarly has to persuade a pagan that a crucified man is worthy of veneration as a God. The passage testifies to the indomitable faith of Paul's generation of Christians. Later generations of Christianity, secure in the meaning of their faith, miss the poignancy of Paul's claim.

One of the most obvious differences between Christianity and other millenarian movements is Christianity's longevity. The normal lifespan of an apocalyptic group is brief.[29] Apocalyptic predictions are usually disproven in some radical way or quashed by the powerful establishment. Christianity differs from this pattern in its long-lived success.

One reason for Christianity's success is its effectiveness in revaluing Scripture. The Christians who revised the expectations about Scripture must have been Jewish Christians of one sort or another. In formulating the new Christian truth, they proved it so effectively that later generations missed the radical surprise everywhere expressed by Jesus' earliest followers. Yet the process was typical of the time.

Another reason for Christianity's success was its originally passive, nonviolent stance, which allowed for a much wider inter-

---

[28]In the Aramaic Targum to Isaiah 53 the rabbis maintain a surprising messianic interpretation where, against the literal meaning of Isaiah 53, the servant Messiah makes all the enemies of God suffer. This is clearly polemic against Christianity inserted into rabbinic commentary.

[29]Gager, *Kingdom and Community*.

pretation of the coming of the Kingdom than did any political messianic group in Judaism. Christianity resembles Rabbinic Judaism in this respect, since both were able to reinterpret the phrase "the Kingdom of God" to refer to the individual's personal commitment of faith rather than to the cataclysmic end of earthly regimes, as the apocalypticists had specified. As it turned out, all overtly political rebellions against Rome were hopelessly doomed to failure. The Christian distaste for Roman rule, like the rabbinic opposition, evolved into a determinedly unenthusiastic compliance with Rome.

Christianity was not notably successful in converting Jews to its message. Its greatest achievement lay in its missionary work among the gentiles. Moreover, the Christianity that spread throughout the Roman Empire had transformed its apocalyptic sectarianism into a religion of personal piety. It had not, however, given up its communal cohesion. Christianity did not so much abandon apocalyptic fervor as channel it into nonapocalyptic areas. The Church maintained that Jesus' resurrection was the beginning of the apocalyptic endtime. Instead of quickening apocalyptic belief itself, the Church transformed that belief into a means to form stable communities. This transformation was effected by Paul, the apostle, who was still very much an apocalypticist but who also laid the groundwork for the theology and fervor that brought Christianity into the wider world.

CHAPTER NINE

What Crucified Jesus?

Ellis Rivkin

Who Crucified Jesus?

It is tragic indeed that the birth pangs of Christianity were occasioned by an event in which Jews were directly implicated. It is tragic because it spawned intense hostility between mother and daughter religions, religions bound by an umbilical cord which can never be severed. As long as the gospels, Acts, the Epistles of Paul, and the other books of the New Testament are read as Holy Scriptures by Christians, the tie to Judaism is a tie that binds. All Christian claims for Christ are grounded in verses from the Old Testament; all Christian claims to be the true Israel are underwritten by proof texts drawn from the Pentateuch; and all Christian claims that Jesus had risen from the dead are embedded in the core belief of the Scribes-Pharisees of Jesus' day. Cut the history and the religion of Israel out of the New Testament, and Christianity vanishes. The Old Testament may be replaced by the New, the Israel of the flesh by the Israel of the Spirit, and the Law by Christ, but the umbilical cord remains.

The umbilical cord remains, yet that tie has been taut with tragedy. Jesus died no ordinary death, in no ordinary circumstances. According to the gospels, he was arrested by order of the high priest; he was tried before a sanhedrin of Jewish notables presided over by the high priest; he was delivered over to Pontius Pilate (see Illus. 11) by the high priest; he was condemned to crucifixion on the charge of claiming to be the King of the Jews; and he was resurrected by God the Father three days after he had breathed his last. Throughout this horrendous process, Jews are in the forefront: the high priest, scribes and elders, the sanhedrin, the hostile crowd calling for crucifixion, the Jews mocking his royal claim as Jesus hung on the cross twisted and dying. How, on hearing or reading this painful and shocking account of a teacher who had healed the sick, commiserated with the poor, exorcised demons, sat with sinners, and preached of God's coming Kingdom, can one respond without pain, sorrow, and bitter anger? And Christians throughout the centuries have responded with pain, with sorrow, and with bitter anger against Jews, who seem to have caused it all.

Crucifixion was a cruel and inhumane act. It would have been cruel and inhumane even were the crucified one guilty of some serious crime. It plumbed the depths of cruelty and inhumanity when it was inflicted on a charismatic, a prophetic visionary, an earnest seeker of salvation and redemption for his people. Those who were ultimately responsible for so heinous a crime are deserving of our righteous wrath, if not of our righteous vengeance.

It is therefore understandable that the disciples of Jesus who witnessed his travail were shocked, outraged, embittered, and unforgiving of those whom they believed to have been responsible. It is also understandable that in the record of Jesus' life, trial, crucifixion, and attested resurrection, there should be so much violent hatred for all those who, in one way or another, had rejected him as the Messiah while he was alive and had rejected him as the Messiah after his disciples had seen him risen from the dead. Were the record otherwise, it would had to have been set down by angels, not beings of flesh and blood.

We cannot therefore shake off this frightening question of responsibility. The New Testament, like the Old, will always be with us. The story will always arouse pain, sorrow, and anger in the hearts of Christians. No surgical procedure can cut away the guts of the gospel story: an arrest, a trial, a crucifixion, and an attestation to a resurrection.

Nor should we dodge the question of responsibility. As seekers of truth, we would wish to know what occurred, why it occurred, and who was responsible for its occurrence. As seekers of reconciliation between the mother and daughter religions, we would wish to build this reconciliation on the facing of facts, rather than on the dissolving of them.

This twofold goal may perhaps be achieved if we shift our focus from the question, Who crucified Jesus? to the question, *What crucified Jesus?*

But that shifting of focus is more easily suggested than done. For we need some source for Jesus' life that is free of the hostile intensity of the gospel story — a source that would provide us the historical Jesus, free of the passionate involvement of those who were certain that he had risen from the dead.

But where shall we find such a source? We have only the gospel record, a record penned with faith, written with passion, and bristling with hostility and resentment. So where are we to turn?

I suggest that we turn to the writings of Josephus — not because he records the life, the trial, the crucifixion, and the resurrection, but because he does not! Josephus was born shortly after Jesus died and was a keen participant and observer of the tumult of the time. As the general in charge of Galilee during the Jews' revolt against Rome, he was actively involved; and he wrote at great length of the road to war, first in *The Jewish War*, then in the last volumes of his *Antiquities*, and finally in his autobiography, *The Life*. As an admirer of Thucydides and Polybius, the grand historians of the Greco-Roman world, Josephus was a penetrative student of political power and a master of historical narrative. As a follower of the Pharisees, he was thoroughly versed in the teachings of the written and the oral Law and was himself a believer in the immortality of the soul and the resurrection of the body. As a committed Jew, he was highly sensitive to the sufferings and helplessness of the Jews pressed in the grip of imperial Rome. Josephus is a precious source, revealing the Roman imperial system as it functioned in Jesus' day; the systems of Judaism prevalent at the time; the revolutionary spasms that convulsed the land; the charismatics, prophets, and would-be messiahs who roamed the hills of Judea and Galilee (see Illus. 5, 7, 8).

Josephus' work lends itself to the ends we are seeking. From his writings we can construct the framework within which Jesus' life, trial, crucifixion, and resurrection were played out. But we can do even more. With Josephus as our guide, we may be able even to resurrect the historical Jesus who for so long has eluded us. By drawing a portrait of a charismatic of charismatics from the intricate web of time, place, structures, and linkages woven for us by Josephus, we may be in a position to compare this portrait with those drawn for us in the gospels. Never was the time more ripe or more ready for a spirit capable of charting a trajectory from life to Life — a spirit whose earthly fate would not be his destiny.

Let us then set off on our odyssey from Who crucified Jesus? to

What crucified Jesus? — an odyssey from human bitterness, hate, and blindness to divine love, reconciliation, and enlightenment.

Render unto Caesar: In Rome's Imperial Grip

The Jewish people had been in the grip of Rome long before the time of Jesus. From that critical moment when the Roman general Pompey had stamped the seal of Rome on Hyrcanus II (63–40 B.C.E.), Jews had exercised little control over their land or their destiny. All who governed Jews, whether puppet kings like Herod (40–4 B.C.E.) or prefects like Pontius Pilate (26–36 C.E.), governed as instruments of the Roman imperium. And Rome's grip loosened not at all in the years that followed the trial and crucifixion of Jesus.

The imperial grip was painful but bearable during those early years when Hyrcanus II and Herod retained the trappings of kingly power. It became less and less bearable in the waning years of Herod's reign, and the frustration, the bitterness, and the resentment of the people began to be expressed in strident defiance and violent demonstrations. It became intolerable when, after Herod's death, Rome dispensed with puppet kings and determined to rule Judea directly through prefects and procurators appointed by the emperor. From that moment on, the Jews were to know no peace, no serenity, no security until the Temple was in ruins, thousands lay slain, and thousands more had been carted off to Rome.

Coponius — the very first "procurator," according to Josephus (but actually a "prefect") — ushered in the new dispensation with an act that set the teeth of the Jews on edge. No sooner had he taken office in 6 C.E. than he ordered a census and an assessment of Jewish property, in order to determine the amount of tribute to be exacted. The Jews were shocked and inclined to resist. Only the pleas of the high priest deterred them from what would have been a tragic confrontation. But two sages, Judas of Galilee and Zadok, a Pharisee, refused to knuckle under. They called on the people to revolt, insisting that God and God alone could be called *despotes*, Emperor. It was blasphemous, they said, to obey the Roman emperor's decrees. "Heaven would be their zealous helper," they reassured the people, "to no lesser end than the furthering of their enterprise until it succeeded — all the more if with high devotion in their hearts they stood firm and did not shrink from the bloodshed that might be necessary" (*Ant* 18.5–6).

The rise of the Fourth Philosophy underscores the blurred line that separated the religious-nonpolitical realm from the religious-political realm. From the point of view of the founders of the Fourth Philosophy, the call for revolution against Rome was inspired by religious, not political zeal. They claimed that it was blasphemous to call any individual *despotes*, lord, master, emperor. Their call to arms was intended to overthrow another Antiochus who was challenging God's claim to be the only God. Such a call to arms had political consequences, but it was not motivated or justified on political grounds. The fact that both Judas and Zadok were sages, not soldiers, and the fact that Josephus dignified this revolutionary movement by setting it beside the schools of thought of the Sadducees, Pharisees, and Essenes as another religious philosophy within Judaism attest to the religious wellsprings of this violent challenge to Rome.

From the point of view, however, of the High Priest Joazar and from the point of view of the leading spokesmen for the Pharisees, the taking of a census, the assessment of property, and the payment of tribute fell within Caesar's domain. For them, paying tribute to the emperor was not equivalent to paying tribute to a god.

Thus when Pontius Pilate became prefect in 26 C.E. and immediately reconfirmed Caiaphas as high priest, he fell heir to a country that had been wracked by continuous violence. It was a battleground where the mettle of the prefect and his high priest was put to the test day-in and day-out. If Pontius Pilate were to make his mark and show himself worthy of advancement in the hierarchy of imperial power, it was essential that he impress the emperor with his ability to maintain law and order in a land which had proven itself to be a seedbed of dissidence, disorder, and violence. Unless, then, Pontius Pilate were shrewd enough to govern this unruly people, his tenure as prefect was bound to be extremely short.

It is evident from Josephus' account that Pontius Pilate was shrewd, tough, ruthless, and successful. His ten years in office testified to his good record in the preserving of law and order. He was able to head off trouble before it reached dangerous proportions. *His key to effective governance was to nip revolutions in the bud by making no distinction between "political" and "religious" dissidents. Dissidence, not motive or rallying cry, was his target.* For him, a charismatic's vision of the Kingdom of God that God himself would usher in was equally as threatening as the revolutionaries' call to rise up against the Romans, for the end result would be the same: Roman rule would be finished. For Pilate, the beginning of wisdom was the fear of revolt, however masked by religious pietudes.

But Pilate could not achieve his objectives unless there were a loyal and able Jewish counterpart as committed to Pilate's strategy as was Pilate himself. In Caiaphas, he found such a counterpart. No previous high priest had ever held this high office for such a long period of time, and no subsequent high priest was ever to best Caiaphas' record. This was no mean achievement. Every prefect and procurator, both prior to and following Pontius Pilate, was free to employ a pliant high priest. Since Herod's day, the high priest had been appointed and dismissed at the whim of the ruler. The high priest's sacred robes were kept under lock and key by the political authorities, to be released only on festivals when he needed them in order to perform his duties. *Held thus firmly in the grip of prefect or procurator, all high priests had to toe the line.*

Yet Caiaphas seems to have been the only high priest who possessed those special qualities that enabled him to serve not just one, but two prefectors. Since he held the office for a full ten years under such a demanding prefect as Pontius Pilate, Caiaphas obviously had the ability to keep the anger of the people from boiling over into violent anti-Roman demonstrations. Caiaphas weathered the storms and held his post throughout Pilate's administration. No major disturbances marred their relationship — an eloquent testimony to the high priest's skill in snuffing out sparks before they burst into flames.

There was one event, however, during the high priesthood of Caiaphas, which reveals the fear and trembling in high places. Although this event occurred outside the political jurisdiction of Pontius Pilate, it reflects the cast of mind of all who exercised authority during those discordant and troublesome times. It involved a charismatic, John the Baptist, who was put to death by Herod the Tetrarch.

John, in Josephus' opinion, was a good man who exhorted the Jews to live righteous lives, to practice justice toward their fellows and piety toward God. When John called the people to join him in baptism, he was urging them to participate in a symbolic act signifying that their souls had already been cleansed by the righteous lives they had lived since heeding his call. There was nothing political in John's teachings. He was a religious charismatic — pure and simple.

Yet as Josephus points out, Herod the Tetrarch was unwilling to accept John for what he was. As long as crowds were aroused by John's sermons, the ruler feared that such eloquence could stir the people to some form of sedition. For John was no ordinary preacher. He could so stir his listeners with his aura that they would willingly follow wherever he might lead. Thus Herod was confronted with a dilemma: If he ignored John, the crowds might become more and more prone to violence in response to some real or imagined provocation. On the other hand, if he put John to death, he might be inviting the very outbreak he was attempting to avoid. It turned out that, in this instance at least, Herod the Tetrarch had made a shrewd decision: The people, though aroused and angry, did not rise up.

The Roman imperial framework, within which Jesus' life, preaching, trial, crucifixion, and attested resurrection took place, is clear enough. At the pinnacle of power and authority was the emperor, who exercised his authority over the Jews either through puppet kings, like Herod, or through prefectors, like Coponius and Pontius Pilate. These imperial instruments, in turn, sought to carry out their responsibilities to the emperor by appointing high priests who were selected for their pliancy rather than their piety. Their function was to serve as the eyes and ears of the puppet king or prefector, so as to head off demonstrative challenges to Roman rule. Of these high priests, only one — Caiaphas — had such piercing eyes and such keen ears that he was able to keep the confidence of the prefectors he served as long as they remained in office.

But even Caiaphas could scarcely have done his job single-handedly. It is thus highly likely that he appointed a council, or sanhedrin, consisting of individuals who were well aware of the dire consequences that would follow any outbreak against Roman authority, however innocent and naive its instigator.

Such a sanhedrin, as is evident from Josephus' usage of the term, could only have been a strictly political body with no religious sanction, authority, or jurisdiction. It was a body appointed by the high priest to help him carry out his political responsibilities to the prefector as the prefector's "eyes and ears." As such, it was a body that could consist of both Sadducees and Pharisees who were at religious loggerheads with one another.

A close reading of Josephus thus enables us to discern the political framework within which the life, ministry, trial, crucifixion, and witnessed resurrection of Jesus were played out. This is the framework presupposed by the gospels, by Acts, and by the Epistles of Paul. The Roman emperor ruled Judea, Galilee, and Samaria by means of puppet kings, governors, prefects, and prefector-appointed high priests. But the Jewish people over whom these instruments ruled proved to be ungovernable.

In such a world — where violence stalked the countryside, death frequented the streets of Jerusalem, and riots disturbed the precincts of the Temple; where every flutter of dissidence sent chills of fear up the spines of puppet kings, governors, prefects, and prefector-appointed high priests — even the most nonpolitical of charismatics took his life in his hands when he preached the good news of God's coming Kingdom. And if his call to repentance were so eloquent that crowds gathered round to hear and to hope, would not the power of his word invite the kiss of death?

Render unto God: The Mosaic of Judaism

Judea was under the control of Rome. The emperor, the prefector, the high priest, and the high priest's privy council — all were tied together by two interests: the preservation of imperial power in the face of any challenge, and the smooth collection of tribute for the enrichment of Rome. All those who functioned in the imperial interest were not motivated by religious, but by political considerations. The high priest was no exception, even though he ministered in the Temple, and he alone was allowed to enter the Holy of Holies on the Day of Atonement to seek God's forgiveness for the sins of all Israel. Yet he himself was, in the sight of God, an arch sinner, for nowhere in the five books of Moses or in the repository of the oral Law, the Mishnah, do we read that a high priest is to be an appointee of any king, prince, or potentate. According to the Pentateuch, the high priesthood was to be reserved for the direct lineal descendants of Aaron, Eleazar, and Phineas.

From the standpoint of God's Law, all high priests who had held office since Herod's day were illegitimate. They had been merely political instruments imposed by regal power and acquiesced to by the leaders of the three divergent forms of Judaism in Jesus' day — the Judaism of the Sadducees, of the Pharisees, and of the Essenes. Though the followers of each of these forms regarded the followers of the others as heretics and rejectors of God's will, Judaism appeared to the Roman authorities as a mosaic with three inlays, which, though distinguishable one from another, were nonetheless of a single design. This was so because, out of desperation, the leaders of each form had committed themselves to two doctrines: the doctrine of the two realms to regulate their relationship to the state, and the doctrine of live-and-let-live to regulate their relationship to one another. In a word, they urged their followers to render unto Caesar what was Caesar's, so that they would be able to render unto God what was God's. And they also, in order to exist amiably side by side with one another, had initiated a policy of peaceful coexistence.

Let us now take a closer look at each of the three inlays — the Sadducees, the Pharisees, and the Essenes — so that we can comprehend how three such divergent forms of Judaism could have appeared to the Roman authorities as a mosaic, rather than as separate, distinct, and mutually exclusive forms of the religion of Israel. For at first glance, the differences that set them apart were far more impressive and fundamental than those that drew them together.

The Sadducees believed that God had revealed one Law only — the five books of Moses; the Scribes-Pharisees believed that God had revealed two Laws — one written and the other oral; while the Essenes believed that God had also revealed his will in books besides the Pentateuch and the other books of the Bible. There were additional significant differences as well: The Sadducees believed that God had endowed Aaron and his sons with absolute authority over God's Law and over his cultus. The Scribes-Pharisees believed that God had endowed first Moses, then Joshua, then the elders, then the prophets, and then themselves with absolute authority over God's twofold Law, the written and the oral. The Essenes kept themselves aloof from the people at large and from the cultus of the day. And finally, while the Sadducees believed that God rewarded the righteous and punished the wicked in this world, the Scribes-Pharisees believed that God rewarded the righteous with eternal life for the soul and resurrection for the body and that he punished the souls of the wicked with eternal suffering in the nether world. As for the Essenes, they believed that the souls of the righteous would enjoy eternal life, but they did not believe in the resurrection of the body. But however severe and tenacious the differences, Sadducees, Scribes-Pharisees, and Essenes all looked to God, not to the Roman emperor, as their Lord. Whereas the governor-appointed high priest and his privy council were harnessed to the imperial chariot, the Sadducees, Pharisees, and Essenes were yoked to God.

In Jesus' day the Scribes-Pharisees were the most luminous inlay within the mosaic of Judaism. It was they who sat in Moses' seat, and it was they who determined the norms by which all public religious functions were carried out in accordance with the provisions of the written and oral Law. Thus the religious calendar of the Temple followed the lunar-solar calendar of the oral Law. The sacrifices in the Temple and the celebrations of the festivals were carried out in accordance with the oral Law. In a word, the oral Law of the Scribes-Pharisees was normative for all Jews, insofar as public manifestations of religion were concerned. The religious activity of the Sadducees and Essenes was confined to their private domains, and their religious teachings were restricted to doctrinal claims and verbal protestations.

This doctrine of the two realms — Caesar's and God's — proved to be attractive to the secular and political authorities. They were willing, therefore, to grant religious autonomy to the Scribes-Pharisees. The implications of this doctrine, however, were to have momentous consequences; for it meant nothing less than a promise on the part of the Scribes-Pharisees that as long as their religious autonomy was not violated, the political authorities were to be given a free hand. Should the political authorities fail to stay within their realm, should they trespass on the realm of the holy and sacred, then the people must rise up in revolt, as they had done when John Hyrcanus and Alexander Janneus had barred the road to eternal life. Or they could resort to passive resistance, willing to martyr themselves rather than yield. This they had indeed done when they refused to be cowed by Pontius Pilate's threats if they persisted in blocking the introduction of the emperor's images into Jerusalem and into the Temple.

This compact was reaffirmed when Coponius, having been appointed prefect in 6 C.E. after Archelaus' death, ordered the census to serve as the basis for the exaction of the imperial tribute. This order, as we have seen, was so bitterly resented by the people that it could easily have sparked a revolt, had not the Scribes-Pharisees stood firmly behind their compact. The exaction of tribute fell in Caesar's domain. It did not bar the road to eternal life. The census-taking was a legitimate exercise of Roman authority and could *not* be challenged on *religious* grounds, no matter how much suffering and hardship the exaction of tribute would impose upon the people. The census was legal, the tribute was legal, its exaction was legal because Roman sovereignty was legal. It was legal because the *doctrine of the two realms* accorded to Caesar all that was Caesar's and to God all that was God's.

The Scribes-Pharisees' adherence to their compact was not without heavy cost. For the first time since they had taken possession of Moses' seat, they found their leadership rejected by a significant number of their followers when Judas and Zadok denounced Coponius' order as being an affront to God's sovereignty. So fundamental indeed was this split with the Scribes-Pharisees that the Fourth Philosophy came to be recognized as a distinctive form of Judaism, alongside those of the Scribes-Pharisees, the Sadducees, and the Essenes.

As for the doctrine of live-and-let-live, the Scribes-Pharisees of Jesus' day had long since given up their earlier efforts to bind the Sadducees to the oral Law. Except for worship in the Temple, adherence to the religious calendar, and conformance to cultic ceremonial acts of a religious and public nature, the private acts and teachings of the Sadducees and their followers had come to be regarded as their own affair. Conflicts between Pharisees and Sadducees were now confined exclusively to doctrinal debate. On a day-to-day basis, Pharisees and Sadducees mingled freely, and Sadducean high priests carried out their Temple functions in accordance with the prescriptions of the oral laws with seeming good grace. Indeed, on such issues as political sovereignty, the Pharisees and Sadducees tended to see eye to eye, since the Sadducees, like the Scribes-Pharisees, had committed themselves to the doctrine of the two realms.

It is thus evident that in Jesus' day, the Pharisees and the Sadducees coexisted peacefully on the religious plane and held similar views on the political plane. Both had adopted a noninterference policy, not only toward each other, but toward every religious group in Judaism, however much it might deviate from their own beliefs. Whatever common concern they shared over religious dissidents whose teachings had dangerous political implications, such concern was political, not religious: Dissidents should be brought before some appropriate political authority — puppet king, governor, or governor-appointed high priest — to be judged on political grounds. Such dissidents, however, were not to be brought before the *Bet Din Ha-Gadol* (Great *Boulē*), the senate of the Scribes-Pharisees, or before any of their lesser bodies, each of which was called simply a *bet din (boulē)*. In Jesus' day, these bodies did not exercise any political jurisdiction, while the religious jurisdiction they did exercise was limited to those Jews who voluntarily followed the teachings of the Scribes-Pharisees. Adhering to their compact with the state, the Scribes-Pharisees steered clear of political involvement; and adhering to their compact with the Sadducees and Essenes, they confined their outrage at religious dissidents to verbal onslaughts.

If, then, a charismatic stirred crowds with his call for repentance, awed crowds by his wonder working, or uplifted crowds with the promise of God's Kingdom to come, then the Scribes-Pharisees might confront him, they might remonstrate with him, they might even denounce him as an emissary of Beelzebul, but they would not — *for they could not* — arrest him and have him brought before either the *Bet Din Ha-Gadol*, or a lesser *bet din*. They could no more haul a charismatic before their religious bodies than they could haul the High Priest Caiaphas, who, as a Sadducee, held far more outrageous religious beliefs than those held by many of the charismatics.

Thus the Judaism in Jesus' day, though it consisted of three main distinctive facets blended together, appeared to the Romans as a mosaic, flashing from all its facets the reassuring message: "Render to Caesar the things that are Caesar's, and to God the things that are God's" (Mk 12:17).

From Out of the Depths They Cried

The mosaic of Judaism was not fractured by the provocations of the ruling authorities. But many Jews found those provocations so painful that they could not submit passively. For them, the situation demanded some alternative to the doctrine of the two realms. It was inconceivable to them that God could be party to such harsh injustices. They believed that God could not and would not remain silent. Although the Pharisees, Sadducees, and Essenes may have drawn a line between the religious and secular realms, God had drawn no such line. Voices began to cry out that God was not neutral and that Caesar's realm was neither safe nor sacrosanct. They believed that God's righteous justice would not be deterred by some imaginary line drawn by men — that God would bring low the haughtiness of emperors and wreak vengeance on their cruel injustices to God's people. Some believed, as did the followers of the Fourth Philosophy, that the wrath of God would be manifested through violent revolutionaries. Others were drawn to charismatic teachers who proclaimed that God himself would sweep away Roman rule and establish his glorious Kingdom in its stead.

For the Roman authorities and the high priest, the revolutionaries offered no real problem. It was not so easy, however, for the authorities to decide what to do about charismatic leaders who preached no violence and built no revolutionary organizations, but rather urged the people to repent and to wait for the coming of God's Kingdom. Were these charismatics harmless preachers, or were they troublemakers? Were their teachings and visions goads to personal righteousness, and therefore apolitical or even nonpolitical? Or were they goads to dissatisfaction and unhappiness with the world that was?

The prophet-like charismatics were preachers, not revolutionaries. They resembled the prophets of old. They did not call upon the people to rise up against Rome, but to look to God, who had the power to perform miracles and move mountains. Yet when John the Baptist preached repentance and not revolt he was put to death by Herod Antipas (4 B.C.E.–39 C.E.) for no other reason than that his eloquence attracted crowds and crowds were dangerous.

Josephus' portrayal of John reveals that there could indeed be a charismatic teacher whose teachings were nonpolitical but could arouse fear in the hearts of the authorities, who were concerned only with the thought that the crowds gathering round him might get out of control and go on a rampage. Thus Herod Antipas deemed it "better to strike first."

The Roman authorities clearly could not risk making a distinction between revolutionaries and charismatics. Both were politically dangerous.

In the Likeness of the Son of Man

Amid the spiritual convulsions of those troubled times, and among the prophet-like preachers and charismatics who were crying out the good news that God would soon redeem his people from bondage, we scan the writings of Josephus in vain for that charismatic of charismatics whom we would have anticipated

finding there — a charismatic so compassionate, so loving, so eloquent, and so filled with the Spirit of God that his disciples would
refuse to accept his death as real. But Josephus shares with us only
the charismatic John the Baptist. Yet, for all his charisma, John
the Baptist failed to arouse in his disciples a love intense enough
or a faith secure enough to evoke his death as but a prelude to
life. However overwhelmed with grief, and however drawn to
his person John's disciples may have been, they did not see him
risen from the dead, even though the Scribes-Pharisees were daily
preaching resurrection, just as they and many other Jews daily
reaffirmed it when they recited the Tefillah (the so-called Eighteen Benedictions), the prayer par excellence, as required by the
twofold Law. John's charisma, however impressive and alluring,
clearly lacked the power to sustain his life beyond the grave.

The sound, the fury, and the tumult of the times cry out for a
charismatic of charismatics. Yet Josephus gives us no such unique
individual. He readies us for a Jesus, but gives us only John the
Baptist. His fleeting allusion to Jesus as the brother of James fades
away as he concentrates on James' fate, not Jesus' resurrection.
Josephus' awareness that Jesus was called the Christ, that James
must have preached him as risen from the dead, remains unartic-
ulated. For whatever reason, Josephus bespeaks John the Baptist,
not Jesus called the Christ.

Josephus' silence stimulates us to try our own hand at paint-
ing a portrait of the missing charismatic of charismatics from the
pigments of the age which Josephus has preserved in his palette.
We ask ourselves: What manner of man would such a charismatic
have been? What qualities must he have had to so endear himself to his disciples that even death itself did not have the power
to pry them apart? What must his likeness have been to so en-
trance his followers that they were open-eyed to see his likeness,
as much alive after death as before? In a word: What qualities
must this unique individual have possessed to make him an even
more powerful and alluring charismatic than John?

Such a charismatic of charismatics would have been a man able
to fuse an Elijah with an Isaiah — behaving like the former and
dreaming like the latter, being both a wonder-worker and a visionary. He would mingle with the poor and lowly and revive their
spirits with his spirit. He would stir them with hope and faith as he
proclaimed that the Kingdom of God was coming. He would look
very much like a prophet of olden times but he would also bear

the likeness of the Son of man, the Anointed, the King-Messiah, ushering in the day of the Lord. He would have stamped on his countenance the image of an Elijah, the image of an Isaiah, and the fused image of the Son of man as both prophet and King-Messiah.

In addition to these, he would have fused within himself the model of a Scribe-Pharisee. This image would have been *sui generis*, for it would have been that of a teacher who *taught* the Word of God, not that of a prophet who *spoke* the Word of God. Unlike the prophets, the Scribes-Pharisees never prefaced their teachings with "Thus saith Yahweh," even though what they taught — the Halakha (oral Law) and the Haggadah (oral lore) — was deemed to be even more authoritative than that which had been uttered by even the greatest of prophets, Moses himself. The laws that God had commanded and which Moses had written down in the Pentateuch had been subordinated to the oral Law of the Scribes-Pharisees; while the moral and ethical injunctions that God had revealed to Moses and to the prophets were themselves dependent upon the meaning assigned them by the Scribes-Pharisees.

If such a charismatic had taught and preached during the years when Pontius Pilate was prefector and Caiaphas was high priest, what would his fate have been? None other, we can be sure, than the fate that had overtaken John the Baptist. If such a charismatic were believed to be an Elijah when he healed the sick, raised the dead, and cast forth demons, his wonder working would have attracted crowds — and crowds, as we know, were dangerous and could get out of hand. If he seemed to be a visionary and, like Isaiah, proclaimed that the Kingdom of God was near at hand, his high hopes would have attracted crowds — and crowds, as we know, were dangerous and could get out of hand. If he bore a likeness to the Son of man, the King-Messiah, his likeness would have attracted crowds — and crowds, as we know, were dangerous and could get out of hand. And if his compassion and love reached and lifted up the wretched, gave hope to the outcast, and reassurance to the faint of heart, such compassion and love would have attracted crowds — and crowds, as we know, were dangerous and could get out of hand.

Crowds were dangerous indeed! So dangerous, in fact, that Herod Antipas had put John the Baptist to death — not because John urged the people to repent, live pious lives, and undergo baptism, but only because his eloquence attracted crowds and crowds were unpredictable and prone to violence. Ever since the young firebrands had torn down the Roman eagle in God's name, violence had become a normal response to Roman provocation. Even the presence of Roman legionnaires in the Temple precincts could not deter crowds from going berserk.

What chance for survival would a charismatic of charismatics have — this man of eloquence, wonder-works, religious fervor, fevered fantasies, messianic pretensions, and sheer charisma — if his person attracted crowds in Jerusalem, where Pontius Pilate and his high priest Caiaphas quaked at every rustle of discontent and every wisp of dissidence? No chance at all! For was this not the same Pilate who had dared to parade the icons of the emperor through the city? Was this not the same Pilate who had dressed his soldiers in civilian garb to mingle with the crowds, so as to provoke them to riot and give him a pretext to cut them down? And was not Caiaphas, whose piercing eyes and keen ears had kept him in office throughout Pilate's prefectorship, the high priest?

With such a pair, can there be any doubt that they would have taken even fewer chances than had Herod Antipas, were a charismatic of charismatics to appear in Jerusalem attracting crowds? Would Pontius Pilate or Caiaphas care a fig for what the man taught or preached? And if the charismatic were attracting crowds because it seemed to many that he was the Son of man, the King-Messiah about to usher in the Kingdom of God, would they not pounce on him swiftly and hasten him to the cross, the ultimate Roman deterrent for keeping revolutionaries and would-be messiahs at bay? For Pontius Pilate and Caiaphas, danger to Rome lurked as much behind the visions of an Isaiah, the prophecies of an Ezekiel, the mantle of an Elijah, or the likeness of the Son of man, as behind the sheathed dagger of a Judas of Galilee.

A charismatic of charismatics would thus have had no chance of survival at all. To the degree that he proved himself to be such a charismatic through his healing of the sick, his casting out of demons, he raising of the dead, his arousing of hopes for the coming of God's Kingdom — to that degree would he attract crowds. And if this charismatic of charismatics actually tested his faith and that of his followers by parading through Jerusalem among crowds who were chanting "the Messiah, the Son of man is among us — Hosanna in the highest," and by appearing in the Temple precincts as a champion of piety and rectitude, Caiaphas would have been provoked to decisive action, lest his failure to act be mistaken as a sign of either permissiveness or fear. With his high priestly office dangling on his detection of sparks of violence before they burst into flames, Caiaphas would lose no time in silencing so ominous a threat to law and order.

Events then would have occurred with blurring rapidity. Caiaphas would have had the charismatic of charismatics brought before his privy council, a sanhedrin of the high priest, and have charged him with undermining Roman authority by his teachings, his preachings, and his actions. For he had taught and preached that the Kingdom of God was near at hand, a Kingdom which, were it to come, would displace the kingdom of Rome. By creating the impression that he might be the Son of man, the King-Messiah who would usher in God's Kingdom, he had, in fact, sought to reign in Caesar's stead. And by stirring up the crowds, parading as he did through Jerusalem and causing a commotion in the precincts of the Temple, he had readied the people for riotous behavior. His teachings, preachings, and actions were bound to sway the loyalties of the Jews: God disapproved of the emperor, God disapproved of the prefect, and God disapproved of the prefector-appointed high priest. The fact that the charismatic of charismatics had taught no violence, had preached no revolution, and lifted up no arms against Rome's authority would have been utterly irrelevant. The High Priest Caiaphas and the Prefector Pontius Pilate cared not a whit how or by whom the Kingdom of God would be ushered in, but only that the Roman emperor and his instruments would not reign over it.

With charges such as these flung at him in the presence of Caiaphas' hand-chosen privy councillors, the fate of the charismatic would be sealed. He had undermined law and order by his words and deeds. He had sowed the seeds of mass demonstrations and contagious violence. These alone were the issues. *Neither his religious teachings nor his beliefs could have been on trial — only their potential political consequences; for the sanhedrin was the high priest's council, which had no function other than to advise the high priest on political matters.* All those who sat on this sanhedrin were committed to the doctrine of the two realms — a doctrine to which Sadducees and Pharisees and Essenes adhered. *As a body appointed and convened by a religious illegitimate, the sanhedrin of the high priest had no authority over religious matters.* Sadducees could sit beside Pharisees only as individuals concerned with preserving the compact with Rome, a compact which guaranteed religious autonomy to the Jews as long as the Jews recognized Roman sovereignty. The high priest's sanhedrin thus could not have been a *bet din (boulē)*; for the issues to be dealt with were political issues, not religious ones.

These then were the questions they would have asked themselves: Were the man's charisma and teachings attracting crowds? What were the chances that the people might go berserk and provoke the prefect into ordering out the troops? Even though the charismatic himself were a man of peace, not of violence; a visionary, not a revolutionary; a gentle and compassionate healer and teacher, not a rabble-rouser, he could release a tempest of violence. Empathy for the charismatic's plight would have been counterbalanced by empathy for the hundreds, if not thousands, who might be butchered by the Roman soldiers if the crowds misheard, misunderstood, or brushed aside the pleas of the charismatic that violence was not what he had meant at all — that God, not the violence of people, would usher in his Kingdom.

The outcome of such a trial would thus have been cut and dry. The high priest, as the eyes and ears of the prefect, was not a free agent. The members of the council, the sanhedrin which he convoked, were likewise not free agents. The charismatic had attracted crowds with his preachings, his wonder workings, and his charisma. As such, he was potentially dangerous. There could be few grounds for hesitancy or mitigation. *If the charismatic either claimed to be or were believed to be the Son of man, the Messiah, the King of the Jews, and if he were preaching the imminent coming of the Kingdom of God, which of necessity would displace the kingdom of Rome, then the case was open and shut.* There was no recourse for the high priest but to advise the prefect that the charismatic of charismatics was in contempt of the emperor and a potential source of disruption and violence, however couched his teachings might be in prophetic imagery and however much he might emphasize that the Kingdom of God was to be brought in by God, not man.

The high priest and the sanhedrin would thus report to the prefect the simple facts: Here is a charismatic of charismatics who attracted crowds; who set off a disturbance in the Temple area, thronged at festival time with highly excitable pilgrims; who was acclaimed as the Messiah, the King of the Jews, as he walked through the streets of Jerusalem; and who called upon the people to prepare themselves for the coming of God's Kingdom — not at some distant time in the future, as the Scribes-Pharisees taught, but at any moment — in the twinkling of an eye.

It would now be up to the prefect to make a final decision as to whether he concurred with the facts and the judgment: Was the charismatic sufficiently dangerous to be crucified as a warning to other charismatics that their religious teachings would be judged by the political consequences that might follow in their wake? *Crucifixion awaited the revolutionary and charismatic alike.*

The fate of charismatics was thus sealed by a process that began with a trial before the high priest and his sanhedrin and ended with the prefect's sentence of death by crucifixion — a process that was political throughout in its intent and purpose. His crime would have been *lèse majesté* — proclaimed to all by the *titulus* above the cross, mocking his pretension to be "the King of the Jews." The charismatic had crossed the line that separated the turf of Caesar from the turf of God. He had crossed over into that no-man's-land where every life was forfeit. He may have been naive, but his political innocence would not spare him. There was a war being waged daily in Galilee, in the streets of Jerusalem, and in the Temple courts. Thousands already had been killed, maimed, burned, and crucified. Thousands more were destined to share the same fate. The people had become ungovernable. From day to day, Pontius Pilate did not know whether he would be prefect on the morrow. Caiaphas knew not at nightfall whether, when morning dawned, he would be high priest. One provocative act, one unguarded moment, one still small voice proclaiming the Kingdom of God — and the people could go wild with a frenzy that would not calm itself until the troops had butchered Jews by the hundreds, if not thousands. With their fate precariously dangling on the edge of each decision, Pontius Pilate and Caiaphas were hardly likely to spare a charismatic of charismatics whose innocence and naiveté had allowed him to stumble over the line that separated God's turf from Caesar's.

The cross would have been the fate that awaited a charismatic of charismatics, but it would not necessarily have been his destiny. For if his disciples had come to believe that he was indeed the Son of man, and if he had bound them tightly to his person by his charisma, then there was every likelihood that their belief in him would have remained unshaken, even though they heard him gasp with his last breath, "God, why hast thou forsaken me?" for at the very core of his teaching would have been his sturdy faith in the good news of the Scribes-Pharisees that souls of the righteous soar up to God the Father, where they await the day of resurrection. Nothing could have been more certain to him than this promise. Resurrection, far from being impossible, was inevitable. And if inevitable, how could it be denied by his disciples, if they saw their Teacher risen from the dead? For them, this would be the proof that he must be the Son of man, the King-Messiah. This was a happening that would confute the Scribes-Pharisees: The charismatic of charismatics must be the Messiah, because he had risen from the dead.

And would not, then, the difference between a charismatic of charismatics such as this man, and a charismatic such as John the Baptist, lie precisely in this: that while the charismatic's life would have ended in death, the charismatic of charismatics' death would have ended in Life?

Jesus, King of the Jews

We have drawn a portrait of a charismatic of charismatics whose life would have ended in Life. We have drawn it primarily from Josephus' writings; Josephus himself did not draw it for us. It is a portrait of a charismatic who would have lived and died and been seen as resurrected. Given the time, the place, the situation, and the mind-set, this portrait is as real as life itself.

But there were those who painted portraits of a charismatic of charismatics who had actually lived — portraits which they believed expressed the very likeness of a remarkable person who had lived, died, and been seen as resurrected while Pontius Pilate was prefect and while Caiaphas was high priest. That charismatic of charismatics whose portrait they painted was "Jesus the Messiah, the Son of man, the resurrected One." Yet though those portraits describe the same man, they so differ from one another as to put us at a loss to know which portrait bears the greater likeness.

We thus find ourselves in a quandary. On the one hand, we have drawn a portrait from Josephus of a charismatic of charismatics who might have lived, died, and been seen as resurrected. On the other hand, we have, in the four gospels of Mark, Matthew, Luke, and John, portraits of Jesus drawn from real life preserved. Yet these portraits are so at variance that we cannot be certain which is most lifelike. Perhaps we can extricate ourselves from our dilemma by placing the portrait of the charismatic of charismatics that we have drawn next to the portraits of Jesus as painted in the gospels.

Let us look first at the Gospel of John to see how markedly different is his portrait of Jesus from that of the charismatic of charismatics drawn from Josephus.

In John, we see a Jesus above time, above place, above constraining frameworks. John sets Jesus off from the Jews as though Jesus himself had been a gentile. He seems unaware that not all Jews were Pharisees and overlooks Jesus' controversies with the Pharisees regarding the binding character of the Traditions of the Elders. Likewise, John's failure to refer to the Scribes, mentioning only the Pharisees, illuminates how little John seems to know or care about the historical setting in which Jesus preached.

John's portrait of Jesus bears little resemblance to our portrait drawn from Josephus — that of a charismatic of charismatics emerging out of the matrix of time, structure, process, and causality.

Not so with the synoptic gospels. The portraits of Jesus found in the gospels of Mark, Matthew, and Luke portray a Jesus who, however much he may have been "out of this world," was part and parcel of it as well. He is pictured as a prophet-like figure, a charismatic of charismatics, the Son of man who enjoys a special relationship to God the Father. In Mark, we are told that there were some people who believed that Jesus was John the Baptist resurrected, and hence endowed with miraculous powers; there were others who believed him to be Elijah; there were still others who believed that he was a prophet like the prophets of old — all images evoking charismatics whom God had endowed with supernatural powers (Mk 6:14–16). And even when Jesus is transfigured, he is pictured as being with Elijah and Moses as one who, like them, had a special relationship with God (Mt 17:3; Mk 9:4; Lk 9:30). Here Jesus is humanized, personalized, and historicized. Jesus becomes credible because he is reminiscent of an Elijah and a Moses. He is not a divine being with no biblical prototype.

The portraits in the synoptic gospels, with all their differences in shading and nuance, stand out in sharp contrast to John's portrait of Jesus. There are clearly discernible features that bear a striking resemblance to the charismatic of charismatics whom we have drawn from Josephus. For the words and deeds of our projected charismatic of charismatics, like those of Jesus, would have evoked images of John the Baptist, Elijah, Moses, and the prophets of old in the minds of those who listened to Jesus and observed his wonder-working powers. So too, Jesus' journey from life to Life as traced in the synoptic gospels is the very trajectory that our projected charismatic of charismatics would have taken — the path of a person of flesh and blood, in whom the Spirit of God dwelled and who became thereby worthy of resurrection.

This human life of Jesus as delineated in the synoptic gospels sets him firmly in the historical matrix of the times. John the Baptist, a real charismatic, is held up as a precursor and a prototype. He is the same good man in the synoptics as in Josephus. He is the voice crying in the wilderness, preaching a baptism of repentance and proclaiming the coming of God's Kingdom — a Kingdom not to be ushered in by him, but by one who is to come after him, one more blessed and more worthy than he. Whereas John baptized with water, he who is to come will baptize with the Holy Spirit (Mk 1:2–4, 7–8; cf. Mt 3:2, 11–12; Lk 3:4–6, 15–18). Mark and the other synoptic gospel writers are telling their readers that while John the Baptist was only a charismatic, Jesus was a charismatic of charismatics.

The synoptic gospels portray Caiaphas and Pontius Pilate as doing exactly what we would have expected them to do, knowing as we do the tragic fate of John the Baptist. We are not surprised, therefore, to learn that Caiaphas moved against Jesus as quietly as he could, lest angry crowds gather; had him brought, as we would have expected, before the high priest's sanhedrin of privy councillors, handpicked for their loyalty to the doctrine of two realms and for their sense of concern for a savage Roman response to any riotous behavior of the crowds, irrespective of its source (Mt 26:3–5, 57–68).

The followers of Jesus thus told it as it had actually happened. *Jesus was brought before the only body that had jurisdiction over those who were charged with breaking or endangering the peace: the high priest's sanhedrin, convoked by him and presided over by him. Despite the hostility they may have harbored for the Scribes-Pharisees, the disciples of Jesus did not report that Jesus had been brought before a* bet din *(boulē), presided over by a teacher of the twofold Law, to be charged with a violation of God's Law. They did not so report because in Jesus' day, all Jews living in Judea and Galilee knew that a charismatic would never be brought before a religious body to stand trial for his life, however deviant his religious teachings.*

The synoptic gospels' accounts are thus historically credible, since they exonerate the *bet din (boulē)* from any role in the trial and crucifixion of Jesus. They bear true witness to the imperial system and its jurisdiction over political issues; to the doctrine of the two realms espoused by the Scribes-Pharisees with respect to the political and religious realms; and to the doctrine of live-and-let-live with respect to divergent forms of Judaism.

The gospels likewise confirm our expectations when they tell us that Jesus was charged with the crime of being the Son of man, the Messiah, the King of the Jews. *For the issue was not a religious issue, even though these images were grounded in the Hebrew Scriptures.* The prophets have envisioned an end of days when all pain and suffering and anguish — even death itself — would be stilled. Isaiah had visualized a King-Messiah, sprung from the stump of Jesse, who would reign in glory. Ezekiel had been addressed by God as the Son of man.

And here lies the tragedy of it all: These images rooted in Scriptures did indeed have political implications. God's Kingdom in was Rome's kingdom out! There was no way Jesus' preaching of God's Kingdom could be disentangled from politics. *The high priest, the high priest's sanhedrin, and the prefect — all were bound to look upon Jesus' teachings as politically dangerous, however free they were of overt political intent.* Jesus' preaching of the coming of God's Kingdom was treasonous in their eyes, as long as that Kingdom had no place for the Roman emperor, his governor, and his prefect-appointed high priest. Only if Jesus were in truth the Son of man and the King-Messiah could the prophetic promise of a messianic age be acknowledged as having been fulfilled in him. But this was dependent on his actually bringing in the Kingdom despite all human efforts to block it. In a word, Jesus would need to prove his claim by living, not by dying.

The synoptic gospels thus confirm that Jesus suffered the fate that would have befallen the charismatic of charismatics we have drawn from Josephus. For the gospels tell us that Jesus was brought before Caiaphas, an appointee of the procurator, and before the high priest's sanhedrin — not before a *bet din (boulē)* of the Scribes-Pharisees — and charged with having claimed to be the Messiah, the King of the Jews. But though the gospels clearly testify that Jesus was tried by a political body, the followers of Jesus may have believed that he had been tried on religious grounds. *For in their eyes, Jesus was the Son of man, God's Anointed — a* divinely, not a humanly crowned King. He was necessarily a fulfillment of God's promise. He was thus, *ipso facto*, a religious, not a political figure.

The high priest and his sanhedrin, however, had no such belief. For them, Jesus was deluded, and his followers were deluded. He was just another would-be messiah whose naive illusions could spark an uprising. It is not surprising, therefore, that Jesus' disciples, who believed him to be the Christ, would attribute religious motives to the high priest and his sanhedrin, since for the disciples, Jesus was exclusively a religious instrument of God, not a political figure. No wonder, then, that the gospels blur the distinction between the political and the religious motivations, of which the high priest and his sanhedrin were always conscious.

The gospels have no surprises for us, either, in their account of the crucifixion or in their attestation of Jesus' resurrection. After all, the *titulus* above the cross spelled out precisely why Jesus was crucified: He was accused of having proclaimed himself "King of the Jews" (Mt 27:37; Mk 15:26; Lk 23:38). *Having been found guilty of treason, was not Jesus fated for crucifixion, the punishment designed especially for those who dared to challenge the authority of Rome?* The *titulus* preserved in the gospels thus leaves us in no doubt as to *why* Jesus was crucified, and *by whom*. And the fact that on either side of him was a revolutionary suffering the same fate evokes for us Rome's determination to eradicate anyone who challenged its rule, whether violent revolutionary or charismatic visionary.

Jesus' last words as reported in the gospels (Mk 15:34) likewise come to us as no surprise. These are words that might very well have sprung to the lips of a charismatic when confronted with the implications of his approaching death. Sharing the belief held by all Jews that the Messiah would bring in the Kingdom of God during his time on earth, a charismatic would realize, when death was imminent, that his messianic hopes had been dashed. Every would-be messiah knew that there was only one test for his claims: Had he, or had he not brought in the Kingdom of God in his lifetime? His own demise, whether by the sword or by the cross, would bring an end to his messianic pretensions. When, therefore, a charismatic found himself at death's door, the frightening thought that God had misled him was bound to well up within him. Twisted with pain beyond endurance, his tragic plight would evoke the psalmist's cry, so expressive of his own feelings of wretched wonder: "My God, my God, why hast thou forsaken me?"

Even the witnessing of Jesus risen from the dead, with the new meaning of the Messiah to which it gave birth, lay deep though dormant in the womb of Pharisaism. After all, the Scribes-Pharisees daily had taught that every righteous individual would some day be rewarded by being raised from the dead. Resurrection was not only possible, but inevitable. This was the very belief the gospels tell us was preached during his lifetime by Jesus himself — the belief that even gained him much praise from scribes who were so pleased with Jesus' artful use of a proof text from Scripture to confute the Sadducees, who did not believe in resurrection (Lk 20:39). The historical Jesus had seeded in the minds of his disciples the absolute certainty that resurrection would someday occur. When, therefore, these disciples saw their master and teacher risen from the dead, their eyes were already open to believe what they saw: Jesus fully alive as the Christ.

We thus find within the gospels a historical Jesus, however subordinated he may be to Jesus the risen Christ, Jesus whose features are identical with those of the charismatic of charismatics drawn from Josephus. As such he is one of those rare spirits who burst into this world, at infrequent intervals, to confront ordinary humans with a life that is out of this world, and a love that is out of this world, and a hope that is out of this world. There are very few who can emulate such a life and such a love. The world closes in and spreads a veil of human frailties over him, leaving, even in the records of his life, only shadows of that life in this world. For had Jesus not been a spirit so rare when he walked among people, would his life not have ended with death, rather than with Life?

What Crucified Jesus?

Throughout the centuries, Jews and Christians have struggled with the gospel legacy. As the only record of Jesus' life, ministry, trial, crucifixion, and attested resurrection, it has been cherished by believing Christians as the story of Moses in the Pentateuch has been cherished by believing Jews. Just as Jesus is reported in the Gospel of Matthew (5:17–18) to have told his followers that he had come not to abolish the Law, but to fulfill it, so Christian ministers have preached to their flocks that not one iota, not one jot of the gospel story will pass away until all that is taught within it is accomplished. So trustworthy indeed was the record for believing Christians that they could offer no more powerful attestation to the veracity of any statement than to affirm it as "gospel" truth.

However, what was gospel truth for Christians was gospel untruth for Jews. Until very recent times, all Jews regarded the gospels as false revelation and looked upon Jesus as a false messiah. For Jews, the gospels seemed to be the source of their tragic experience with Christians, not only throughout the Middle Ages but into modern times as well. Jews found in the gospels the source of the harassments, the humiliations, the pogroms, and the expulsions that have plagued them to this day, the day of the Holocaust. Indeed, there are many Jews who are convinced that anti-Semitism will never pass away until every jot and tittle of the gospel stories is erased. As long as Christians read in the gospels Jesus' denunciation of the Scribes-Pharisees as hypocrites, white-washed tombs, vipers, and sons of hell (Mt 23:13–33); as long as Christians read as gospel truth the cry "Crucify him," shouted by the Jews before Pilate (Mk 15:13; cf. Mt 27:22, Lk 23:21, Jn 19:6), or the insistence of the Jews that Pilate should crucify Jesus because "We have a law, and by that law he ought to die, because he has made himself Son of God" (Jn 19:7); just so long will anti-Semitism be "the cross" that Jews living among Christians will be forced to bear.

Some salvation for Jews seemed to be at hand with the spread of critical biblical scholarship in the nineteenth and twentieth centuries. Non-Jewish scholars, many of them Christians, subjected the gospel accounts to scrutiny and concluded that however much truth they might contain, the gospel stories fall far short of being "the gospel truth." Although some of those non-Jewish scholars may have been anti-Semitic, and most of them looked upon Christianity as a higher stage of religion than Judaism, they nonetheless opened the sluice gates for challenge of the gospels. Indeed, some went so far as to raise the question as to whether a Jesus had actually lived. If the gospels then were not "gospel truth," the harsh anti-Jewish passages in the New Testament could be ascribed to the long, tortuous process by which the earliest traditions about Jesus were amplified, expanded, even negated by the changing needs of the Christian communities as they spread into the gentile world. Jesus' hostility toward Jews that emanates from the gospels could be mitigated by transferring that hostility from Jesus to the gospel writers, writers who had attributed to the historical Jesus the hostile feelings of a later age.

Yet there are empirical facts that cannot be dissolved. Only were we to agree with those few scholars who question whether there was a Jesus, could we dodge the facts that Jesus was tried, crucified, and seen by his followers as resurrected during the prefectorship of Pontius Pilate and the high priesthood of Caiaphas. And if these bare facts are true, then the question of responsibility is certain to be raised again and again. For Jesus was no ordinary man, and his crucifixion and attested resurrection were no ordinary events. His life, his trial, his crucifixion, and the faith in his resurrection launched a religion of enormous profundity and power. For his followers, his life, trial, crucifixion, and rising from the dead were facts before which all other facts must bow. And of all these facts *for faith*, the fact of his resurrection is the fact nonpareil, for without that belief, however visualized, there would have been no Christianity. Had Jesus' life ended with death, his fate would have been no different from that of John the Baptist — no matter how many withered arms he had healed, how many demons he had exorcised, or how many wretched he had comforted. It was only because his life ended in Life that Christianity was endowed with life. But without the claim that he was the Son of man, the King-Messiah, and without the crucifixion that followed from that claim, there could have been no resurrection. So whatever the findings of critical scholarship, a triad of facts — trial, crucifixion, attested resurrection — undergird Christianity.

The collision between Jews and Christians over the facts that revolve around Jesus as the Messiah, and around Jesus' resurrection, is a collision that should no longer be necessary. Although the wish to spread the good news about Jesus and the good news about Judaism is not only understandable but desirable, the likelihood that Jews will ever accept the resurrection as a fact, or that believing Christians will ever be convinced that the resurrection did not occur, is remote indeed. As faith communities, Judaism and Christianity follow paths that diverge.

But when it comes to the trial and crucifixion, collision between Jews and Christians would seem to be inevitable. The gospels have drawn up a bill of indictment, an indictment that is bound to provoke this question: "Who crucified Jesus?" And once the question is thus phrased, we instinctively focus on the persons responsible. And those persons are seen to be, with the exception of Pontius Pilate, Jews. *But should our focus shift from casting blame on persons to casting blame on the time, the place, and the situation, we may be able to view the issue in a new light.* Perhaps it was not *who* one was, but *what* one was, that is the crux. *For it emerges with great clarity, both from Josephus and from the gospels, that the culprit is not the Jews, but the Roman imperial system.* It was the Roman emperor who appointed the governor (prefect or later procurator); it was he who appointed the high priest; and it was the high priest who convoked his privy council. It was the Roman imperial system that exacted harsh tribute. It was the actions of Roman governors that drove the people wild and stirred Judea with convulsive violence. And it was the Roman imperial system that bred revolutionaries and seeded charismatics.

It was the Roman imperial system that was at fault, not the system of Judaism. The Sadducees, Scribes-Pharisees, and Essenes pushed no one to violent revolt, sowed no soil to breed charismatics. Neither biblical writ nor oral Law allowed for the high priest to be elevated into or tossed out of the high priestly office at the whim of puppet king or arrogant governor. Nor was there to be found in either the written or oral Law any provision for the high priest to convoke a sanhedrin for any purpose whatsoever. So far removed in that day were the Sadducees, Scribes-Pharisees, and Essenes from punitive actions against those who might preach aberrant ideas, that the Scribes-Pharisees allowed Sadducean high priests to enter the Holy of Holies on the Day of Atonement, provided they followed Pharisaic procedures. And they allowed Sadducees to preach their "heretical" views, provided they did not act them out publicly.

And insofar as the *bet din (boulē)* of the Pharisees was concerned, it exercised jurisdiction only over those who freely chose to follow the teachings of the Scribes-Pharisees; over the conduct of public worship; and over the liturgical calendar. Not only was the *bet din* a *boulē* and not a sanhedrin, but it was presided over by a *nasi*, not the high priest, and it consisted exclusively of teachers of the twofold Law. Had there been no Roman imperial system, Jesus would have faced the buffetings of strong words, the batterings of skillfully aimed proof texts, and the ridicule of both Sadducees and Scribes-Pharisees, but he would have stood no trial and been affixed to no cross.

And what is striking is that the gospels confirm that no institution of Judaism had anything to do with the trial and crucifixion of Jesus.

We find in the gospels that the high priest was appointed in violation of both the onefold and the twofold Law; that the high priest's sanhedrin convoked by him had no warrant from either the onefold or the twofold Law; that the governor was appointed by Rome, with no sanction from either the onefold or the twofold Law; and that the penalty of crucifixion was nowhere provided for in either the onefold or the twofold Law. One searches in the gospels for the *bet din (boulē)* of the Scribes-Pharisees; for the *nasi* who presided over it; for the procedures spelled out by either the written or the oral Law; or for the specific written or oral law that Jesus had violated — but all in vain.

What we do find is that Joseph of Arimathea, a member of the *boulē* — *not* the sanhedrin — seeks to give Jesus a Jewish burial (Mk 15:43; cf. Lk 23:50); that the Nasi Gamaliel urges the sanhedrin to let Peter and his associates go free (Acts 5:34ff.); that Paul disrupts a sanhedrin when the Pharisees support his belief in resurrection (Acts 23:6–10); and that Jesus is seen risen from the dead, as the core teaching of the Scribes-Pharisees allowed.

It is true that the gospels portray the Scribes-Pharisees as challenging Jesus' claims, and it is true that the Scribes-Pharisees are pictured as cooperating with the authorities, but that is a far cry from having religious jurisdiction. The Scribes-Pharisees confronted the Sadducees with no less angry, harsh, even vituperative words — but words only. And as for the Scribes-Pharisees' cooperation with the authorities, such cooperation was not a result of concern over the religious consequences, but the tragic *political* consequences that could befall the entire Jewish people.

And those political consequences around 30 C.E. could be devastating indeed. Thousands of Jews had lost their lives only a few years before in the aftermath of the pulling down of the golden eagle. Uncounted others had been slain in bloody encounters between religiously motivated prefects and puppet kings. Rulers in Jesus' day knew that prophetic visions were not to be trifled with, just as they had known it in the days of Jeremiah. Frightened by the crowds drawn to Jesus' charisma, and absolutely certain themselves that Jesus was not the Messiah and that the Kingdom of God was not at hand, some Scribes-Pharisees may have voiced their concern for the tragic consequences that might follow, should the crowds get out of hand and go on a rampage. They reasoned, even as Herod Antipas had reasoned, that it was risky to take chances when the stakes were so high. There may have been a sharing of these concerns — concerns that did not arise from the religious content of Jesus' teachings, but from their political implications for the authorities. The Scribes-Pharisees, after all, were committed to *both* the doctrine of live-and-let-live in the religious sphere and the doctrine of the two realms in the political sphere.

It was this doctrine of rendering to Caesar the things that are Caesar's and to God the things that are God's that was the gut issue. It was a doctrine that the Scribes-Pharisees, the Sadducees, and the Essenes all subscribed to because it held out the hope of the preservation of the people of Israel as a people of God. The essence of that designation was *the Covenant* that had been made with God — not with the Roman emperor. And that Covenant called for obedience to God's revealed Law: the written Law, for the Sadducees; the written *and* the oral Law, for the Scribes-Pharisees; the written Law and many other holy writings, for the Essenes. As long as that Covenant could be kept, the issue of political sovereignty was irrelevant. After all, had not the Aaronide priests, for more than two centuries, tended the altar and preserved the Covenant under the imperial sway — first of the Persians, then of Alexander, then of the Ptolemies? If the preservation of God's Covenant required subservience to Roman rule, the payment of tribute to Rome, or helpless inaction as Roman legions repressed unruly crowds, then this was but a small price to pay for spiritual survival. It was not by might or by power, but by the Spirit, that the people of God were to be sustained.

Render to Caesar the things that are Caesar's and to God the things that are God's became no less a fundamental doctrine in early Christianity. Indeed, it was Jesus himself who enunciated it (Mk 12:17; cf. Mt 22:21, Lk 20:25). Jesus did not call on his followers to withhold tribute from Rome, nor did he call on them to overthrow Roman rule by force. God, not man, would usher in the Kingdom. *Jesus, like the Scribes-Pharisees, adhered to the doctrine of the two realms throughout his entire earthly life.* And his earliest followers likewise adhered. For once it became evident that Jesus' second coming was to be delayed, the early Christians pleaded with Rome to extend to them the same religious autonomy it had extended to the Jews. As long as the emperor did not obstruct Christians from believing that their Lord and Master had risen from the dead, and as long as they did not prohibit the peaceful spreading of the good news among the Jews and pagans of the empire, Christians leaders were willing to urge their followers to pray for the welfare of the emperor, even as the Jews up until the Revolt of 66–70 offered sacrifices and prayers for his well-being. The problem for the early Christians was not their unwillingness to make such a compact, but the emperor's unwillingness. When that willingness eventually was forthcoming from Constantine, Christian leaders responded with swiftness and relief.

And the reason? The very same that had motivated the Sadducees, the Scribes-Pharisees, and the Essenes. The Christians were *the* people of Christ. They were the true Israel, a people who, like the people of Israel, were sustained not by might or by power, but by the Spirit of God. They were a people sojourning in this vale of tears while longing for the eternal life that awaited them beyond the grave. Even when the Church became a worldly power, it never ceased preaching the good news that each Christian would find true salvation in the bosom of Christ — not in the bosom of king or emperor.

When therefore the Scribes-Pharisees sought to preserve the people of God by setting aside Caesar's turf for Caesar and God's turf for God, they were pointing the way for the Christians to come. *And just as the Scribes-Pharisees were wary of charismatics and would-be messiahs lest their visions unleash violent consequences, so the Christian leaders proved to be wary when this or that individual announced the second coming of Christ.* There was this difference, however: The Scribes-Pharisees could voice their concern, but they had no coercive power, for the state in Jesus' day was not a "Jewish" state as the states of the Middle Ages were "Christian" states. Only the governor or the governor-appointed high priest and his sanhedrin could judge the potential danger inherent in the teachings of a charismatic, order his arrest, bring him to trial, and render a judgment. And the governor had the right to make the final decision as to that charismatic's fate. From perceived threat until final judgment, political factors alone weighed in the balance. Whatever link there may have been between the Scribes-Pharisees and the political authorities, it was a link that derived from the doctrine of the two realms, not a link that derived from Jesus' "heretical" teachings.

If, then, we are to assess responsibility, we once again find ourselves laying it at the feet of the Roman imperial system, a system which had made the doctrine of the two realms necessary for the survival of Judaism. The times were no ordinary times; the tempests, no ordinary tempests; the bedlam, no ordinary bedlam; the derangements, no ordinary derangements. The chaos that gave birth to a charismatic like Jesus was the very chaos that rendered clarity of judgment impossible. The Roman emperor held the life or death of the Jewish people in the palm of his hand; the governor's sword was always at the ready; the high priest's eyes were always penetrating and his ears always keen; the soldiery was always eager for the slaughter. Jewish religious leaders stumbled dazed from day to day, not knowing what they should do or not do, say or not say, urge or not urge. Everyone was entangled within a web of circumstance from which there was no way out. Whatever one did was wrong; whatever one thought was belied; whatever one hoped for was betrayed. Thrashing about in a world gone berserk, and in abysmal ignorance of the outcome of any decision or action, one did what, in one's human frailty, one thought was the right thing to do. The emperor sought to govern an empire; the governor sought to hold anarchy in check; the high priest sought to hold on to his office; the members of the high priest's sanhedrin sought to spare the people the dangerous consequences of a charismatic's innocent visions of the Kingdom of God, which they themselves believed was not really at hand; the Scribes-Pharisees sought to lift up the eyes of the people from the sufferings of this world to the peace of life eternal; the followers of Jesus sought to make sense of the confusion and terror that enveloped the last days of the life of their Master and Teacher.

It is in this maelstrom of time, place, and circumstance, in tandem with impulse-ridden, tempest-tossed, and blinded sons of men, that the tragedy of Jesus' crucifixion is to be found (see Illus. 14, 15). *It was not the Jewish people who crucified Jesus,* and it was *not the Roman people — it was the imperial system,* a system that victimized the Jews, victimized the Romans, and victimized the Spirit of God.

And Jesus understood. Twisted in agony on the cross — that symbol of imperial Roman cruelty and ruthless disregard of the human spirit — Jesus lifted his head upward toward God and pleaded, "Father, forgive them; for they know not what they do" (Lk 23:34).

CHAPTER TEN

Christianity and Judaism

Hans Küng

Introduction

Jesus is by no means merely an ecclesiastical figure. Sometimes he is even more popular outside the Church than inside it. But, however popular he is, what is immediately evident — when we look at the real Jesus — is his *strangeness*. And historical analysis, however uncongenial, arduous, or even superficial it may seem to some, can help to ensure that this strangeness will not be concealed: that he is not simply fitted into our personal or social requirements, habits, wishful thinking, cherished ideas; that he is not appropriated into the world outlook, moral theories, and legal opinions of Church authorities or theologians, not played down in the Church's rites, creeds, and feasts. The all-important point is to *let Jesus speak without restriction*, whether this is congenial or not. Only in this way can he himself come closer to us in his strangeness. Obviously this does not mean the mechanical repetition of his words, the recital of as many biblical texts as possible, preferably in a long-familiar translation. Nonetheless, an interpretation that is relevant in the proper sense of the word is possible only at a certain distance from him. Strictly speaking, I must at the same time keep at a distance from myself, from my own thoughts, ideas, valuations, and expectations. Only when it becomes clear what he himself wanted, what hopes he brought for the people of his own time, can it also become clear what he himself has to say to the people of the present time, what hopes he can offer for humankind today and for a future world.

The Sufferings of the Past

What is there about this Jesus that seems strange to us? Here we shall be occupied first of all only with a single — but admittedly basic — feature of his nature. Jesus was a human being, a fact that has always been more or less clearly asserted in Christendom. But there has not been the same readiness to admit that Jesus was a *Jewish* human being, a genuine Jew. And for that very reason he was only too often a stranger to both Christians *and* Jews.

Jesus the Jew

Jesus was a Jew, a member of a small, poor, politically powerless nation living at the periphery of the Roman Empire. He was active among Jews and for Jews. His mother Mary, his father Joseph, his family, his followers were Jews. His name was Jewish (Hebrew *Yeshu'a* [see Illus. 1], a later form of *Yehoshu'a* ="Yahweh is salvation"). His Bible, his worship, his prayers were Jewish. In the situation at that time he could not have thought of any proclamation among the gentiles. His message was for the Jewish people, but for this people in its entirety without any exception.

From this basic fact it follows irrevocably that without Judaism there would be no Christianity. The Bible of the early Christians was the "Old Testament." The New Testament Scriptures became part of the Bible only by being appended to the Old. The gospel of Jesus Christ everywhere quite consciously presupposes the Torah and the Prophets. The Christians too hold that the same God of judgment and grace speaks in both Testaments. Christianity does not share this special affinity with Buddhism, Hinduism, or Confucianism, and not even with Islam, despite biblical influences on it. Christianity has this unique relationship only with Judaism; it is a relationship of origin, resulting in numerous common structures and values. At the same time the question also immediately arises, why it was not Judaism — despite its universal monotheism — but the new movement emerging from Jesus (i.e., "Christianity") that became a religion for all humankind.

It is precisely between those who are most closely related that the bitterest hostility can exist. One of the saddest features of the history of the last two thousand years is the hostility that has prevailed almost from the beginning between Jews and Christians. It was mutual, as is so often the case between an old and a new

religious movement. It is true that the young Christian community at first seemed to be no more than a particular religious group
within Early Judaism, professing and practicing a special conception of religion, but incidentally maintaining its connection with
the Jewish national community. But the process of detachment
from the Jewish people was rooted in the profession of faith in
Jesus. It was very quickly set in motion with the formation of
a gentile Christianity free from the Law. The gentile Christians
soon formed the overwhelming majority and their theology lost
any immediate reference to Judaism. After a few decades the process was completed with the destruction of Jerusalem and the end
of Temple worship in 70 C.E. In a dramatic history the Church had
thus been changed — quantitatively and qualitatively — from a
Church of Jews into a Church of Jews and gentiles and finally a
Church of gentiles.

At the same time the Jews who rejected Jesus and the claims of
his earliest followers began to be hostile to the young Church. For
their part they thrust the Christians out of the national community and persecuted them. This rejection is illustrated particularly
by the sufferings of Saul the Pharisee, who, even as the Apostle
Paul, constantly upheld the special election of the people of Israel. It was perhaps already in the second century that the cursing
of "heretics and Nazarenes" was included in the main rabbinical prayer, recited daily (Eighteen Benedictions). In short, at an
early date Jews and Christians were at cross-purposes with each
other. The intellectual discussion was reduced more and more
to wrestling for proof-texts for or against the fulfillment of the
biblical promises in Jesus.

A History of Blood and Tears

The centuries following the third century witness predominantly to a history of blood and tears.[1] Once in control of the

---

[1] The range of Christian-Jewish literature is immense. Worthy of mention are the series
of specialist works (*Judaica, Studia Delitzschiana, Studia Judaica*) and periodicals (*Freiburger
Rundbriefe, Der Zeuge, The Bridge, The Hebrew Christian, Cahiers sioniens*). Particularly important are the collections: *The Christian Approach to the Jew: Addresses Delivered at the
Pre-Evanston Conference at Lake Geneva, Wisconsin* (New York, 1954); H. J. Schultz (ed.),
Juden-Christen-Deutsche (Stuttgart, Olten, Fribourg, 1961); W. D. Marsch and K. Thieme
(eds.), *Christen und Juden: Ihr Gegenüber vom Apostelkonzil bis heute* (Mainz, 1961); D. Gold-
schmidt and H. J. Kraus (eds.), *Der ungekündigte Bund: Neue Begegnung von Juden und
christlicher Gemeinde* (Stuttgart, 1962); O. Betz, M. Hengel, and P. Schmidt (eds.), *Abraham
unser Vater: Juden und Christen im Gespräch über die Bibel*, Festschrift for O. Michel (Ley-

state, Christians forgot too quickly the commitments they had made to mercy and toleration when they were persecuted by Jews and gentiles. Christian hostility to Jews was not at first racial, but religious. It would be more correct on the whole to speak of anti-Judaism than of anti-Semitism (for others, notably Arabs, too, are Semites). In the Imperial Constantinian Church, what had been pre-Christian, pagan anti-Judaism was given a "Christian" stamp. And although in subsequent times there were also examples of

den, Cologne, 1963); W. P. Eckert and E. L. Ehrlich (eds.), *Judenhass — Schuld der Christen?* *Versuch eines Gesprächs* (Essen, 1964); K. T. Hargrove (ed.), *The Star and the Cross: Essays on Jewish-Christian Relations* (Milwaukee, 1966); K. H. Rengstorf and S. von Kortzfleisch (eds.), *Kirche und Synagoge: Handbuch zur Geschichte von Christen und Juden. Darstellung mit Quellen,* 2 vols. (Stuttgart, 1968, 1970); W. Strolz (ed.), *Jüdische Hoffnungskraft und christlicher Glaube* (Freiburg, Basel, Vienna, 1971); C. Thoma (ed.), *Judentum und Kirche: Volk Gottes* (Zürich, Einsiedeln, Cologne, 1974). The October issue of *Concilium,* 1974 (no. 10, vol. 8) is devoted to the theme of Christians and Jews, with an introduction by H. Küng and parallel contributions from Jews and Christians: L. Jacobs and W. D. Davies; J. Heinemann and C. Thoma; R. Gradwohl and P. Fiedler; S. Sandmel and J. Lochman; A. Neher and A. T. Davies; J. J. Petuchowski and J. Moltmann; D. Flusser and B. Dupuy; U. Tal and K. Hruby.

Recent works on the problems: K. Barth, *Church Dogmatics* (Edinburgh, New York, 1957, 1961, 1962), vol. 2.2, §34, pp. 195–305; vol. 3.3, pp. 210–28; vol. 4.3, pp. 876–78; C. Journet, *Destinées d'Israël* (Paris, 1944); H. Schmidt, *Die Judenfrage und die christliche Kirche in Deutschland* (Stuttgart, 1947); J. M. Oesterreicher, *The Apostolate to the Jews* (New York, 1948), J. Jocz, *The Jewish People and Jesus Christ* (London, 1949; Naperville, 1954); *A Theology of Election: Israel and the Church* (London, 1958); P. Démann, *La catéchèse chrétienne et le peuple de la Bible* (Paris, 1952); C. Dix, *Jew and Greek* (London, 1953); W. Maurer, *Kirche und Synagoge: Motive und Formen der Auseinandersetzung der Kirche mit dem Judentum im Laufe der Geschichte* (Stuttgart, 1953); L. Goppelt, *Christentum und Judentum im 1. und 2. Jahrhundert* (Gütersloh, 1954); G. Hedenquist et al., *The Church and the Jewish People* (London, Edinburgh, 1954); F. Lovsky, *Antisémitisme et mystère d'Israël* (Paris, 1955); E. Sterling, *Er ist wie Du: Aus der Frühgeschichte des Antisemitismus* (Munich, 1956); H. U. von Balthasar, *Einsame Zwiesprache: M. Buber und das Christentum* (Cologne, Olten 1958); H. Gollwitzer, *Israel — und wir* (Berlin, 1958); G. Jasper, *Stimmen aus dem neureligiösen Judentum in seiner Stellung zum Christentum und zu Jesus* (Hamburg, 1958); F. W. Foerster, *Jews — A Christian View* (New York, 1962); W. Sulzbach, *Die zwei Wurzeln und Formen des Judenhasses* (Stuttgart, 1959); E. Peterson, *Frühkirche, Judentum und Gnosis* (Freiburg, 1959); M. Barth, *Israel and the Church* (Richmond, 1969); K. Kupische, *Das Volk der Geschichte* (Berlin, 1960); H. Diem, *Das Rätsel des Antisemitismus* (Munich, 1960); D. Judant, *Les deux Israël* (Paris, 1960); *Israel en de Kerk* (A study commissioned by the general synod of the Dutch Reformed Church) (Gravenage, 1959; German translation: *Israel und die Kirche* [Zürich, 1961]); G. Dellinger, *Die Juden im Catechismus Romanus* (Munich, 1963); G. Baum, *Die Juden und das Evangelium* (Einsiedeln, 1963); W. Seiferth, *Synagoge und Kirche im Mittelalter* (Munich, 1964); Augustine Cardinal Bea, *Die Kirche und das jüdische Volk* (Freiburg, 1966); F.-W. Marquardt, *Die Entdeckung des Judentums für die christliche Theologie. Israel im Denken Karl Barths* (Munich, 1967); C. Thoma, *Kirche aus Juden und Heiden* (Vienna, 1970); J. Brosseder, *Luthers Stellung zu den Juden im Spiegel seiner Interpreten* (Munich, 1972); P. E. Lapide, *Ökumene aus Christen und Juden* (Neukirchen/Vluyn, 1972). Cf. also the numerous manuals and books on the history of the Jews and the works of Jewish authors outstanding for their interpretation of the Jewish position (L. Baeck, S. Ben-Chorin, M. Buber, H. Cohen, E. L. Ehrlich, A. Gilbert, J. Klausner, F. Rosenzweig, H. J. Schoeps, P. Winter); finally, the articles on Judaism and Judaeo-Christianity in the encyclopedias. On the whole question of the relationship between the Church and the Jews see Küng, *The Church,* CI, 1 and 4.

fruitful collaboration between Christians and Jews, the situation of the Jews became increasingly difficult, particularly after the high Middle Ages. Jews were slaughtered in Western Europe during the first three Crusades and Jews in Palestine were exterminated. Three hundred Jewish communities were destroyed in the German Empire from 1348 to 1349; Jews were expelled from England (1290), France (1394), Spain (1492), and Portugal (1497). Later came the horrifyingly virulent anti-Jewish speeches of the elderly Luther. Persecution of Jews continued after the Reformation, there were pogroms in Eastern Europe, and so on. It must be admitted that, during these periods, the Church probably slew more martyrs than it produced. All of this anti-Judaism is incomprehensible to the modern Christian.

It was not the Reformation, but humanism (Reuchlin, Scaliger), then pietism (Zinzendorf), and particularly the tolerance of the Enlightenment (with its declarations of human rights in the United States and in the French Revolution) that prepared the way for change and, up to a point, also brought it about. The complete assimilation of European Jews at the time of their emancipation admittedly did not entirely succeed, but came nearest to doing so in America. It would be presumptuous to attempt to trace here the terrible history over many centuries of the suffering and death of the Jewish people, culminating in the Nazi mass insanity and mass murder which claimed a third of all Jewry as its victims. The word "deplore" in the Declaration of the Second Vatican Council — like a corresponding declaration of the World Council of Churches,[2] more a beginning than an end — sounded terribly weak and vague after all these horrors. Even this statement was nearly prevented by the Roman Curia, quick to react to Hochhuth's problem-charged novel, *The Deputy*, but still too concerned with political opportunism and persistent anti-Jewish feeling to give diplomatic recognition to the State of Israel.

In view of this situation — still far from being resolved — and of a veiled anti-Judaism in Rome and Moscow, unfortunately also in New York and elsewhere, it must be clearly stated that Nazi anti-Judaism was the work of godless, anti-Christian criminals. But Nazi anti-Judaism would not have been possible without the almost two thousand years' pre-history of "Christian" anti-Judaism;

---

[2]*Memorandum of the First Assembly of the World Council of Churches on the Christian Approach to the Jews* (Amsterdam, 1948); since then the World Council has repeatedly expressed its views on the Jewish question.

moreover, this deep-seated anti-Judaism prevented Christians in Germany from organizing a committed and energetic resistance on a broad front.

Although some Christians were also persecuted and others — in Holland, France, and Denmark — gave effective help to Jews, it must be noted in order to define more precisely the question of guilt that none of the Nazi anti-Jewish measures were new. Special distinguishing clothing, exclusion from professions, prohibition of mixed marriages, expropriation, expulsion, concentration camps, massacres, burnings — all these things existed in what were called the "Christian" Middle Ages (see, for example, the measures adopted by the great Fourth Lateran Council in 1215) and at the time of the "Christian" Reformation. Only the racial argument was new, prepared by the French Count Arthur Gobineau and the British-born Houston Stewart Chamberlain and put into practice in Nazi Germany with horrifyingly thorough organization, technical perfection, and a dreadful industrialization of murder. After Auschwitz there can be no more excuses. Christendom cannot avoid a clear admission of its guilt.

Future Possibilities

Must the sufferings of the past, however, be the sufferings of the future? The awareness that started with the Enlightenment and had its effect particularly in the United States in the nineteenth century has meanwhile stamped itself on the whole of Christendom.

Increasing Understanding

The most recent, most terrible catastrophe to affect the Jewish people and the reemergence of the State of Israel — which Christians had not expected and which is the most important event in Jewish history since the destruction of Jerusalem and the Temple — have shaken anti-Jewish "Christian" theology. Pseudotheology had reinterpreted the Old Testament salvation history of the Jewish people as a New Testament history of a curse on the Jewish people, overlooking the permanent election of this people asserted by Paul and relating it exclusively to Christians as the "new Israel." With the Second Vatican Council the new awareness also came to prevail in the Catholic Church.[3] The idea of a collective guilt on the part of the Jewish people of that time or even of the present in regard to the death of Jesus was expressly rejected by the council. No one dares any longer to take seriously the old widespread prejudices that Jews are "money-men," "poisoners of wells," "Christ killers," "deicides," "cursed and condemned to dispersion."

It is easier now to perceive the psychological motives operative in anti-Judaism. Most noteworthy are the following: group hostility, fear of being the odd man out, search for scapegoats, contrary ideals, personality structure disturbance, and mass emotionalism.

The old excuses offered shamefacedly or shamelessly have become obsolete: "The Jews too have made mistakes"; "We must understand the spirit of the age in which these things happened"; "The Church itself was not involved"; "One had to choose the lesser evil."

We are beginning therefore to recognize that the Jews are in many respects an enigmatic community linked by a common destiny and with an amazing power of endurance: a race, a single-language global community, a religious community, a state, a nation, and yet not really any of these. They are a community linked by a common destiny, involved in a religious mystery in which this "people of God" is acknowledged by devout Jews and devout Christians alike to have a special vocation among the peoples of the world. Christians must at least take note of the fact that from this perspective — despite the cruel sacrifices involved for Arabs whose ancestors have lived in Palestine for centuries — the movement for their return to their "promised land" has a religious significance for many Jews.

Whatever Christians of Arab descent (for whom one must have sympathy) may think about the State of Israel, a Church which — as so often in the past — preaches love and sows hatred, proclaims life and yet prepares death, cannot invoke Jesus of Nazareth to support its attitudes. *Jesus was a Jew and all anti-Judaism is a betrayal of Jesus himself.* The Church has stood too often between Jesus and Israel. It prevented Israel from recognizing Jesus. It is

---

[3] Second Vatican Council, *Declaration on the Relationship of the Church to Non-Christian Religions*, 1965. A declaration of the French Bishops' Committee for relations with Judaism on the position of Christians in regard to Judaism (1973) goes much further. It was published with a commentary by Kurt Hruby in *Judaica* 29 (1973) 44–70.

high time for Christendom not merely to preach "conversion" to the Jews, but to be "converted" itself: to the *encounter* which has scarcely begun, to a not merely humanitarian but *theological discussion* with Jews, which might be an aid not merely to a "mission" or capitulation, but to understanding, mutual assistance, and collaboration.

Indirectly, perhaps, such an encounter might even help increase understanding between Jews and Christians on the one hand and Muslims on the other, for we cannot ignore the fact that Muslims in virtue of their origin are closely linked with both Jews and Christians through a common belief in God the Creator and in the resurrection of the dead with reference to Abraham and Jesus, both of whom have an important place in the Koran. After all that has happened, the conditions are more favorable than they have ever been for a genuine discussion between Christians and Jews, to whom Christianity, Islam, and humankind as a whole owe the incomparable gift of strict monotheistic belief. These conditions must include an unconditional acknowledgment of the religious autonomy of the undoubtedly rigorous and exacting Jewish partner.

A. Long before Hitler's time, in *Christendom* as a whole and among exegetes, particularly in German-speaking and Anglo-Saxon countries, a new openmindedness had been established toward the Old Testament in its autonomy and its agreement with the New Testament. The importance of the rabbinical commentators for the understanding of the New Testament has likewise been recognized. We have begun to see that there are powerful aspects of Hebrew thought that are fully comparable to that of the Greek and hellenistic world: greater historical dynamism; total alignment; devout and joyous acceptance of the world, the body, and life; hunger and thirst for justice; and orientation to the future Kingdom of God. All this has helped to overcome the Neo-Platonic, Neo-Aristotelian, Scholastic, and Neo-Scholastic incrustation of Christianity. For the official Catholic Church the declaration of Vatican II on the Jews became "the discovery or rediscovery of Judaism and the Jews both in their intrinsic value and in their meaning for the Church" (J. Oesterreicher).[4]

B. The mental situation of *Judaism* has likewise changed very much, particularly since the restoration of the State of Israel: the

---

[4]J. Oesterreicher, *The Rediscovery of Judaism* (South Orange, N.J., 1971).

decreasing influence of casuistic legalist piety, especially among the younger generation, and the increasing importance of the Old Testament by comparison with the former universal validity of the Talmud. What is most typically Jewish has been brought home to Christians by the great minds of Jewry in this century: women like Simone Weil and Edith Stein; men like Hermann Cohen, Martin Buber, Franz Rosenzweig, Leo Baeck, Max Brod, Hans Joachim Schoeps; and more indirectly from Sigmund Freud, Albert Einstein, Franz Kafka, and Ernst Bloch. And thus the way has been prepared today for a common investigation by Jewish and Christian scholars both of the Old Testament and the rabbinical works *and*, up to a point, of the New Testament (as a testimony also of the history of the Jewish faith). This affinity has also been made clear in a more lively and creative development in worship on both sides, an affinity that goes far beyond literary criticism and philology. There is no doubt about the fact that Jews by virtue of their Judaism can discover dimensions of the New Testament that often enough escape the Christian. All things considered, despite numerous inhibitions and difficulties, there is a growing awareness of a common Jewish-Christian *basis* that is not merely humanitarian but *theological*. Jews too are asking today for "a Jewish theology of Christianity and a Christian theology of Judaism" (J. Petuchowski).[5]

The theological discussion between Christians and Jews, however, has proved to be infinitely *more difficult* than that between separated Christians, who at least have a common basis in the Bible. But the conflict between Christians and Jews cuts right across the Bible and splits it into two Testaments, of which the former prefer the "New" and the latter the "Old." And can we ever overlook the real point of the controversy? The very person who seems to unite Jews and Christians also separates them abysmally: the Jew Jesus of Nazareth. Can Jews and Christians ever reach agreement about him? It seems that more is involved here than "two ways of faith" (M. Buber). For Jews to give up their unbelief in regard to Jesus seems just as unlikely as for Christians to cease to believe in Jesus. For then the Jews would no longer be Jews and the Christians no longer Christians.

---

[5] J. J. Petuchowski, in an introduction to the German translation of Oesterreicher's book, *Die Wiederentdeckung des Judentums durch die Kirche* (Meitingen, Freising, 1971) p. 34.

Discussion about Jesus?

The dispute seems hopeless. Is there really any point in Jews and Christians discussing Jesus of Nazareth? But the question could be put in another way. Would there not be advantages to both sides if the Christian readiness for understanding were met on the Jewish side with a movement to break down mistrust, skepticism, and rancor toward the figure of Jesus and instead to arrive at a more historical-objective judgment, to spread genuine understanding and perhaps even regard for his person? Immense progress has been made in recent times. A long list could be produced of authors and their books on Jesus of Nazareth published recently in the State of Israel.[6] There are undoubtedly numerous Jews who would at least accept the "Jesus of culture" even though they reject the "Jesus of religion."[7] The *cultural* significance of Jesus is therefore asserted. And it is in fact very difficult for a modern Jew to share fully in Western cultural life without constantly encountering Jesus, even if it is only in the great works of Bach, Handel, Mozart, Beethoven, Bruckner, and of Western art as a whole.

This, however, still leaves open the question of the *religious* significance of Jesus. If today the religious significance of Judaism is being subjected by Christians to a new appraisal, should not Jews on the other hand face up to the question of the religious significance of Jesus? Even in the nineteenth century there was a considerable Jewish tradition that attempted to take Jesus seriously, as a genuine Jew, even as a great witness of Jewish faith. And at the turn of the century, Max Nordau, the faithful collaborator of Theodor Herzl, the founder of the Zionist movement, wrote: "Jesus is the soul of our soul, as he is flesh of our flesh. Who then would want to exclude him from the Jewish people?"[8]

In the first half of the present century there followed the first thorough studies of the figure of Jesus on the Jewish side: the var-

---

[6]See P. E. Lapide, *Jesus in Israel* (Gladbeck, 1970); W. P. Eckert, "Jesus und das heutige Judentum" in F. J. Schierse (ed.), *Jesus von Nazareth* (Mainz, 1972) pp. 52–72. See also the work by G. Lindeskog, *Die Jesusfrage im neuzeitlichen Judentum* (reprinted Darmstadt, 1974; especially the postscript to this reprint); R. Gradwohl, "Das neue Jesus-Verständnis bei jüdischen Denkern der Gegenwart" in *FZPT* 20 (1973) 306–23. A survey of the image of Jesus in Jewry over the ages is given by Schalom Ben-Chorin in *Jesus im Judentum* (Wuppertal, 1970).

[7]S. Sandmel, *We Jews and Jesus* (New York, 1965) p. 112; see the same author, *A Jewish Understanding of the New Testament* (Cincinnati, 1956).

[8]Cited as in S. Ben-Chorin, *Bruder Jesus: Der Nazarener in jüdischer Sicht* (Munich, 1967).

ious publications of Claude G. Montefiore[9] and especially Joseph Klausner's work,[10] certainly the best-known book on Jesus by a Jew and one which, as a result of its use of material from Talmud and Midrash, can be described as the beginning of the modern Hebrew quest for the historical Jesus. It was the important Jewish thinker Martin Buber who first described Jesus as the "elder brother," to whom "belongs an important place in Israel's history of faith," who "cannot be fitted into any of the usual categories."[11] The Jewish scholar David Flusser draws attention to the fact that in Jesus we encounter a real, flesh-and-blood Jew talking to Jews: from Jesus a Jew can learn how to pray, fast, love his neighbor, and comprehend the meaning of the Sabbath, God's Kingdom, and the judgment.[12] Schalom Ben-Chorin's book *Brother Jesus: The Nazarene from the Jewish Viewpoint* develops along such lines: "Jesus is certainly a central figure of Jewish history and the history of the Jewish faith, but he is also a part of our present and future, no less than the prophets of the Hebrew Bible whom we can also see not merely in the light of the past."[13]

Here, however, the *limit* to a Jewish acknowledgment of Jesus the Jew also becomes clear. For all his understanding of the figure of Jesus, Schalom Ben-Chorin writes in the same book, "I feel this brotherly hand which grasps mine, so that I can follow him," but adds, "It is *not* the hand of the Messiah, this hand marked with scars. It is certainly not a *divine*, but a *human* hand in the lines of which is engraved the most profound suffering.... The faith of Jesus unites us, but faith in Jesus divides us."[14] But does not this very hand with its wounds call for an explanation, a deeper exploration?

It is not impossible that in the future more Jews will come, with a struggle, to acknowledge Jesus as a great Jew and witness of faith, and perhaps even as a great prophet or teacher of Israel. The gospels rightly have a unique fascination for numerous Jews. They show to the Jew many possibilities lying within the Jewish faith itself. And cannot Jesus be understood almost as a *personal symbol*

---

[9] C. G. Montefiore, *The Synoptic Gospels* (London, 1927 [2nd ed.]; revised edition, 2 vols., New York, 1968).

[10] J. Klausner, *Jesus of Nazareth* (originally in Hebrew; London, 1925).

[11] M. Buber, *Zwei Glaubensweisen* (Zürich, 1950) p. 11.

[12] D. Flusser, "In What Sense Can Jesus Be a Question for Jews?" *Concilium* 10.8 (1974); Flusser, *Jesus* (New York, 1969).

[13] S. Ben-Chorin, *Bruder Jesus: Der Nazarener in jüdischer Sicht*, p. 14.

[14] Ben-Chorin, *Bruder Jesus*, p. 12.

of Jewish history? The Jew Marc Chagall constantly depicted the sufferings of his people in the figure of the Crucified. We might see it in this way: Does not the history of this people with its God, this people of tears with life, of lamentation with confidence, culminate in this one figure, Jesus? Is not his history a striking sign of the crucified and risen Israel?

In all this, however, there remains the one disturbing question: Who is Jesus? More than a prophet? More than the Law? Is he even the Messiah? A Messiah crucified in the name of the Law? Must the discussion come to a complete end at this point? Here perhaps the Jew particularly could help the Christian to conduct the *discussion* on Jesus afresh, as we suggested, not from above, but *from below*. This would mean that we Christians too should strive to consider Jesus from the standpoint of his Jewish contemporaries. Even his Jewish disciples had to start out first of all from Jesus of Nazareth as man and Jew and not from someone who was already obviously the Messiah or even the Son of God. It was only in this way that they could raise at all the question of the relationship of Jesus to God. And for them, even later, this relationship did not consist of a simple identification with God, which might have meant that Jesus was God the Father. Perhaps Jews could also help us Christians to understand better those central New Testament statements on Jesus and particularly his honorific titles, which have an obvious background in Early Judaism.

Be that as it may, if we start out from Jesus of Nazareth as man and Jew, we shall be able to go *a good part of the way together* with unbiased Jews like my distinguished colleagues in this volume. And it may be that in the end of our journey together, Jesus will appear remarkably different from what the long Jewish-Christian disputes have led us to expect. The only plea we are making at the moment is once more for openmindedness which does not permit the unavoidable preconception — whether Christian or Jewish — to become a prejudgment. We are not asking for neutrality but certainly for objectivity in the service of the truth. At a time of fundamental reorientation of the relationship between Christians and Jews, we shall have to remain open to all future possibilities.

Annotated Bibliography

James H. Charlesworth

In order to draw attention to the vast literature now available, I have annotated the following bibliography. It is selected and focused on major publications, especially on books published since 1980. Some classics are listed that do not deserve to be called "Jesus research"; they are included because of their prominence. For reviews of scholarly publications on Jesus from 1965 through 1980 the reader is directed to W. G. Kümmel's articles in *Theologische Rundschau* 40 (1975) 289–336; 41 (1976/1977) 198–258, 295–363; 43 (1978) 105–61, 232–65; 45 (1980) 48–84, 293–337.

Borg, M. J. *Conflict, Holiness & Politics in the Teachings of Jesus*. Studies in the Bible and Early Christianity 5. New York, Toronto, 1984. An impressively penetrating probe into the world of pre-70 Palestine, with an astute demonstration of the importance of holiness in Early Judaism and the necessary link between Jesus' powerful movement and politics.

Bruce, F. F. *The Hard Sayings of Jesus* (The Jesus Library). London, 1983. A solid and honest study of Jesus' harsh sayings by one of the finest classically-trained NT specialists.

Bruce, F. F. *Jesus and Christian Origins Outside the New Testament*. Grand Rapids, Mich., 1974, 1984. An authoritative introduction to references to Jesus outside the canon.

Carmody, D. L., and J. T. Carmody. *Jesus: An Introduction*. Belmont, Calif., 1987. A wide-ranging introduction to Jesus, and a comparison of him with others like Moses, Buddha, Confucius, and Muhammad; for college classes.

Charlesworth, J. H. "The Historical Jesus in Light of Writings Contemporaneous with Him," *Aufstieg und Niedergang der Römischen Welt*

II, 25 (1982) 2, pp. 451–76. A demonstration of Jesus' Jewishness by highlighting the appearance of the concept "the Kingdom of God" in early Jewish documents.

Charlesworth, J. H. "Jesus and Jehohanan: An Archaeological Note on Crucifixion," *ExpT* 84 (1973) 147–50. A study of the crucifixion of Jesus in light of the archaeological insights derived from the remains of a man crucified in, or near, Jerusalem before 70.

Charlesworth, J. H. *Jesus within Judaism.* Garden City, New York, 1988. An attempt to assess the reasons for the emergence of Jesus research, and to posit Jesus within Judaism.

Charlesworth, J. H. "Research on the Historical Jesus," *Proceedings of the Irish Biblical Association* 9 (1985) 19–37. Clarification of the new trend to take seriously the fruitfulness of Jesus research.

Cornfeld, G. *The Historical Jesus: A Scholarly View of the Man and His World.* New York, London, 1982. The best work on the new insights from archaeology on the Jesus of history; marred somewhat by a failure to observe the redactional quality of the gospels.

Crossan, J. D. *In Fragments: The Aphorisms of Jesus.* New York, Cambridge, 1983. Dedicated to Jesus research, Crossan examines Jesus' brief wisdom sayings and develops a method for distinguishing between authentic and inauthentic aphorisms.

Dunn, J. D. G. *The Evidence for Jesus.* Philadelphia, 1985 (actually the publication date is "March 10, 1986"). An insightful book, focused on replying to the 1984 British TV series "Jesus: The Evidence." Addressed to a lay audience, this work is not a study of the historical Jesus. It is a solid, at times brilliant, somewhat conservative discussion that has one major thrust: to show Christians how to move from reading the gospels incorrectly so that the original purpose and intent of the evangelists can be discerned.

Dunn, J. D. G. *Jesus and the Spirit: A Study of the Religious and Charismatic Experience of Jesus and the First Christians as Reflected in the New Testament.* Philadelphia, 1975. Dunn, who is rapidly becoming a widely influential thinker, writes an informed book, which *inter alia* demonstrates how Jesus spoke ecstatically and how early Christian prophets spoke as if they were Jesus, creating sayings of Jesus.

Flusser, D. *Die rabbinischen Gleichnisse und der Gleichniserzähler Jesus. 1. Teil: Das Wesen der Gleichnisse.* Judaica et Christiana 4. Bern, 1981. A significant corrective to NT scholars who tend to read Jesus' parables as if this literary form were not found in Early Judaism.

Gerhardsson, G. *The Origins of the Gospel Traditions.* Philadelphia, 1979. Gerhardsson further develops his well-known position, that Jesus' sayings were studied and preserved by a group of Jews — the *collegium* of "the Twelve " — who memorized his teachings. His reflections are informed and should be carefully studied. He allows for the creative character of early Christian teaching and points out some major flaws in Form criticism. Nevertheless, his arguments are sometimes forced, and he concentrates almost solely on Rabbinics.

Goppelt, L. *Theology of the New Testament*, translated by J. Alsup, edited by J. Roloff. 2 vols. Grand Rapids, Mich., 1981, 1982. See especially vol. 1, subtitled *The Ministry of Jesus in Its Theological Significance*. A major corrective to Bultmann's claim that Jesus was a presupposition of NT theology; weak on the historical background of Early Christianity, but full of significant theological insights.

Green, M. *The Empty Cross of Jesus* (The Jesus Library). Downers Grove, Ill., 1984. A confessional and theological reflection on the death of Jesus.

Griffiths, M. *The Example of Jesus* (The Jesus Library). Downers Grove, Ill., 1985. Designed for spiritual reflection.

Gruenler, R. G. *New Approaches to Jesus and the Gospels: A Phenomenological and Exegetical Study of Synoptic Christology*. Grand Rapids, Mich., 1982. Gruenler attempts to demonstrate how phenomenology (as developed by Wittgenstein, Polanyi, and Marcel) adds a necessary sensitivity and perspective to the study of Jesus and Christian Origins. As I attempted to show in the 1960s, one of the most important phenomenologists for New Testament research is Merleau-Ponty.

Hagner, D. A. *The Jewish Reclamation of Jesus: An Analysis and Critique of the Modern Jewish Study of Jesus*. Grand Rapids, Mich., 1984. A reliable discussion of why and how Jewish scholars today have taken up the study of Jesus of Nazareth.

Harnisch, W. (editor). *Gleichnisse Jesu: Positionen der Auslegung von Adolf Jülicher bis zur Formgeschichte* (Wege der Forschung 366). Darmstadt, 1982. Nineteen major articles on Jesus' parables are reprinted.

Harvey, A. E. *Jesus and the Constraints of History*. Philadelphia, 1982. Harvey perceptively sees and illustrates that great thinkers, like Jesus, must wed their message to the norms and constraints of the particular social, historical, and linguistic situation.

Hengel, M. *Between Jesus and Paul: Studies in the Earliest History of Christianity*, translated by J. Bowden. London, 1983. One of the most influential scholars today, Hengel contends that Jesus was eschatologically enthusiastic, was convinced of his messianic relationship with God, and was aware that God's Kingdom was dawning with his activity.

Hengel, M. *The Charismatic Leader and his Followers*, translated by J. C. G. Greig (Studies of the New Testament and its World). Edinburgh, 1981. An unusually informed work; Hengel demonstrates that Jesus was neither a rabbi nor an eschatological prophet: "Jesus' 'charisma' breaks through the possibilities of categorization in terms of the phenomenology of religion. The very uniqueness of the way in which Jesus called individuals to 'follow after' him is an expression of this underivable 'messianic' authority" (p. 87).

Hengel, M. *Crucifixion: In the Ancient World and the Folly of the Message of the Cross*, translated by J. Bowden. London, 1977. A significant study of the manner of Jesus' execution.

Higgins, A. J. B. *The Son of Man in the Teaching of Jesus* (SNTS Monograph Series 39). Cambridge, 1980. Higgins' thesis is that Jesus' authentic "Son of man" sayings are those that reflect his expectation of being vindicated after death through his exaltation before God in order to fulfill the functions of the Son of man, specifically to judge and to bring salvation.

Hoffmann, R. J. *Jesus Outside the Gospels*. New York, 1984. Claiming that the intracanonical gospels are "the missionary propaganda of the cult of Christ" (p. 7), Hoffmann turns to extracanonical references to Jesus. Unfortunately much of this book is reactionary, even polemical, against the consensus of modern scholars (and of Christianity); the following statement is preposterous: "We cannot be certain whether he [Jesus] was 'crucified *under* Pontius Pilate,' . . . or was stoned as a heretic by his fellow Jews . . . " (pp. 127–28).

Jonsson, J. *Humour and Irony in the New Testament: Illuminated by Parallels in Talmud and Midrash*, with a foreword by K. Stendahl (BZRG 28). Leiden, 1985. A significant study of Jesus' use of humor; see especially pp. 166–99.

Kretz, L. *Witz, Humor und Ironie bei Jesus*. Freiburg im Breisgau, 1982 (2nd edition). An informative insight into Jesus' use of humor.

Lapide, P., and U. Luz. *Jesus in Two Perspectives*, translated by L. W. Denef. Minneapolis, 1985. Lapide, a Jew, posits three arguments: Jesus did not claim to be the Messiah, he was not rejected by Israel but was warmly received by the majority of Jews, and he did not reject Israel. Luz, the Christian, tends to agree with Lapide's conclusions; but he wisely points out that the main insightful questions that are important for "a Jewish-Christian discussion concerning Jesus are not raised . . . " (p. 123). He astutely points out that such a discussion cannot begin in a vacuum; and he sees far better than Lapide the diversity and complexity of such issues in first-century Palestine.

Leroy, H. *Jesus: Überlieferung und Deutung* (Erträge der Forschung 95). Darmstadt, 1978. A solid review of research on the quest for the historical Jesus, from Schweitzer through the late 1970s.

Lindars, B. *Jesus Son of Man: A Fresh Examination of the Son of Man Sayings in the Gospels in the Light of Recent Research.* Grand Rapids, Mich., 1983. Lindars, Rylands Professor of Biblical Criticism and Exegesis at Manchester University, contends that Jesus used "Son of man" to identify himself with humanity. His reflections are important and informed: they do help us understand a dimension in some of Jesus' authentic Son of man sayings, but specialists have now shown that the Parables of Enoch (1 Enoch 37–71) are Jewish and pre-70. Hence, the Son of man as a heavenly, apocalyptic figure was part of Jewish theology in Jesus' time.

Mackey, J. P. *Jesus the Man and the Myth: A Contemporary Christology.* 1979, 1985. A gifted theologian addresses to a wide audience his assessment of "the central problems and the tentative solutions which have accrued in recent times to the perennial quest for the spirit of Jesus" (p. 2).

Maier, J. *Jesus von Nazareth in der Talmudischen Überlieferung* (Erträge der Forschung 82). Darmstadt, 1978. This book is one of the major studies of Jesus in light of the Talmud, by a distinguished and careful scholar. Maier rightly claims in light of early Jewish traditions that the distinction between "the historical Jesus" and the "proclaimed Christ" is based on false dichotomies. He also perceptively argues that *Antiquities* 18 contains a Christian reworking of an authentic reference to Jesus by Josephus. But, see the major corrections to Maier's book by D. Goldenberg, "Once More: Jesus in the Talmud," *The Jewish Quarterly Review* 73 (1982) 78–86.

Marsh, J. *Jesus in His Lifetime.* London, 1981. An attempt to tell with integrity the story of Jesus "to the typical 'twentieth-century man.' "

Marxsen, W. *The Beginnings of Christology,* translated by P. J. Achtemeier and L. Nieting, with an introduction by J. Reumann, Philadelphia, 1979. Brilliantly and powerfully, Marxsen argues (contra Bultmann, but consonant with Moule) that "Jesus is always the one who is proclaimed — even when he himself appears as the proclaimer" (p. 81). For Marxsen the Palestinian Jesus Movement (my term) was shaped by a Christ kerygma which is profoundly post-Easter, and a Jesus kerygma which is definitely pre-Easter.

Meyer, B. F. *The Aims of Jesus.* London, 1979. This Roman Catholic scholar contends that a new approach to the historical Jesus is fruitful, and that Jesus intended to restore Israel. Jesus' focal point was the proclamation of the imminence of God's Reign, which "meant the imminent restoration of Israel . . . " (p. 221).

Moule, C. F. D. *The Origin of Christology.* Cambridge, New York, 1977. In this important work Moule argues that Christology developed out of authentic Jesus traditions, and that the genesis of Christology is found in "the impact made by him on those who knew him during his ministry . . . and the impact made by him after the resurrection . . ." (p. 5). Christology interpenetrates Jesus research.

Neill, S. *The Supremacy of Jesus* (The Jesus Library). Downers Grove, Ill., 1984. The focus is on Jesus as a historic figure; confessional but informed.

O'Neill, J. C. *Messiah: Six Lectures on the Ministry of Jesus: The Cunningham Lectures 1975–76.* Cambridge, 1980, 1984. O'Neill is engaged in Jesus research, and his thoughts are insightful and refreshingly independent.

Pelikan, J. *Jesus through the Centuries: His Place in the History of Culture.* New Haven, London, 1985. An erudite study by the Sterling Professor of History at Yale University, who rightly emphasizes that Jesus was a Jew and that the "first attempts to understand and interpret his message took place within the context of Judaism, and it is likewise there that any attempt to understand his place in the history of human culture must begin" (p. 11).

Perrin, N. *Jesus and the Language of the Kingdom: Symbol and Metaphor in New Testament Interpretation.* Philadelphia, 1976. A significant examination of Jesus' teaching; see next annotation.

Perrin, N. *Rediscovering the Teaching of Jesus* (New Testament Library). London, 1967. Perrin was one of the most brilliant and influential thinkers during the 1960s and 1970s, during the waning years of the so-called new quest. Moving out from under the influence of Jeremias to Bultmann, but hindered by a second-hand knowledge of first-century Palestinian Judaism, he tenaciously held to the position that one can recover Jesus' authentic words. He developed widely influential methods to attempt this task, although the result was to render most of Jesus' sayings inauthentic.

Ramsey, M. *Jesus and the Living Past: The Hale Lectures 1978.* Oxford, New York, 1980. The former Archbishop of Canterbury affirms the necessity of employing honest and rigorous historical criticism in the study of Christian origins, and wisely evokes Bishop Lightfoot's famous dictum: "Though the gospel is capable of doctrinal exposition, and though it is eminently fertile in moral results, yet its substance is neither a dogmatic system nor an ethical code, but a person and a life" (p. 25). For Ramsey the event of Jesus includes the pre-crucifixion life of Jesus, as well as the passion and resurrection, and it must be seen "not as antecedent to the event of the Church but as one event with the origin of the Church " (p. 32).

Riches, J. *Jesus and the Transformation of Judaism.* London, 1980. For Riches the essential "pressing question" concerns Jesus' purpose, and for him it is that "Jesus advocated powerfully and originally the virtues of patience, forgiveness, and long-suffering love" (p. x). But, these virtues were characteristic of religious Jews and of the Jewish ethical writings (see *The Old Testament Pseudepigrapha*, edited by J. H. Charlesworth, vol. 2, and Ben Sira). Riches tends to talk about ideas and gives us little insight into first-century intellectual history; also, he tends to exaggerate the creativity and uniqueness of Jesus, without really pausing to listen to the other first-century Jews.

Riesner, R. *Jesus als Lehrer: Eine Untersuchung zum Ursprung der Evangelien-Überlieferung*, 2nd edition (WUNT 2.7). Tübingen, 1984. This young German NT scholar claims that the Jesus traditions were preserved and protected by a School of Jesus, which antedates the cross, since Jesus, as other Jewish teachers, gathered around himself a circle of scholars and students.

Rivkin, E. *What Crucified Jesus?* Nashville, 1984. Rivkin, Adolph S. Ochs Professor of Jewish History at Hebrew Union College-Jewish Institute of Religion in Cincinnati, demonstrates by a study of first-century Palestinian history, especially through Josephus' writing, that Jesus' power and charisma were a threat to the Roman imperial system. It was that "what," not the "who" — the Jews — which caused Jesus' death. This is a marvelous book and opens up windows for seeing Jews and Christians as "brothers."

Sanders, E. P. *Jesus and Judaism*. Philadelphia, 1985. Sanders is very influential today, because of his work on Paul. His *Jesus and Judaism* is the most important work on Jesus published in the 1980s, although he unfortunately tends to read back into first-century Palestine the "normativeness" of post-Jamnaic Judaism.

Sanders, E. P. (ed.). *Jesus, the Gospels, and the Church: Essays in Honor of William R. Farmer*. Macon, Ga., 1987. See especially the section on "Jesus and the Gospels," with essays by D. Daube, D. L. Dungan, B. Gerhardsson, C. F. D. Moule, P. Parker, B. Reicke, and E. P. Sanders.

Schillebeeckx, E. *Jesus: An Experiment in Christology*, translated by H. Hoskins, New York, 1979. A powerful, highly influential statement of the possibility of dialogue among the historian, the exegete, and the theologian, because behind the kergymata lives "the concrete person Jesus of Nazareth," which is "the one and only basis for an authentic christology" (p. 82).

Sloyan, G. S. *Jesus in Focus: A Life in its Setting*. Mystic, Conn., 1983, 1984. Sloyan sees Jesus as a mystic, an unconventional teacher, and an outsider who taught and lived out holiness and love. The book is informed by the best in the world's great religions, is engagingly written, and is a persuasive statement why the Jesus story is possible and necessary.

Tambasco, A. J. *In the Days of Jesus: The Jewish Background and Unique Teaching of Jesus.* New York, 1983. This little book contains the acknowledgment that the gospels are not biographies; but it is confessional, posits false options ("...the apostles were interested in ...'Who *is* Jesus, alive and present to us?' and not 'Who *was* Jesus?'" p. 7), is dated (p. 50), and is simplistic: "God had, as a matter of fact, come to humanity with a new kingdom and was showing himself through Jesus as 'Dad'" (p. 71). Affirmations about Jesus' unique teachings are the means for distorting his Jewish background.

Theissen, G. *The Shadow of the Galilean: The Quest of the Historical Jesus in Narrative Form,* translated by J. Bowden. Philadelphia, 1987. Writing engagingly, this perceptive scholar moves the reader through the charged events of Jesus' time through the eyes of a fictitious character, Andreas.

Theissen, G. *Sociology of Early Palestinian Christianity,* translated by J. Bowden. Philadelphia, 1978. The book is the first attempt in the second half of this century to apply the methods and perspectives of sociology to the Jesus movement; it is not Theissen's best work. One of the controversial claims made by Theissen is that a sociology of the Jesus movement makes a contribution to solving some of the problems in the quest for the historical Jesus, because "it suggests that we should assume a continuity between Jesus and the Jesus movement and in so doing opens up the possibility of transferring insights into the Jesus movement to Jesus himself" (p. 4).

Trocmé, E. *Jésus de Nazareth: Vu par les témoins de sa vie* (Bibliothèque Théologique). Neuchâtel, Switzerland, 1971. A brilliant, but idiosyncratic, study of Jesus' influence on the diverse social strata of Palestinian Jews by a master NT scholar.

Vermes, G. *The Gospel of Jesus the Jew: The Riddell Memorial Lectures.* Newcastle upon Tyne, 1981. In the late 1960s this Jewish scholar began his own quest for the historical Jesus; here he presents a prolegomenon to Jesus' teachings. A first-century Jewish holy man (a Galilean Hasid), Jesus calls for repentance, announces the coming of the Kingdom of God, is "uniquely aware of his filial relation to the Father," and seeks to inculcate in others the self-same relationship.

Vermes, G. *Jesus the Jew: A Historian's Reading of the Gospels.* London, 1973, 1981. An attempt to understand Jesus' place in history by reading the Jewish sources as well as the NT. Jesus is portrayed as one of the Galilean miracle workers, like Honi and Hanina ben Dosa.

Wenham, D. (ed.). *Gospel Perspectives: The Jesus Tradition Outside the*

Gospels, vol. 5. Sheffield, 1984. Contains fourteen important studies by scholars, significant for the study of the transmission and preservation of Jesus traditions.

Wilder, A. N. *Jesus' Parables and the War of Myths: Essays on Imagination in the Scriptures*, edited by J. Breech. Philadelphia, 1982. This collection of essays, all but one previously published, reveals the eschatological dimensions of Jesus' parables, by interpreting them through literary and rhetorical criticism. Wilder is a most distinguished and gifted New Testament theologian.

Wilson, I. *Jesus: The Evidence*. London, 1984, 1985. This challenging book, considered by many readers to be provocative, is highly influential (but certainly not to scholars). It is the text behind a far too popular three-part London Weekend Television program (see the important correctives in Dunn's *The Evidence for Jesus*); but it is more serious, sensitive, and balanced than the TV series.

Yaseen, L. C. *The Jesus Connection: To Triumph over Anti-Semitism*. New York, 1985. Designed for the public, intended to show that Jesus, and many other admired individuals, were Jews, and that "Jesus was a defender, not a denigrator, of Judaism" (p. 2).

Zimmermann, A. F. *Die urchristlichen Lehre* (WUNT 2.12) Tübingen, 1984. Against Dibelius and Bultmann, but with Riesenfeld and Gerhardsson, Zimmermann contends that the transmission of Jesus' sayings was controlled by a Christian rabbinate.

Index of Names

Index of Passages